REPRESENTING PEOPLE WITH DEMENTIA

A Practical Guide for Criminal Defense Lawyers

ELIZABETH KELLEY, EDITOR

Foreword by Andrea D. Lyon

AMERICAN BAR ASSOCIATION

Cover design by Amanda Fry/ABA Design

Printed in the United States of America.

26 25 24 23 22   5 4 3 2 1

A catalog record for this book is on file with the Library of Congress.

Contents

Foreword

It is a tautology to say that an attorney has a duty to zealously represent her client. But what if doing so means exploring what the client doesn't want explored? In the context of a capital case, it may mean developing mitigation against the client's wishes. In an insanity defense it might mean exploring the client's mental health, despite him insisting there is nothing wrong with him.

What about dementia? What if you begin to see that the client is having difficulty remembering or recounting matters? In things you have discussed with her, what if she does not remember discussing them? If you leave an interview with your client unconvinced that the nods of agreement were in any way knowing, what then?

Well, in this context it might mean exploring the possibility of dementia with your client and appropriate mental health professionals, even though it will not likely be welcome. Unfortunately, as a society we generally view mental illness as a moral failing, and while that is changing for the better, talking to a client, relative, or friend about what this subject is fraught with.

Take for example a client I will call Steven. Steven was a very intelligent, well-read client, who had taught himself three languages in prison, read voraciously, and had opinions both legal and philosophical about most everything—opinions he could and would back up.

Then there was a stroke. He still believed internally that he was making sense. He would discuss his situation with the same emphasis and enthusiasm he had always shown, but wasn't making any sense. When I would try to "translate," he would get frustrated and angry, would yell at me, and abruptly end our meetings.

I didn't know what to do. The medical staff at the prison shrugged their shoulders and said essentially—it's a stroke, what do you expect? Nothing was being done to try to rehabilitate him, to assess his cognitive functioning, or anything more than keeping him relatively clean. I was, eventually, able to get him some help and he slowly began to recover verbal functioning (it turned out he had a form of aphasia) and meaningful communication became possible again.

Now I realize not all dementia comes from a stroke, and that it is not always suddenly just there in such a dramatic and obvious way. This decline happens slowly and may not be clear for a long time. But the issue for advocates and evaluators is how to identify people who have dementia, or may have it; how to talk about such a sensitive issue with your client or patient; and what your obligations are once it is established they have diminished cognitive functioning.

Perhaps the best legal framework to think about this is what is used when assessing whether a client is "fit for trial." It doesn't require much to be fit; first, the client must understand the case he or she is involved in; and, second, he or she must be able to communicate with counsel. Most of us who have had issues with unfit clients find that this is a harder set of questions to answer than it might first appear. What, for example, does "understand" mean in this context? If I have a client in jail, he may understand that fact, and that he has a case against him, but does he understand enough to be able to make decisions about the case? To discuss strategy? To be able to see how he could win? Could lose? Whether to risk going to trial and getting convicted of more than he would after a plea? These concepts are hard enough to understand even if your client isn't impaired, but are increasingly fraught when your client is impaired.

Worse, can the client communicate with counsel? And by communicate I do not mean "talk," I mean express him or herself, respond appropriately to what you say, and digest information?

Let me tell you a story about communicating with words, but without meaning: the execution of Ricky Ray Rector. After killing a man in a restaurant and fleeing, and three days on the run, he agreed to turn himself in to the authorities, but instead he shot the police officer who had negotiated his surrender in the back. He then shot himself in the head in a suicide attempt. The attempt effectively resulted in a lobotomy. The U.S. Supreme Court denied review in his case regarding whether he was "fit" to be executed. In other words, could he understand what was going to happen to him and why? Then Arkansas Governor Bill Clinton made a point of returning to Arkansas to oversee Rector's January 24, 1992, execution during the U.S. presidential campaign, in order to appear sufficiently tough on crime.

Now, Mr. Rector could talk, and we know this because when he ordered his last meal, he asked the warden to save his dessert for after the execution.[1] Again, this isn't the classic dementia situation, but it illustrates the challenges in representing someone who is cognitively impaired.

In this timely book, experts weigh in on subjects from understanding dementia, to working with experts and clients, and to the realities someone with dementia faces in jail or prison. There is much to learn here, much we all *need* to learn.

—Andrea D. Lyon

1. Frady, Marshall (February 22, 1993). "Death in Arkansas". *The New Yorker*.

Introduction

Those of us who have been practicing criminal defense have noticed a gradual greying of our clientele. At the same time, various professional listservs post inquiries about how to handle a case involving an older offender who perhaps can't remember the circumstances of his or her offense or who simply wouldn't survive prison.

This gradual greying may well turn into a silver tsunami for the criminal justice system. First of all, the general population is getting older and living longer. With that comes not only physical challenges, but also cognitive challenges like dementia, which may lead to irresponsible conduct. Second, because of draconian prison sentences including lengthy mandatory minimums and three-strikes laws, our current prison population is getting older.

Representing People with Dementia: A Practical Guide for Criminal Defense Lawyers, is modeled after my earlier books, *Representing People with Mental Disabilities: A Practical Guide for Criminal Defense Lawyers* and *Representing People with Autism Spectrum Disorders: A Practical Guide for Criminal Defense Lawyers*. The reason for this book on dementia is three-fold: first, there is a growing recognition that people with dementia become involved with the criminal justice system and need vigorous, informed, compassionate advocacy; second, there is a need for practical, easily digestible information for lawyers about this non-traditional criminal defendant; and third, this book is an attempt to get in front of the curve.

Many of the traditional goals of the criminal justice system are inappropriate, if not impossible, to achieve when it comes to people with dementia. Certainly, jail or prison would incapacitate a person with dementia, but locking such a person up is expensive because of the medical treatment required, and their behaviors could be disruptive for institutional staff as well as the inmate population. Because dementia is a progressive and irreversible disease, rehabilitation is unrealistic. In terms of deterrence, to the degree that other potential offenders are incapable of controlling their behavior, they cannot be deterred. And as a civilized and compassionate society, do we really want to punish someone who may have until this point in their lives been productive and law-abiding and who, simply put, may not be long for this world, or whose final years will be spent enveloped in the cloudlike fog of dementia?

Similarly, the criminal defense lawyer will have to master new skills in order to best serve this population. Competency is the threshold issue in every case, but regarding people with dementia, this is a real concern. Related to this is the fact that restoration of competency is likely impossible. Finding an expert may not be enough. Rather, the expert must be knowledgeable about the various kinds of dementia. Indeed, the criminal defense lawyer representing someone with dementia will likely need to have a team of different experts. The chapters in this book are intended to address these as well as other challenges.

Theoretically, readers can open this book to any chapter. However, the material in that chapter may necessarily overlap with material in one or more other chapters. Whenever possible, cross-references are provided. Additionally, you may want to read chapters in sets. For instance, you might read chapter 2, titled Competency, in conjunction with chapter 3, Restoration. Similarly, the general chapter on jail and prison conditions is made particularly real and human by the following chapter which details the decline in prison of a fictional prisoner.

The chapters are relatively short (as far as legal works go). Although the chapters lack the footnotes traditionally seen in legal writing, attribution is given when appropriate, and complete citations are available by contacting the author or authors. The back of the book contains a list of suggested works arranged by chapter heading if you would like to further explore a topic. As with the chapters, the works cited may overlap one another in terms of content.

I have written a brief introduction to each chapter to put the topic into context or to raise a point not covered by the author. As editor, this is my attempt to weave together the different voices and perspectives of a diverse group of writers.

This book was one of my Pandemic Projects. Thanks are due to a host of people. It was inspired by conversations I had with Dr. Eric Y. Drogin about the aging of our clients and their attendant cognitive issues. Dr. Drogin is the author of two chapters in this book. As importantly, I appreciate the contributions of my authors. I am grateful that they shared their expertise and embraced the parameters of this project. I also acknowledge the individuals who peer reviewed chapters: Dr. Timothy Allen; Donna Lee Elm, Esq.; Cindy Arends Elsberry, Esq.; Dr. Manesh Fozdar; Richard Ginkowski, Esq.; and Justin Murphy, Esq. I am grateful to Audra Thramer, a law student at the University of Oregon for her assistance in providing much-needed and much-appreciated technical support. And finally, I thank the American Bar Association for once again, supporting another of my writing adventures. In particular, I thank Bryan Kay, Susan Lorimor, and John Palmer.

In February 2019, the United States Supreme Court decided the case of *Madison v. Alabama*, 586 U.S. 718 (2019). Vernon Madison was scheduled to be executed by the State of Alabama, but suffered advanced dementia which rendered him incapable of having any understanding of why he would be executed. The Court ruled that the Eighth Amendment protections extended to people like Mr. Madison who were suffering from cognitive issues like dementia which made him incompetent to be executed. As Bryan Stevenson, Mr. Madison's attorney and the author of the critically acclaimed *Just Mercy* stated at the end of his oral argument, "The Eighth Amendment isn't just a window. It's a mirror. And what the Court has said is that our norms—our values—are implicated when we do things to really fragile, really vulnerable people. . . . Dementia in this case renders Mr. Madison frail, bewildered, vulnerable, in a way that cannot be reconciled with executing him because of his incompetency."

There are too many people like Mr. Madison in our criminal justice system. And more will be coming. Thankfully, statistically, not all will be in a place as grim as a Death Row. But nonetheless, the criminal justice system as a whole is not the place for someone with dementia. Jail, or worse, prison, would be absolute torture. This book is an attempt to help those who, because of dementia, are fragile, bewildered, and vulnerable—and to give their attorneys the tools to obtain a fair and just resolution of their case.

— Elizabeth Kelley

Chapter

1

What Is Dementia?

Dr. Marc Blatstein and Fay F. Spence

Many attorneys use the terms "Alzheimer's" and "dementia" interchangeably. Few attorneys know that there are at least a dozen kinds of dementia. Each kind presents differently, but all share the same quality: Each is irreversible.

This chapter, by Dr. Marc Blatstein and Attorney Fay Spence, is an excellent primer for criminal defense lawyers representing a person with dementia. The chapter is a survey of the different kinds of dementia, and describes the symptoms and possible strategies for their management. The chapter also lays a foundation for subsequent chapters and topics in this book.

In the coming decades, representing people with dementia will become increasingly common for criminal defense lawyers, either because of the growing population of older citizens who are charged with a crime or because of the aging of our current prison population due to lengthy mandatory or life sentences. (Also important are the people suffering from frontotemporal dementia (FTD), which can afflict people as early as their forties.) It is therefore imperative that we understand the terminology in order to effectively and zealously advocate for our clients with dementia.

• • •

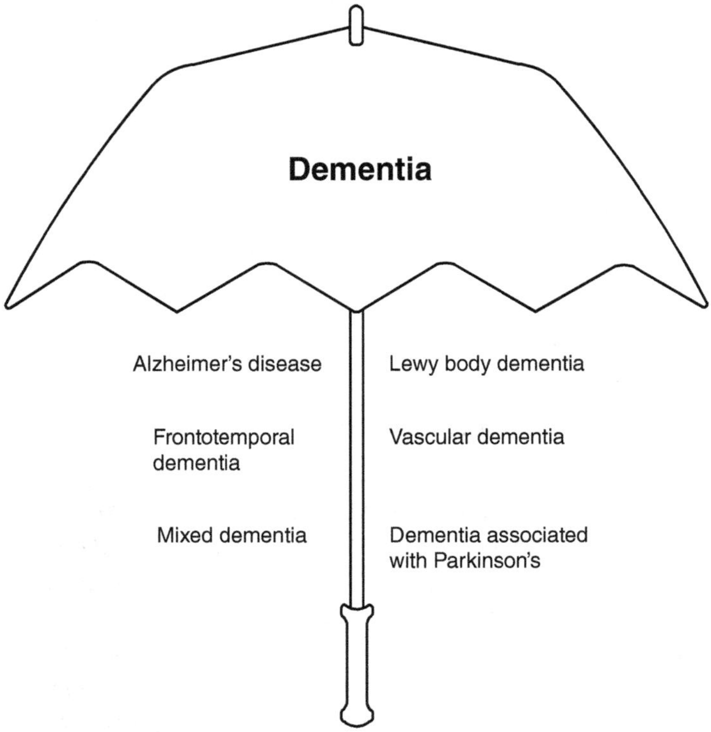

FIGURE 1.1 Types of Dementia
Source: Adapted from *What Is Dementia?* by Alzheimer's Association, Copyright 2021, https://www.alz.org/alzheimers-dementia/what-is-dementia.

A Starting Point

A good starting point for discussing the incarceration of defendants with dementia is understanding that Alzheimer's disease is a specific degenerative brain disease that is caused by complex brain changes following cell damage, whereas dementia is a more general term for a combination of symptoms, such as loss of memory and other mental abilities caused by physical changes in the brain; this loss is severe enough to interfere with daily life (or Activities of Daily Living, ADL) (Alzheimer's Association [AA], 2021; Miller, 2020). While Alzheimer's is the most common of the dementias, accounting for 60 to 70 percent of all dementia cases, frontotemporal dementia (FTD) is most associated with criminal activity (Miller, 2020; Shugart, 2015).

Recently, the *Diagnostic and Statistical Manual of Mental Disorders (DSM-5)* (American Psychiatric Association [APA], 2013) included dementia within the category of "Major Neurocognitive Disorders (MND)" (Sousa, et al., 2020). A determination that a person's impairments are likely caused by dementia is appropriate if the following are present:

- Recent decline in attention and cognitive functioning, which includes learning, memory, perception, and problem solving, that is
  1) Documented by a person familiar with the patient, or
  2) Documented by neuropsychological testing or clinical assessment (Miller, 2020).
- The cognitive deficits affect activities of daily living, such as paying bills or taking correct medications (Miller, 2020).
- The cognitive deficits do not occur exclusively in the context of a delirium (Miller, 2020).
- Other disorders have been ruled out, such as major depression or schizophrenia (APA, 2013, p. 604; Miller, 2020).
- A definitive diagnosis "can only be made postmortem via autopsy of the brain" (Miller, 2020).

Because dementia progressively affects the nerve cells impacting a person's ability to remember, reason, and make rational judgments, having a defendant with dementia who is facing incarceration requires an innovative defense strategy that attempts to get the defendant the care that they require. The defense must emphasize that the defendant has abnormal, declining brain changes that will affect the defendant's ADL: dressing, eating, paying bills, interpersonal relationships, following orders, and interacting with others. This begs the question of how to provide the best treatment for the defendant while also protecting society. The court will need to understand the necessary medical care *and* mental health care and where these can be obtained, as well as the most economical way to meet the defendant's needs and still protect society. The goal is to seek treatment and supervision within the community, protective care within the Federal Bureau of Prisons (BOP), or placement in a secured mental health facility.

Frontotemporal Dementia (FTD): Most Commonly Associated with Criminal Activity

Many psychiatrists (including forensic) are unfamiliar with frontotemporal dementia (FTD), or lack experience diagnosing this disease (Shugart, 2015). Therefore, consulting an expert neuropsychiatrist experienced in working with this neurodegenerative disorder is critical. Counsel should supply the neuropsychiatrist's report and opinion to the probation officer preparing the pre-sentence report (PSR). If the probation officer does not include that opinion in the PSR, counsel must provide it to the court when objecting to the PSR, because the information is critical for the court to consider, and if the defendant is to be incarcerated, the information must get to the institution's placement unit. Some of the references that follow may prove to be good starting points.

While the most common type of dementia is Alzheimer's (Alzheimer's Society United Against Dementia [ASUAD], 2021), criminal behavior is more common in patients with FTD. Documented evidence may prove important as part of the defense. "Judicial evaluations of criminality in the demented individual might require different criteria than the classic 'insanity defense' used in the American legal system; these individuals should be treated differently by the law" (Liljegren et al., 2015, p. 300).

In more than 30 percent of patients with FTD (a conservative estimate), criminal behavior is the first visible indicator (Shugart, 2015). The literature reports that the first offenses commonly committed by people with FTD include stealing, exposing themselves to children, sexually harassing others, and leaving the scene of an accident (Mendez, 2010; Shugart, 2015). Empirical studies suggest that neurological brain dysfunction is a contributing causative factor in more than 90 percent of homicide offenders and over 75 percent of sex offenders (Mendez, 2010). In a German study of 83 dementia patients, more than half of those with behavioral variant FTD (also known as semantic dementia) reported criminal behavior, compared to only 12 percent of Alzheimer disease patients (Shugart, 2015). Although FTD can occur at any age, the average age of its onset is the mid-to-late fifties, with men and women equally susceptible (Mendez, 2010). Neurologists and psychiatrists aware of FTD are increasingly urging legal professionals to think seriously about the brain whenever someone commits a crime, especially when a person's first crime is committed after age 50 (Shugart, 2015).

In his 2010 article in the *Journal of the American Academy of Psychiatry and the Law Online*, Mendez provided four patient histories as representative of criminal behavior in persons with FTD. The first patient, a man in his sixties, began following children home from school and trying to touch them. He had never previously engaged in this behavior. When he exposed himself to his neighbor's children, he was arrested. He did not deny his actions, which he described in detail, and he agreed that such acts are wrong and harmful. Yet he also stated that he did not feel that he was causing harm when he engaged in that behavior (Mendez, 2010).

The second patient that Mendez described was a woman in her fifties, who began stealing merchandise and going behind counters to take items, even when she personally knew the merchants. When her behavior was pointed out to her, she admitted knowing that they were wrong. She also had other behavioral changes. She had become disinhibited, making excessively personal or familiar comments about others, and she frequently made puns and burst into laughter (Mendez, 2010).

A third patient, a man in his fifth decade, was detained after grabbing a woman's buttocks. On previous occasions, he had repeatedly made lewd comments. After his arrest, he acknowledged that his egregious behaviors were inappropriate and said he understood why he got into significant trouble because of his actions (Mendez, 2010).

The fourth patient, a man in his early fifties, left the scene of a hit-and-run accident without concern. The police stopped him a short distance away from the scene, and he admitted his involvement and knew that it was wrong to leave the scene but did not feel the need to stop at the time. His family reported that for two years before the accident, he had begun passing gas and belching in public without embarrassment and appearing partially clothed in front of others (Mendez, 2010).

Mendez (2010) emphasizes that all four were aware that their actions were wrong and understood their potential consequences, but they proceeded with them anyway, in an "impulsive, and often compulsive" manner. The behavior is not consistent with what we recognize as reasonable behavior, which makes it imperative for the court to understand the effect of degenerative brain injury on a defendant's behavior. The defense attorney must ensure that he or she provides this information to the court, through a medical expert, so that the court can consider the effect of brain injury on the defendant's moral capacity and moral cognition (Mendez, 2010). Without this understanding, the court and others will perceive the offender as a remorseless sociopath.

When there is no previous diagnosis of FTD, the early involvement of a neurologist is critical to document the history of changes in the defendant's behaviors before his or her arrest, so that a diagnosis can be made if the offender appears to be suffering from FTD (Mendez, 2010). Even with such a diagnosis, the defense will have an uphill battle in persuading the court to consider this a mitigating factor when the disease has not been documented before the client's arrest. Educating the judiciary generally about the effects of dementia on criminal behavior is also important, so that a judge does not hear of this for the first time in a specific case, where he or she is likely to be more skeptical.

Because of FTD patients' ability to recall and describe their crimes and to understand intellectually that the behavior is wrong, FTD will not provide a valid insanity defense in American courts (Shugart, 2015). Shugart (2015) notes, as a matter of policy, that a person with FTD in Germany's criminal justice system is not protected from prosecution, but his or her dementia is considered in setting the penalty. When a person with dementia and the resultant diminished capacity to control impulses poses a danger to others, he or she is generally placed in a forensic psychiatry unit or closed ward of a nursing home, not prison (Shugart, 2015).

In the federal system, depending on the nature of the offense for which an inmate is convicted, the inmate may be referred to a specific program in the BOP. Because indecent exposure, public urination, and other sexually inappropriate behavior are frequent early symptoms of FTD, an inmate may be expected to attend a sex offender program in the BOP. Would being convicted of a sex crime be the best legal charge for someone with dementia? As it will be forever on their record, and will do nothing to change their future behavior, is there a better option that protects the inmate as well as society?

If a defendant's FTD has progressed to the point of memory deterioration, counsel should consider whether these programs are appropriate options, as an inmate can say things in a prison treatment setting that are ultimately used to their detriment later. Combined with the complete lack of a cure for dementia, the risk may well outweigh any benefit to be gained from any program participation. (*See* Chapter 7, Early Onset Dementia/ Frontotemporal Dementia.)

Other Types of Dementia

Legal practitioners should be aware of other types of dementia as well, including Wernicke-Korsakoff syndrome, Creutzfeldt-Jakob disease, Lewy body dementia, Parkinson's disease dementia, vascular dementia, and mixed dementia.

Wernicke-Korsakoff Syndrome

Wernicke-Korsakoff syndrome resembles dementia and is caused (with rare exceptions) by drinking too much alcohol (ASUAD, 2021). The alcohol prevents the body from absorbing enough thiamine (vitamin B1). Over time, the person may develop Wernicke encephalopathy, an intense inflammation and swelling of the brain. The symptoms of Wernicke encephalopathy usually include disorientation, confusion, and memory loss, and may also include one or more of the following: difficulty controlling eye movements, poor balance, and malnourishment. Unfortunately, the symptoms are often mistaken for alcohol withdrawal if a person appears intoxicated. Treatment for the encephalopathy includes large doses of vitamin B injections and cessation of alcohol consumption. If not treated quickly, the long-term Korsakoff syndrome develops, with many of the same symptoms as dementia (ASUAD, 2021).

The symptoms of Korsakoff syndrome include difficulty understanding new information or learning new skills, changes in personality, lack of insight into one's condition, confabulation, and loss of executive functioning skills (ASUAD, 2021). An example of lack of insight is that the person may believe that his or her memory is working well, but, in fact, there are large, obvious gaps in the person's memory. Confabulation occurs when the person's brain fills in the missing gaps of memory with things that did not happen; this is not purposeful lying, as the person believes the memory is real. Damaged executive functioning skills result in difficulty concentrating, planning, making decisions, or solving problems (ASUAD, 2021).

Closely related to Korsakoff syndrome is alcohol-related brain damage (ARBD), which is caused by damage to and death of nerve cells in the brain, damage to blood vessels, and malnutrition (including lack of thiamine, or vitamin B1) as a result of long-term alcohol consumption and/ or binge drinking (ASUAD, 2021). Some consider Wernicke-Korsakoff syndrome to be a subset of ARBD. In addition to the symptoms of Korsakoff syndrome, a person with ARBD will have trouble with motivation, controlling emotions, setting goals, staying focused, and understanding how other people are thinking and feeling. ARBD is considered one of the younger-onset dementias, with average age of diagnosis being between 40 and 50. ARBD affects men more often than it does women, but women with ARBD are likely to be diagnosed much earlier, because women are more susceptible to the damaging effects of alcohol (ASUAD, 2021).

Unlike other forms of dementia, ARBD does not always get worse over time (ASUAD, 2021). If the person stops drinking alcohol, gets good nutritional treatment, and receives good support, then they may be able to make a partial or full recovery, regaining much of their memory and cognitive skills, allowing them to function independently. With such treatment, about 25 percent of patients with Korsakoff syndrome will make a good recovery; 50 percent will make partial recovery but will still need extra support to manage some aspects of their lives. The remaining 25 percent will not recover and may require long-term care in a residential facility (ASUAD, 2021).

Creutzfeldt-Jakob Disease (CJD)

Creutzfeldt-Jakob disease (CJD) is caused by an abnormally shaped protein, known as a *prion*, infecting the brain (ASUAD, 2021). The exact cause of the buildup of prions in the brain is unknown, but it is not believed to be hereditary nor infectious. A rare disease, CJD affects about one person in a million each year, usually over age 40. The symptoms usually progress quickly, within a few weeks or months, starting with minor memory loss, mood changes, and apathy, progressing to shakiness and jerky movements, stiff limbs, incontinence, and loss of movement and/or speech. A newer variant of CJD is commonly known as mad cow disease. Symptoms may be managed with medication, but the disease is incurable. This type of dementia is not associated with criminal activity.

Lewy Body Dementia

Lewy bodies, named after the doctor who first identified them, are tiny deposits of alpha-synuclein, a protein that appears in nerve cells in the brain (ASUAD, 2021). Why they appear and how they cause dementia is not well understood, though they are associated with low levels of the neurotransmitters acetylcholine and dopamine and with a loss of connection between nerve cells, causing cellular death. Lewy bodies at the base of the brain are a main feature of Parkinson's disease, causing impaired motor skills. As Parkinson's progresses, a patient is at high risk of developing Parkinson's disease dementia, especially if that person has had the disease for several years or if he or she developed it later in life. Lewy bodies in the outer layers of the brain are linked with cognitive symptoms, including dementia. Dementia associated with Parkinson's disease or with other Lewy body dementia is not associated with criminal behavior (ASUAD, 2021).

Vascular Dementia

Vascular dementia is the most common form of dementia other than Alzheimer's disease (Miller, 2020). This is caused by reduced blood supply to the brain from damaged blood vessels. The lack of blood flow results in loss of oxygen and nutrients to the brain. When damaged blood vessels leak or get blocked, no blood reaches the brain cells, and the cells die. Death of brain cells interferes with memory, rational thinking, and reasoning. When these cognitive functions are compromised enough to impact a person's daily life, or ADLs, then the person has vascular dementia (ASUAD, 2021).

Mixed Dementia

Mixed dementia is another way of saying that a person is suffering from two or more types of dementia simultaneously (Miller, 2020). The most common type of mixed dementia is Alzheimer's disease and vascular dementia, followed by Alzheimer's disease and Lewy body dementia. If the person has more symptoms of one disease than the other, then the dementia with the greater number of symptoms is called the predominant disease (ASUAD, 2021).

• • •

Dr. Marc Blatstein had a successful foot and ankle practice for 30 years, providing quality patient care. Over a decade ago he received a felony conviction of one year and one day due to insurance coding and for which he took full responsibility. There was never any question regarding the quality of patient care, and his medical license has been current for more than 30 years. This has provided him an extensive health care background, which allowed him to experience firsthand how the system at times failed defendants. His experience and medical knowledge have provided him a clear understanding of the medical and mental health care issues, along with security requirements, that defendants face and the BOP requires. This comprehensive understanding provides him the skills necessary to help mitigate sentences while suggesting appropriate prison placement options that would be acceptable to all parties.

Dr. Blatstein maintains an active medical license and is the founder of Physician Presentence Report Service, LLC. He can be contacted at info@PPRSUS.com, (240) 888-7778, or through his website: https://pprsus.com/federal-sentencing/.

Fay F. Spence is an attorney with more than 30 years of experience in criminal law, including 13 years with the Federal Public Defenders Office for the Western District of Virginia as First Assistant Public Defender and then as Senior Litigator. She currently serves as a pro se law clerk for the U.S. District Court for the Western District of Virginia. She can be reached at fayspenceatty@msn.com.

Citations available from author(s) by request.

Chapter

2

Competency

Dr. Kaustubh Joshi and Dr. Richard Frierson

The following chapters—Chapter 2, Competency, by Dr. Kaustubh Joshi and Dr. Richard Frierson, and Chapter 3, Restoration, by Dr. Joette James and Dr. LaFaye Marshall—should be read together. Competency to proceed is the threshold issue in any criminal case and is a concept that follows the defendant throughout the life of a case, including sentence and even execution. But as the Competency chapter illustrates, competency evaluations of elderly defendants may differ from evaluations of younger adults because of a neurocognitive disorder other than dementia, other medical or psychological symptoms, or simply lack of experience with the criminal justice system.

Both chapters note that because dementia is a progressive disease, the legal concept of restoration for this population is usually impossible to meet. Both chapters give practical advice about how counsel can best work with experts during competency evaluations of people who might likely have dementia. The Competency chapter lists the records, discovery materials, and collateral sources of information necessary for a thorough evaluation. The Restoration chapter emphasizes that a team of experts, including a neuropsychologist or neuropsychiatrist, is necessary for demonstrating to the court and the prosecutor the defendant's cognitive decline. Both chapters contain abundant references to medical literature that will help lawyers explain to the courts and prosecutors why people with dementia cannot satisfy the two prongs of their jurisdiction's equivalent of the Dusky standard—the ability to understand the nature of the proceedings and the ability to assist counsel.

• • •

In 2019, while individuals aged 65 and over accounted for approximately 16.5 percent of the U.S. population (Kaiser Family Foundation, 2019), they only accounted for 1.46 percent of total arrests in the United States (Federal Bureau of Investigation, 2019). However, they may be slightly overrepresented in subgroups arrested on certain criminal charges. For example, they account for 1.74 percent of all arrests for murder and non-negligent manslaughter, and 1.68 percent for all arrests for aggravated assaults (Federal Bureau of Investigation, 2019). They are less likely than their younger counterparts to be arrested for burglary (0.65 percent), drug offenses (0.63 percent), larceny (1.24 percent), or other property crimes (Federal Bureau of Investigation, 2019). The subgroup of elderly defendants referred for pretrial psychiatric evaluation are most likely referred for a competency to stand trial (CST) evaluation and are most likely facing trial for a violent offense (Frierson & Srinivasan, 2018).

The most common diagnoses encountered in elderly criminal defendants are alcohol use disorder and/or major or mild neurocognitive disorder (Rosner, Wiederlight, Harmon & Cahn, 1991). With the 2013 publication of the American Psychiatric Association's *Diagnostic and Statistical Manual of Mental Disorders (DSM-5)* (2013), dementia is now subsumed under a new category named *major neurocognitive disorder. Mild neurocognitive disorder* (which is also found in DSM-5) can be conceptualized as "pre-dementia" or a less severe level of cognitive impairment compared to major neurocognitive disorder. In elderly defendants, major neurocognitive disorder may account for up to 90 percent of forensic opinions that elderly defendants lack competency to stand trial (CST), and alcohol-induced major neurocognitive disorder (significant cognitive decline attributed to long-standing alcohol use) may be the most common etiology of neurocognitive disorder encountered in elderly criminal defendants (Frierson, Shea & Shea, 2002). Major neurocognitive disorder may be seen in up to 30 percent of elderly defendants referred for a CST evaluation (Heinik, Kimhi & Hes, 1994). With these statistics in mind, this chapter examines CST evaluations of elderly defendants.

Legal Overview

Criminal defendants are presumed to be competent to stand trial. It is estimated that approximately 20 percent to 30 percent of evaluated defendants are found incompetent to stand trial (Nicholson & Kugler K, 1991;

Cooper & Zapf, 2003). CST evaluations may be requested by the defendant's attorney, the prosecutor, or the judge at any point before or during the trial process. As defendants have the constitutional right to be competent to stand trial, every state and the federal government has a process that allows criminal courts to obtain an evaluation of the defendant's CST. In all U.S. jurisdictions, statutes or case law prohibit using information obtained during a CST evaluation to prove criminal responsibility, unless defendants place their mental state at the time of the alleged incident(s) at issue (Mossman et al., 2007). Because many mental illnesses (e.g., schizophrenia, depression) can fluctuate in symptom severity over time, court officers (defense attorneys, prosecutors, and judges) should be alert to circumstances that could affect the defendant's competency to stand trial during the course of criminal proceedings (*Drope v. Missouri*, 420 U.S. 162 [1975]), even if a defendant was previously deemed competent to stand trial. Due process does not require the State, once it provides a defendant access to procedures for undergoing a CST evaluation, to persuade the trier of fact that the defendant is competent to stand trial (*Medina v. California*, 505 U.S. 437 [1992]). In addition, the burden of proof is on the defendant to prove incompetence to stand trial by a preponderance of the evidence standard (*Cooper v. Oklahoma*, 517 U.S. 348 [1996]).

Evaluators of CST should be familiar with the statutorily defined CST standard in the jurisdiction where the trial will take place (Mossman et al., 2007). These statutes are based on the principles outlined in *Dusky v. United States*, 362 U.S. 402 (1960): the test for competency to stand trial is "whether [a defendant] has sufficient present ability to consult with his lawyer with a reasonable degree of rational understanding and whether he has a rational as well as factual understanding of the proceedings against him." This standard involves the defendants' ability to understand the criminal process and their ability to assist their attorneys in their own defense. CST evaluations are "here and now" evaluations in that they hinge on the defendant's present mental state.

This is in contrast to criminal responsibility evaluations (also known as insanity evaluations), which refer to the defendant's mental state at the time of the alleged offense(s). CST evaluations examine the defendants' capacity to stand trial and not their willingness to stand trial (Melton et al., 2018). In addition, this standard requires only that defendants have a reasonable degree of rational understanding and not a perfect understanding (Melton et al., 2018). Finally, the presence of a mental illness (e.g., major neurocognitive disorder) alone does not automatically mean a defendant lacks trial competency; the symptoms of the mental illness have to specifically interfere with a defendant's ability to understand legal proceedings and work with an attorney in the preparation of a defense. Although the *Dusky* standard does not specifically state that a mental disease or defect is necessary to find a defendant incompetent to stand trial, most state statutes require a mental disorder as the basis for a finding of trial incompetency. Since states have slight variations in their CST standards, it is important for the evaluators to be familiar with the specific language that defines trial competency in the jurisdiction where the defendant will stand trial.

Competency to Stand Trial Evaluations

Prior to conducting a CST evaluation, the evaluator should ensure that the defendant has retained counsel or been appointed counsel (if he or she doesn't already know), and that the defense counsel is aware of the evaluation (American Academy of Psychiatry and the Law, 2005). If cognitive impairment or other symptoms interfere with an elderly defendant's ability to understand the nature and purpose of the evaluation and the limitations of confidentiality, the evaluator may make the defendant's counsel aware and extend an offer to have defense counsel present during the evaluation (Frierson & Srinivasan, 2018). Prior to evaluating defendants for CST, evaluators typically review discovery material. This material includes, but is not limited to, information about the charges the defendants are facing, including arrest warrants, police incident reports, witness statements regarding the alleged offense(s), crime scene reports, autopsy reports, law enforcement body-worn camera footage, statements that defendants have given or provided law enforcement, and the defendant's National Crime Information Center (NCIC) report. This information allows the evaluators to assess the defendant's ability to understand the legal charges and relevant evidence in the case (Frierson & Srinivasan, 2018). Having the court provide the evaluators the reasons that the CST evaluation was ordered is extremely helpful to understanding the concerns the court has about the defendant's trial competency. Additionally, information from the defense counsel about their interactions with the defendant may also be helpful.

Evaluators also benefit from reviewing jail records, prior inpatient and outpatient mental health treatment records, medical records, and school records. These may reveal mental health diagnoses or medical concerns that could potentially impair an elderly defendant's trial competency. While an elderly defendant's medical records may be voluminous, evaluators usually focus on records documenting recent functioning, as trial competency is a "here and now" determination (Frierson & Srinivasan, 2018). Jail records may also contain information about the defendant's functioning in the jail setting and the presence of behavioral disturbances while incarcerated that may recur in a courtroom setting (Frierson & Srinivasan, 2018). Additionally, if defendants present with cognitive deficits, evaluators usually attempt to obtain collateral information from a spouse, family members, and/or jail personnel about the duration of their deficits, previous medical workup, and the impact of such deficits on their daily functioning (Frierson & Srinivasan, 2018).

A "factual understanding" of the court proceedings involves a defendant's understanding of several factors: the legal charges that the defendant is facing, the seriousness of the charges, the possible sentences if convicted, the roles of various court personnel (judge, defense attorney, prosecutor, jury), the possible pleas that could be entered, the concepts of evidence and witnesses, and the process involved in plea bargaining (Scott, 2018). Most of these tasks require crystallized abilities (i.e., information and skills gained from experience) and may be more resistant to impairment in normal aging and in the earlier stages of neurocognitive disorders (Frierson & Srinivasan, 2018). Additionally, defendants may provide inadequate answers about the legal process due to a lack of knowledge about, or experience within, the legal system as opposed to an impaired ability to understand this information (Scott, 2018). Lack of knowledge alone does not equate to trial incompetency. In these situations, evaluators should educate defendants and later ascertain where the defendants have the capacity to learn and retain the information (Scott, 2018). Memory deficits seen in neurocognitive disorders can affect the ability to learn and retain information.

A "rational understanding" involves a defendant's abilities to problem solve within the legal system, to weigh the strengths and weaknesses of the evidence, to weigh the likelihood of conviction or acquittal, to consider possible defenses and their likelihood of success, to follow trial testimony, and to use various points of information in legal decision-making (Frierson & Srinivasan, 2018; Melton et al., 2018). These abilities require fluid intelligence (i.e., flexible reasoning and problem solving) and are more susceptible, along with processing speed, to impairment from neurocognitive disorders (Craft, Cholerton, & Reger, 2003; Frierson & Srinivasan, 2018).

"Sufficient present ability to consult with their attorney" involves assessing their abilities to work with defense counsel, to appreciate their legal situation as a criminal defendant, to rationally consider a mental illness defense, to have sufficient memory and concentration to understand trial events, to maintain appropriate courtroom behavior, to provide a consistent and organized account of the offense (although reported amnesia for an offense does not necessarily prevent a finding of competency to stand trial), and to formulate a basic plan of defense (Scott, 2018). These skills require orientation, memory, abstraction, concentration, calculation, and a lack of disturbance of thought process (i.e., possess organized thinking) or thought content (i.e., no delusions about offense) (Frierson & Srinivasan, 2018). Orientation, attention, concentration, and memory are instrumental to alertness in the courtroom and to the ability to follow trial testimony. Organized thought process is crucial for defendants to converse rationally and provide important information to their attorney. These skills, along with a rational understanding, may be more sensitive to impairment in elderly individuals with neurocognitive disorders or delirium (Frierson & Srinivasan, 2018).

Elderly defendants may present with amnesia for the alleged offense(s) for various reasons, with the most common cause being substance use at the time of the crime (Stout & Farooque, 2008). Amnesia for criminal acts is not an automatic bar to a finding of trial competency. In *Wilson v. United States*, 391 F.2d 460 (D.C. Cir. 1968), the D.C. Circuit Court of Appeals outlined a two-stage process when considering an amnestic defendant's competence to stand trial. First, the trial court must predict whether the defendant's reported amnesia would render them competent or incompetent to stand trial (Scott, 2018). If they are found competent to stand trial, the trial judge conducts a post-trial inquiry involving a review of six factors to determine whether the defendant's amnesia actually impaired their ability to participate during the trial process: (1) the effect of the amnesia on the defendant's ability to consult with and assist their attorney; (2) the effects of the amnesia on the defendant's ability to testify; (3) how well the evidence could be extrinsically reconstructed, including evidence relating to the alleged offense and any plausible defense; (4) the extent to which the government assisted the defense in this reconstruction; (5) the strength of the prosecution's case, including the possibility that the defendant could, but for the amnesia, establish an alibi or other defense; and (6) any other facts and circumstances that would indicate whether or not the defendants had a fair trial (*Wilson v. United States*, 391 F.2d 460 (D.C. Cir. 1968)).

Neurocognitive Disorders' Impact on Trial Competency

Cognitive deficits seen in neurocognitive disorders involve impairments in various cognitive domains such as complex attention, executive function, learning and memory, understanding and expressing language, motor skills, and recognition of emotions (American Psychiatric Association, 2013). The degree of cognitive impairment seen in major neurocognitive disorders can fluctuate over time, including within a 24-hour period. Defendants evaluated for trial competency may perform very well during the morning but poorly later in the day due to a phenomenon known as "sundowning." Sundowning involves emergence or worsening of cognitive impairments in the late afternoon or early evening (Canevelli et al., 2016). As such, individuals with cognitive impairments may require multiple evaluations at different times during the day to reach a more accurate opinion about their trial competency. Due to the possibility that criminal trials can last many days or weeks, depending on the jurisdiction, an inability to maintain cognitive functioning and follow trial processes throughout the entire day may warrant either an opinion of lack of competency to stand trial or a recommendation for abbreviated trial days (Frierson & Srinivasan, 2018).

In addition to cognitive deficits, delusions (i.e., fixed false beliefs that are not amenable to change despite evidence to the contrary) have been known to occur in certain types of major neurocognitive disorders (e.g., in Alzheimer's disease, Parkinson's disease) and can appear before cognitive decline is apparent (Cipriani et al., 2014). Persecutory delusions (i.e., fixed false beliefs that one is going to be harmed, harassed, and so forth by an individual, group, or another entity) are the most common delusions and often consist of beliefs of spousal infidelity or abandonment, which can lead to violent acts against the spouse (Frierson & Srinivasan, 2018).

Delusional disorder (without cognitive impairment) generally occurs in mid- to late life and can present in the context of a forensic evaluation (Lacro, Harris, & Jeste, 1993). Possessing delusions does not automatically impair an elderly defendant's trial competency. Evaluators investigate the impact of the delusion(s) on the defendant's ability to communicate with their attorney and on their legal decision-making. If delusions are not related to the alleged offense(s), and if defendants are otherwise able to understand trial proceedings and work with their attorneys, then the delusions may not affect their competency to stand trial (Frierson & Srinivasan, 2018). Even when delusions relate to the specific act(s) charged (e.g., persecutory delusions possessed by the defendant toward the alleged victim of a murder or an assault), those delusions may or may not impair trial competency. If an elderly defendant insists that their attorney present the delusion(s) in court as the truth, then that defendant lacks trial competency. If they understand that others do not believe their delusions, and if they do not have an urgency to convince others, then they retain trial competency despite possessing such delusions (Frierson & Srinivasan, 2018).

Competency to Stand Trial Evaluation Outcomes

Up to 50 percent of cases of elderly defendants referred for a CST evaluation are adjudicated incompetent (Frierson & Srinivasan, 2018). Evaluators are usually asked to render an opinion as to whether trial competency can be restored with psychiatric treatment. Although state procedures differ by jurisdiction, defendants cannot be involuntarily hospitalized indefinitely for competency restoration purposes. The U.S. Supreme Court ruled that defendants "cannot be held more than the reasonable period of time necessary to determine whether there is a substantial probability that he [they] will attain that capacity in the foreseeable future" (*Jackson v. Indiana*, 406 U.S. 715 [1972]). Prediction of restorability is sometimes difficult, and the presence of neurocognitive disorders may significantly decrease the likelihood of successful restoration because of the lack of effective treatments to reverse cognitive decline in neurocognitive disorders (Frierson & Srinivasan, 2018).

Older age of the defendant, independent of a diagnosis, is also a predictor of not being capable of being restored (Colwell & Gianesini, 2011). This could be due to the age-related burden of chronic medical conditions and other comorbid psychiatric conditions or to cognitive difficulties that do not reach the threshold for a diagnosis of major neurocognitive disorder (Frierson & Srinivasan, 2018). Individuals deemed incompetent to stand trial who were not restored had significantly more psychotic symptoms as well as higher levels of cognitive impairment, including lack of orientation, executive functioning impairments, distractibility, and thought derailment (Gay, Vitacco, & Ragatz, 2017). At least one study of competency restoration revealed that the type of major neurocognitive disorder (e.g., Alzheimer's disease versus vascular disease, etc.) did not affect restoration rates (Morris & Parker, 2009). Overall, restoration rates were low and likely due to the fact that major neurocognitive disorders are progressive illnesses, with deficits due to these disorders typically worsening over time (Frierson & Srinivasan, 2018). However, in cases with serious alleged criminal offenses, courts may decide that attempting restoration is warranted, even if the likelihood of restoration is low. (*See* Chapter 3, Restoration.)

Conclusion

It is important that lawyers, judges, law students, and other nonmedical professionals understand that CST evaluations of elderly defendants can differ compared to CST evaluations of younger defendants due to the various factors explained in this chapter. Elderly defendants have a higher risk of developing cognitive impairments. It is crucial to understand whether an elderly defendant's CST deficits are likely the direct result of a major neurocognitive disorder, other medical or psychiatric symptoms, or a lack of legal knowledge or experience (Morris & Parker, 2009). Elderly defendants may have intact cognitive functioning, but could possess delusions about court personnel or have delusions about the victim of their offense that impair their ability to rationally assist an attorney. Most major neurocognitive disorders are progressive and there is currently no cure for many of them, thus competency restoration is unlikely to be successful. While major neurocognitive disorders and age are negative predictors of competency restoration, evaluators' opinions about the probability of competency restoration should be based on a careful assessment of defendants' history and their functional capacity at the time of the evaluation (Morris & Parker, 2009).

• • •

Kaustubh G. Joshi is Associate Professor of Clinical Psychiatry and Assistant Program Director of the Prisma Health/University of South Carolina School of Medicine Forensic Psychiatry Fellowship. He received his medical degree from University of Medicine and Dentistry of New Jersey–New Jersey Medical School, completed his psychiatry residency at the University of Texas Health Science Center of San Antonio, and completed his forensic psychiatry fellowship at Palmetto Health–University of South Carolina School of Medicine. Dr. Joshi has authored or co-authored several peer-reviewed articles and book chapters on various topics in psychiatry and forensic psychiatry. He is board certified in psychiatry and forensic psychiatry. Dr. Joshi's email is kaustubh.joshi@uscmed.sc.edu.

Richard L. Frierson is Alexander G. Donald Professor of Clinical Psychiatry, Vice Chair for Education, and Director of the Forensic Psychiatry Fellowship, Department of Neuropsychiatry and Behavioral Science at the University of South Carolina School of Medicine, Columbia, South Carolina. He received his medical degree from the University of South Carolina School of Medicine in Columbia, and completed his psychiatric residency and forensic psychiatry fellowship at the William S. Hall Psychiatric Institute, also in Columbia. Dr. Frierson has held several local, state, and national leadership positions in clinical and academic settings, including being President of the American Academy of Psychiatry and the Law, the largest professional organization of forensic psychiatrists in North America. He has edited three textbooks and authored or co-authored dozens of peer-reviewed articles and book chapters on various topics in psychiatry and forensic psychiatry. He is board certified in psychiatry and forensic psychiatry. Dr. Frierson's email is richard.frierson@uscmed.sc.edu.

Citations available from author(s) by request.

Chapter

3

Restoration

Dr. Joette James and Dr. LaFaye Marshall

"Competency to stand trial (CST)," "adjudicative competence," and "procedural competence," are terms used within the psychological literature to discuss a defendant's ability to participate in court processes. CST is one component of the adjudicative process, while the term "procedural competence" describes the entirety of the defendant's court processes, which includes CST as well as other interactions with the court during the process of criminal proceedings, such as competency to waive *Miranda* rights, competency to be sentenced, and competency to be executed.

The historical underpinnings of procedural competence lie in important principles such as those outlined within the Sixth Amendment. In addition to a speedy public trial and an impartial jury, the amendment highlights the importance of a defendant's ability to be cognizant of the allegations made against him/her, challenge opposing witnesses, attain favorable witnesses, and assist in his/her defense (U.S. Const. amend. XI).

As delineated by Polizzi and Draper (2015), the impetus for the established blueprint for CST is "to prevent a mentally incompetent defendant from participating in the adjudication process." In 1960, the Supreme Court of the United States (SCOTUS) provided a standard for the determination of CST. In the case of *Dusky v. United States*, 362 U.S. 402 (1960), the defendant, Milton Dusky, was accused of transporting a minor across state jurisdictions. Although the evaluating psychiatrist opined that Dusky displayed symptoms indicative of schizophrenia, which impaired his ability to assist in his defense, the judge found that Dusky's orientation to "time and place," and recollection of minor aspects of the case rendered him competent. Following an appeal, the case was eventually heard by SCOTUS.

In their decision, SCOTUS determined that Dusky's orientation and memory were an insufficient means to determine his ability to stand trial, and the true determination of competency required delineation of components essential to the adjudicative process. To that end, the *Dusky* standard for competency required that a defendant have "sufficient present ability to consult with his lawyer with a reasonable degree of rational understanding, and whether he has a rational as well as factual understanding of the proceedings against him." This standard has been fully adopted in federal court, and either wholly or partially adopted at the state level. A defendant entering court proceedings is usually assumed competent; however, concerns regarding competency can be raised and at any point in the proceeding. While questions regarding competency can be raised by any parties relevant to the case, concerns regarding competency are often raised by the defendant's attorney (Kruh & Grisso, 2009).

Competency and Functional Deficits

According to Grisso (2014), one of the primary objectives of a competency evaluation is to identify the functional deficits experienced by the defendant with respect to the adjudicative process. Although the *Dusky* standard uses such terms as "factual" and "rational," it does not precisely define the functional abilities required for competence. Grisso operationalizes these terms through four organizing concepts: understanding, appreciation, reasoning, and communication.

Understanding corresponds to the notion of factual knowledge as it relates to the nature and procedures of the criminal justice system (the factual understanding of the proceedings, according to *Dusky*); for example, the awareness of the roles of various individuals in court, such as the defense attorney, as well as an understanding of the nature of one's charges and "guilty" or "not guilty" pleas.

Appreciation, related to the *Dusky* idea of rational understanding, is the ability to apply knowledge of the court system to one's own case and circumstances and is often compromised by the fixed delusions associated with serious psychiatric illness, or by developmental immaturity, which limits the capacity to think abstractly. For example, a defendant may understand the judge's role as an impartial arbiter, but believe her to be the devil, and thus biased or even intending harm.

Reasoning refers to logical information processing and decision-making, required, for example, when weighing the pros and cons of a plea agreement. Similarly, an adolescent's immature executive functioning capacities may lead him to believe that a plea of "not guilty" can only be entered when one has no participation in the offense.

Finally, *communication*, in Grisso's organizing scheme, related to the *Dusky* notion of assistance to counsel, is the capacity to act as an active participant in one's defense, able to receive information, express wants and needs clearly, and conform behavior to the decorum expected in the courtroom setting.

Importantly, the latter principle, assisting in one's defense, has underpinnings in *Drope v. Missouri* (1975). In this decision, the U.S. Supreme Court opined that the Missouri courts unsuccessfully considered evidence of Drope's incompetence, particularly the connection between his mental illness and the ways in which it compromised his competency (Polizzi & Draper, 2016).

To that end, deficits in each of these four areas, which lead to an incompetent to stand trial (IST) finding, have typically been associated with one or a combination of these three common causes: mental/psychiatric illness; developmental disability, most often intellectual disability (formerly known as mental retardation); and developmental immaturity (Grisso, 2014).

First, research indicates that *psychiatric illness* is typically associated with an IST finding. Specifically, Pirelli, Gottdiener, and Zapf (2011) found that psychotic disorder was the predominant diagnostic classification. Moreover, Hubbard, Zapf, and Ronan (2003), as cited in Roesch, Zapf, and Hart (2010), found that defendants who are found IST are "significantly more likely to be single, unemployed, charged with a minor offense, and diagnosed with a psychotic disorder (p. 37).

It is important to highlight jurisdictional differences in the psychiatric terms related to competency. As we previously noted, states have either wholly or partially adopted *Dusky* standards. As outlined within Reisner and Piel's (2018) article, the "psychiatric component in competence to stand trial evaluations may vary by jurisdiction both by legal term used and determination of threshold symptoms or disorders" (p. 88). The authors provide examples in the states of Alabama, Alaska, and Arizona to illustrate that the terminology used to define the "psychiatric component" varies from explicit to vague and generalizable. For example, while Arizona's competency law refers IST as a result of "a mental illness, defect, or disability," Alabama's law references the "mental condition of the defendant." This ambiguity can result in misinterpretation of the statute and have harmful consequences for the defendant (p. 88).

Second, defendants diagnosed with an *intellectual disability* can present with procedural incompetence. It is important to highlight that defendants with intellectual disability comprise 40 percent of the adult defendants who are involved in criminal proceedings (Wall & Christopher, 2012), and as compared to the percentages of those with psychotic disorder (i.e. 45 to 65 percent), represent only a small number (i.e., 12 percent to 36 percent) of defendants deemed IST (Mossman et al., 2007). The initial case report by Kalbeitzer and Benedetti (2008) highlighted that the defendant's cognitive functioning, as measured with the Full Scale IQ, does not in and of itself qualify a defendant as incompetent; instead, the true underpinnings of incompetence in defendants with intellectual disability can lie in their impairments in communication, social judgment, conceptualization, decision-making, and problem solving.

Third, *developmental immaturity* relates to a juvenile's ability to possess procedural competence. As noted in Kruh and Grisso (2009), the developing brain of adolescents in and of itself can result in IST, absent a serious mental illness. Empirical findings in the field of cognitive neuroscience indicate significant changes in both the structure and function of the brain during the adolescent period (i.e., roughly ages 11 through 18 to 21). These changes involve both the prefrontal cortex, involved in impulse control, decision-making, and problem solving, as well as aspects of the limbic system, associated with emotionality and risk/reward contingencies. Early adolescence is characterized by an increased prioritization of risk over reward, while the systems governing inhibition of impulses are fully developed much later, likely in the mid-third decade of life. Given the tendency of adolescents toward immediate rewards, they are more likely to have impairments in modulating impulses, strategic planning, problem solving, and anticipating future consequences. To that end, the physiologically underdeveloped brain, in concert with lacking psychological capacities, frequently results in an IST finding in juveniles.

Evaluating Incompetency to Stand Trial in Older Adults

Unfortunately, much less attention has been paid to cognitive impairment as a functional impediment to competence to stand trial in older adults. This is particularly concerning, since statistics show that the number of older adults in the criminal justice system has been steadily increasing. For example, according to data collected by the Bureau of Justice Statistics (BJS, 2016), the number of individuals aged 55 or older sentenced to more than one year in state prison increased 400 percent between 1993 and 2013, from 26,300 (3 percent of the total state prison population) in 1993 to 131,500 (10 percent of the total population) in 2013. This increase likely reflects many factors, chief of which are harsher sentencing laws resulting in longer prison terms. Regardless of the reason, however, the presence of an increasing number of older adults at all levels of the criminal justice system, in concert with an aging population (i.e., approximately one in five individuals will be over the age of 65 by 2030; Center for Disease Control, 2003), will likely result in a greater need for competency evaluations of older adults, a not insubstantial number of whom may present with impairment in cognitive functioning.

The topic of cognitive impairment in the geriatric population is complex, as the reasoning, thinking, and perceptual abilities of older adults are particularly vulnerable to small changes in physiological variables. For example, delirium (an acute onset condition characterized by significant fluctuations in attention, awareness, orientation, and psychomotor behavior) following a urinary tract infection is much more common in older adults than it is in younger adults or children. Further, depression in older adults is less likely to manifest in sadness or mood instability; depressed older adults more often present with physical and cognitive symptoms such as sleep difficulties and forgetfulness. As such, for the purposes of CST evaluations in this population, it is important for the forensic mental health professional to be aware of and to investigate reversible causes of cognitive impairment leading to IST in older adults, which includes systemic infections and depression, but also other medical conditions such as liver or kidney disease, diabetes, vitamin deficiencies, cardiac conditions, and thyroid abnormalities, as well as potential side effects from medications.

The most common cause of irreversible cognitive impairment in older adults, however, remains dementia. The dementias are a family of conditions that reflect abnormal brain functioning and are progressive and degenerative in nature. They have an insidious onset and involve a gradual progression of impairment in cognitive domains such as memory, language, attention, mental processing speed, visuospatial functioning, and executive functioning. Alzheimer's disease is the most common type of dementia, and according to the Alzheimer's Association, accounts for approximately 60 percent to 80 percent of all dementias (Alzheimer's Association, 2021a). Alzheimer's disease is initially characterized by anterograde amnesia, in which the individual loses the ability to form new memories; long-term memory remains intact in Alzheimer's until the late stages of the disease. The neuropathology of Alzheimer's is characterized by twisted, insoluble protein fibers found within brain cells (neurofibrillary tangles), as well as extracellular neuritic plaques composed of dying cells and beta-amyloid protein (Cullum & Liff, 2014).

Vascular dementia, which is caused by blood vessel disease (e.g., occlusion of vessels leading to inadequate blood flow) and/or hemorrhagic lesions in the brain, is the second most common cause of dementia. Early symptoms of vascular dementia include deficits in attention, processing speed, and motor functions. Frontotemporal dementia, Lewy body dementia, and dementias associated with Parkinson's disease and Huntington's disease are less common types of dementia, together making up about 5 percent to 10 percent of all cases (Alzheimer's Association, 2021b). Dementias can vary in neuropathology and type and onset of cognitive symptoms; for example, socially inappropriate behavior, loss of manners, and impulsivity are often early signs of frontotemporal dementias (Bush, 2014). In mixed dementia, the neuropathological changes of more than one type of dementia occur simultaneously. The most common type of mixed dementia combines the neurofibrillary tangles and neuritic plaques seen in Alzheimer's with the blood vessel changes associated with vascular dementia.

The primary risk factor for Alzheimer's, and all dementias, is age. Approximately 5 percent of individuals over the age of 65 have symptoms consistent with Alzheimer's disease, and prevalence rates double every four to five years, such that it is estimated that between 25 percent and 50 percent of people over the age of 85 meet criteria for the disease (Cullum & Liff, 2014). Currently, more than six million Americans live with

Alzheimer's, and that number is expected to reach nearly 13 million by 2050 (Alzheimer's Association, 2021c). One in three older adults will die from complications related to the disease or another dementia (e.g., aspiration, pneumonia, cardiovascular failure, etc.), more than the number of deaths resulting from breast and prostate cancer combined (Alzheimer's Association, 2021). There is no cure for Alzheimer's, or dementias more generally, and it is a diagnosis of exclusion, since the neuropathology of Alzheimer's, as described earlier, can only be confirmed on autopsy. In 2013, the *Diagnostic and Statistical Manual of Mental Disorders (DSM-5)*, the primary classification scheme for psychological and psychiatric conditions, renamed the dementias as neurocognitive disorders, which can, dependent upon the number of cognitive domains affected, be labeled "mild" or "major" (American Psychiatric Association, 2013).

In 10 percent to 15 percent of adults over the age of 65, Alzheimer's is preceded by mild cognitive impairment (MCI), a less severe condition. In the most common type of MCI, Amnestic MCI, Single Domain, documented focal memory deficits based upon formal neuropsychological evaluation exist alongside memory complaints reported by the individual (or often someone close to the patient, such as a spouse), but testing does not reveal gross deficits in any other cognitive domain, and activities of daily living (e.g., banking, driving, food preparation) remain intact (Cullum & Liff, 2014). The course of Alzheimer's typically occurs over a 5- to 15-year timespan, with a mean duration of illness being seven years. In Stage 1 (one to three years) the individual can function relatively independently in familiar surroundings yet experiences impairments in initiative, recent memory, and learning. Stage 2 (two to ten years) is characterized by rapid forgetting, word-finding challenges, slower speech patterns, topographical disorientation, mood changes (e.g., irritability, agitation secondary to forgetfulness), and difficulty with more complex tasks, such as bill payment. In Stage 3, cognitive impairment becomes profound and more global, with individuals at this stage often needing 24-hour supervision and care. At this stage, associated behavioral and psychological symptoms of dementia may emerge, such as sleep disturbances, hallucinations, and wandering at night (Cullum & Liff, 2014). Understanding the phenomenon of MCI, the staging of Alzheimer's, and its course is likely to be important when considering the functional deficits of an individual undergoing a CST evaluation. (*See* Chapter 1, What Is Dementia?)

Research on the relationship between dementia and IST is sparse, as the bulk of the competence to stand trial literature has focused on IST due to serious psychiatric illness. Heinik et al. (1994) examined 57 criminal defendants over the age of 60 who were evaluated for CST. Among those, 50 percent were deemed IST; 30 percent were diagnosed with dementia, 25 percent were diagnosed with psychosis, and 28 percent were diagnosed with a personality disorder. Frierson et al. (2002) also examined 57 consecutive pretrial older adults who underwent CST evaluations (21 were found IST and 36 were found CST). In their study, the researchers found that those deemed IST tended to be older and more likely to be diagnosed with dementia. IST was associated with deficits in orientation, memory, abstraction, concentration, calculation, and thought processes. The trial-related deficits most associated with IST opinions were failure to understand *Miranda* warnings, legal charges, potential penalties, roles of court officers, pleas, plea bargaining, and the inability to consult with an attorney and demonstrate self-protective behavior. Interestingly, the ability to maintain appropriate behavior in the courtroom did not distinguish between the two groups.

Miller (2020) conducted a case law review of CST spanning the years 2002 through mid-2019 in the United States where dementia was an issue. She examined 90 cases almost equally distributed across federal and state jurisdictions. While information about age was limited, the age of the average defendant at the time of evaluation was 69.30 years. Miller found that the defense was most likely to raise the issue of competency, and that 69 percent of the defendants underwent one or two competency evaluations. When defendants had one expert evaluation, the courts agreed with competency recommendations most of the time (i.e., 86 percent). However, when there were two separate expert evaluations, agreement regarding diagnosis and competency recommendations declined significantly (55 percent for diagnosis and 45 percent for competency recommendations), and in cases of disagreement, the judges tended to side with the prosecution and court-appointed experts.

Miller also found that when a diagnosis of dementia was accepted by the courts, 67 percent of the individuals charged with a crime were deemed to be incompetent (much higher than the rate seen in CST cases not involving older defendants). Courts tended to rely upon clinical descriptions in order to make determinations of competency, however, such descriptions typically occurred only when multiple evaluations were performed. Further, the diagnosis most often rendered was dementia not otherwise specified (NOS), which tended to obscure an understanding of the causes and the specific impairments underlying an IST finding. In addition to the expected finding of the positive relationship between age and IST, Miller's data also showed a link between high levels of education and an IST determination. As she noted, higher levels of education are likely to make salient the significant decline from a baseline and expected level of functioning. Personal, statutory, and violent crimes were more likely to result in an IST finding (versus financial and drug-related crimes). Finally, in 15 percent of the cases, a determination of malingering was made, which Miller interpreted as highlighting the need for the inclusion of performance validity testing in CST evaluations.

Given the available research, we propose a multi-pronged approach for the evaluation of CST in older adults for which the question of cognitive impairment has been raised. First, a team approach of specialists is required, all of whom should have the training and clinical expertise necessary to work effectively with older adults. Although a dementia diagnosis can only be definitive upon autopsy, according to Cullum and Liff (2014), a clinical diagnosis is correct about 85 to 90 percent of the time when a comprehensive evaluation has been conducted. (See Chapter 2, Competency.)

An exciting new area of research in Alzheimer's disease has been the development of early pathological biomarkers for the disease that identify brain abnormalities prior to the onset of significant clinical symptoms; for example, there have been some studies that have effectively utilized positron emission topography (PET) to image amyloid deposits, though this work is still in its infancy (Sperling et al., 2011). Cullum and Liff (2014) recommend that a comprehensive evaluation include cranial magnetic resonance imaging (MRI), neurologic examination, biomarker/blood chemistry studies, a careful clinical history, and neuropsychological evaluation.

A clinical history is critical in characterizing the onset and type of symptoms experienced in order to document the magnitude of the decline from a previous level of functioning, stage the disease, and assist in determining as closely as possible the dementia type. A geriatric psychiatrist may be a useful clinical adjunct to the evaluation process, particularly as a psychiatrist may be able to determine the presence of any co-occurring mood, anxiety, thought, or personality disorders, whether as primary conditions or as secondary behavioral and psychological signs and symptoms of dementia.

In addition, a thorough medical evaluation should focus on ruling out reversible and treatable causes of cognitive impairment (e.g., hormonal imbalances, systemic infections), as described earlier in this chapter. In their paper on restoration of CST in the geriatric population, Heck and Herrick (2007) presented two hybrid case studies of older adult clients. In one case, that of 73-year-old Mr. A, arrested after a four-hour standoff with the police, a thorough medical evaluation conducted by his internist and psychiatrist concluded that he was medically stable and free from chronic illnesses. Yet his social isolation and deteriorated self-care (e.g., sometimes wearing clothes soaked in urine or feces for days), which had declined over a period of five to six years, suggested dementia. This was confirmed by neuropsychological testing that revealed significant impairments in short-term memory encoding, executive functioning, and visuospatial skills. Mr. A was diagnosed with dementia and found "unrestorably incompetent to stand trial" by his psychiatrist, based on the delineation of a degenerative cognitive process. The judge agreed and the charges were *nolle prossed*.

In the second case study, Mr. B, a 69-year-old mostly wheelchair-bound man, was charged with felony assault of a roommate whom he was accused of striking several times with a broken-off piece of his wheelchair, eventually causing the other man to suffer a fatal subdural hematoma. He presented to the local jail with consistent problematic behaviors that included pacing in his cell, refusing food, sleeping minimally, periodic lethargy, physical aggressiveness, tangential speech, and alternations between alert and drowsy states. Mr. B was initially diagnosed with Alzheimer's and prescribed medication designed to slow the dementing process by a physician unfamiliar with his history. However, during an admission to a geriatric psychiatric facility, unusual lab values pointed toward a urinary tract infection causing delirium. After several weeks of treatment for the infection, Mr. B was determined to have returned to his cognitive baseline. A subsequent evaluation by his attending psychologist revealed that he was CST. The cases of Mr. A and Mr. B highlight the complex nature of cognitive impairment in older adults and emphasize the need for a thorough evaluation of differential diagnoses, particularly as an incorrect diagnosis can have serious repercussions in the criminal justice context.

While it is critical to identify treatable causes of dementia in older adults facing the criminal justice system, the literature indicates that reversible dementias comprise less than 10 percent of all neurodegenerative conditions (Demakis, 2018). Obtaining a thorough description of clinical symptoms will assist the forensic mental health professional in elucidating the relationship between symptomatology and functional deficits in legal competency standards. Clarity of the clinical profile is also important in that Miller's research (2020) suggests that judges tend to base their competency determinations largely on these descriptions. As such, it will be important to include a neuropsychologist as part of the CST evaluation team. A comprehensive neuropsychological evaluation is not only necessary to investigate and confirm reported clinical symptoms, but also to establish a cognitive baseline in the form of objective testing results. Given the degenerative nature of dementias, multiple evaluations may also be necessary to track the disease as it progresses.

Depending on the timeline of the CST evaluation, the availability of several neuropsychological evaluations over time (e.g., six months, a year) may be another useful tool for the forensic mental health professional in differentiating dementia from other factors impacting competence as well as a means of highlighting the dynamic nature of competency in this population. Further, given the much higher probability of secondary gain present in all forensically based evaluations, a neuropsychological evaluation should incorporate multiple measures of performance validity in order to rule out dissimulation.

Once the forensic mental health professional has gathered the information just described, the competence to trial evaluation itself should be guided as much as possible by the five objectives outlined by Grisso (2014), namely, the functional, causal, interactive, conclusory, and dispositional. For example, a symptom profile of prominent deficits in recent memory, as associated with Alzheimer's, is likely to cause functional impairment in a defendant's ability to recall important facts of the case. Additionally, the functional impairment may negatively impact the ongoing communication with his/her attorney necessary to track the case as it progresses and make decisions along the way. Deficits in reasoning and abstract thought, present in all dementias, and particularly after two or three years of symptom onset, are highly likely to impair a defendant's ability to appreciate and apply a factual understanding of the case to his/her own situation and to engage in complex decision-making, for example, regarding plea agreements.

Causes of dementia can be difficult to determine, particularly in the case of mixed dementias in addition to the current limitations in precise visualization of neuropathology. However, excluding other causes of cognitive impairment will likely strengthen the connection between the symptoms and functional impairment in the abilities necessary for legal competence. The forensic mental health professional should pay particular attention to the ways in which cognitive impairment due to dementia impact the defendant's functional abilities given the specific demands of the defendant's case. For example, the progressive nature of dementia may mean that the defendant's CST status will fluctuate over the course of a lengthy pre-trial process, or that a particularly complex case will present a greater challenge to the cognitively impaired older adult than a relatively straightforward one.

Competency Remediation in Specialized Populations

Defendants diagnosed with mental/psychiatric illness and/or a developmental disability, and who are developmentally immature represent a specialized population of individuals who will likely have impairments in understanding the court processes and participants.

Prior to a formal discussion regarding competency services within these specialized populations, it is important to note the differences between the terms "competency restoration" and "competency remediation." Most research related to competency applies the term "restoration" to describe the services afforded to a defendant to aid them in learning about the court participants and processes. As described by Kruh and Grisso (2009), the term "restoration" is inappropriate as it implies that the defendant possessed the core competency and functional skills of understanding, appreciation, reasoning, and communication prior to the instant offense. In fact, research has consistently demonstrated that defendants within specialized populations have deficits in one or more of the key competency and functioning areas, and that competency services are used to remediate or teach key skills. Although jurisdictions vary on their use of the term "restoration," we prefer the term "competency remediation" instead of "competency restoration," and will use the former term within our discussion.

First, defendants with psychiatric illness vary; thus for the purposes of this chapter we will focus on competency restoration with individuals with serious mental illnesses such as psychotic disorders. According to 2021 research, over 50,000 individuals are referred for competency evaluations in the United States per year, and a majority of those found incompetent are diagnosed with a psychotic disorder (Cochrane, Laxton, Mulay, & Herbel, 2021).

Research has consistently found that defendants with psychotic disorders were more likely to be found incompetent due to pronounced neuropsychiatric deficits such as impairments in problem-solving, abstract thinking, memory, and orientation (Schwalbe & Medalia, 2007). For example, Pirelli, Gottdiener, and Zapf's (2011) meta-analysis found that defendants diagnosed with psychotic disorder were "eight times more likely to be found incompetent than defendants without a psychotic disorder diagnosis." Concomitantly, incompetence and remediation within this population has been impacted on the dynamic interplay of psychotic symptoms, neuropsychiatric deficits, and socioeconomic status, employment, education, and elevated numbers of psychiatric hospitalizations (Danzer, Wheeler, Alexander & Wasser, 2019; Pirelli, Gottdiener, & Zapf, 2011; Schwalbe & Medalia, 2007; Zapt & Roesch, 2011).

A judicial decision of incompetence likely results in psychiatric hospitalization for the psychotic individual. As noted by Melton et al. (2018), although the U.S. Supreme Court case of *Jackson v. Indiana*, 406 U.S. 715 (1972) limits a defendant's commitment to a psychiatric hospital to "a reasonable period of time necessary," efforts to remediate the individual are predicated on the state's interpretation of the decision.

According to Cochrane et al. (2021), most defendants are able to proceed within six months with the use of a psychotropic medication regimen. Prior to administration of the regimen, the authors note that the psychotropic medication must be deemed psychiatrically and medically efficacious; have minimal impact on cognitive functioning such as problem-solving, reasoning, and memory, which could impact assisting in one's defense; and "no alternative, less intrusive treatment" exists

(p. 1202). Overall, research has found that the administration of psychotropic medications, specifically antipsychotics, have resulted in competency restoration/remediation.

Second, across decades, defendants with intellectual disability have been noted as particularly vulnerable to the legal system. The U.S. Supreme Court decision in *Atkins v. Virginia*, 536 U.S. 304 (2002), as cited in Melton et al. (2018), not only discussed the "diminished capacities" of this special population but also aimed to ban execution of a defendant with such diagnosis. Their cognitive limitations in problem solving, abstraction, memory, and judgment may result in a judicial determination of incompetence. Warren et al. (2006) found that defendants diagnosed with an intellectual disability were more than three times more likely to be found incompetent and were more likely to display impairments in both the rational and factual components of the *Dusky* standard. It is noted that admission to a psychiatric hospital is likely to gain restoration/remediation; however, research indicates that the hospital setting is "unfit to meet their unique treatment needs" (Wood et al., 2019, p. 3).

Efforts at remediation in defendants with an intellectual disability are often stymied, as "group psychoeducation is likely to require cognitive skills beyond those of the typical individual with ID" (Wood et al., 2019, p. 3), and administration of psychotropic medications may be unethical or inefficacious. Resultantly, research has found that use of instruction tailored at improving the defendants' literacy, comprehension, and memory have been helpful in remediation. Moreover, the Slater method, as defined by Wall and Christopher (2012), is an individualized, module-based training program that can be delivered inpatient or in the community. Designated case managers, psychologists, or social workers present the defendant with training on "purpose of training and review of charges, pleas, and potential consequences; courtroom personnel; courtroom proceedings, trial and plea bargaining; communicating with the attorney, giving testimony, and assisting in the defense; and tolerating the stress of proceedings" (p. 368). Defendants are evaluated on a bi-yearly basis with the option of continued training up to two years. Wall and Christopher (2012) found that the application of the Slater method resulted in a notable increase in remediation versus those without the treatment (61.1 percent versus 16.7 percent).

Finally, developmental immaturity as seen in juvenile offenders notably impacts competency. Similar to defendants with an intellectual disability, there is exhaustive research in the area of juveniles and competency to proceed. And this research has been spearheaded by Grisso, who opined that the term "competency remediation" is most clinically appropriate for this specialized population given their developmental immaturity (Kruh & Grisso, 2009, p. 12).

Research has found that juveniles who are diagnosed with neurodevelopmental disorders, including an intellectual disability, and/or major mental health disorders are likely to be found incompetent to proceed (Stepanyan, Sidhu, & Bath, 2016). Although research has demonstrated that most juveniles can attain competency, a singular factor, age, appears to predicate competency in juveniles (Grisso, et al., 2003). Importantly, Warren et al. (2019) found that competency remediation was more successful in juveniles who were ages 14 to 16, as compared to those between the ages of 8 and 10 (i.e., 44 percent versus 7 percent). Moreover, 50 percent of juveniles diagnosed with only with an intellectual disability, 44 percent diagnosed with a mental illness and an intellectual disability, 13.5 percent of those diagnosed with a mental illness and borderline intellectual functioning, and 7 percent with only mental illness were found incompetent and unrestorable.

Competency Restoration in Older Adults

Finally, the forensic mental health professional offering a conclusory opinion of IST (or following a court determination of IST) will need to provide the court specific dispositional information related to the likelihood of competence restoration. It should be stated at the outset that there is scant data related to CST restoration in older adults with dementia. Morris and Parker (2009) did not find a relationship between competency restoration and dementia subtype. However, their research was limited by the relatively small size of the sample; lack of indicators of dementia severity for specific subtypes, such as Alzheimer's; and lack of diagnostic specificity generally (i.e., diagnoses of dementia not otherwise specified). In addition, the procedures for competency restoration were not described in detail. The authors did note that more than half of older adults in their sample were successfully restored to competence. These findings emphasize the point that the diagnosis of dementia in and of itself does not preclude competency restoration (Demakis, 2018).

Although there is not yet adequate research to support these hypotheses, individuals with mild cognitive impairment and/or who are in the early stages of dementia, when activities of daily living are generally unimpaired and functional independence remains intact, are the most likely to be amenable to restoration. Such individuals may benefit from a cognitive remediation program, such as the Neuropsychological Educational Approach to Remediation (NEAR) as described by Medalia and Freilich (2009). Originally designed as a group treatment approach for patients with severe psychiatric illness, such as schizophrenia and bipolar disorder, NEAR has been modified and individualized to address cognitive impairment in Alzheimer's. The program is behaviorally based and applies concepts from learning theory (e.g., errorless learning procedures in which difficulty level is carefully titrated) to promote task engagement and remediate critical executive functioning skills such as attention, memory, and problem solving. Cognitive remediation programs such as NEAR may thus be useful in addressing some of the underlying neurological impediments that lead to the functional deficits in legal competency in older adults with less severe forms of cognitive impairment.

There are also several FDA-approved medications (e.g., donepezil, rivastigmine, galantamine) that slow the rate of cognitive decline in individuals with Alzheimer's and can be given in early and moderate stages of the disease. In some patients, the delay in cognitive deterioration can be as much as 12 to 18 months (Cullum & Liff, 2014). Nevertheless, these medications vary in their efficacy across patients, and there is no way to know which patients will have a positive response.

When competency restoration is not possible, dispositional decisions related to IST older adults are likely to be complex. As noted by Frierson et al. (2002), once an older adult is found IST, there are few appropriate resources available from a health care standpoint. For example, inpatient psychiatric facilities are unlikely to be equipped to provide appropriate treatment to an individual with a degenerative brain disorder, boarding homes may not be able to provide the high levels of supervision plus clinical services needed for these clients, and nursing homes may be hesitant to accept individuals with a history of serious legal charges. All of these factors highlight the critical need for research into the area of criminal competencies of older adults with dementia, especially as the population of the United States continues to age.

• • •

Dr. LaFaye F. Marshall is a nationally credentialed psychologist, licensed in Maryland, Washington, D.C., Virginia, and Pennsylvania. She is also a Certified Sex Offender Treatment Provider. Dr. Marshall obtained a bachelor of arts degree in psychology from James Madison University; a master of arts degree in psychology from The Catholic University of America in Washington, D.C.; and a doctoral degree in clinical psychology from Argosy University in Washington, D.C. Dr. Marshall maintains a thriving private practice, Dr. LaFaye Marshall & Associates, LLC, with offices in Maryland and Pennsylvania. Her clinical and research interests include the neurobiological underpinnings of psychopathy, forensic evaluations, and threat assessment. Concomitant with her clinical experiences, Dr. Marshall has served on the faculty at Marymount and Loyola University, lecturing on topics related to psychopathology and forensic assessment. Currently, she supervises doctoral students at the Loyola University Clinical Centers in Baltimore, Maryland. Dr. Marshall is a Clinical Member of the Association for the Treatment of Sexual Abusers (ATSA) and holds memberships with the Association of Threat Assessment Professionals (ATAP) and the Society for Personality Assessment (SPA). Finally, one of Dr. Marshall's most valued accomplishments is the recognition of her business in the community. In 2016, she was awarded the Greater Baltimore Committee Bridging the Gap Award, which honors minority- and women-owned firms for their business achievements and efforts to strengthen minority business development. Dr. Marshall can be reached at drlfmarshall@gmail.com.

Dr. Joette James completed her doctoral degree in clinical psychology at Northwestern University in Chicago; her internship at Harvard Medical School/Boston Children's Hospital in Boston, Massachusetts; and a two-year postdoctoral fellowship in pediatric neuropsychology at Children's National Medical Center (CNMC) in Washington, D.C. After completing her postdoctoral fellowship, Dr. James was employed at CNMC as a staff neuropsychologist for seven years, where she participated in the training of graduate students, interns, and postdoctoral residents. During that time she also served as the chief neuropsychologist at HSC Pediatric Center, a sub-acute rehabilitation facility in Washington,

D.C., affiliated with CNMC. She held an appointment as an Assistant Professor in the Departments of Pediatrics and Psychiatry and Behavioral Sciences at George Washington University. Dr. James is board-certified in clinical neuropsychology by the American Board of Professional Psychology (ABPP) and currently serves on the DC Board of Psychology. Dr. James provides customized clinical assessments for individuals of all ages with neurodevelopmental disorders, including Autism Spectrum Disorders (ASD), Attention-Deficit/Hyperactivity Disorder (ADHD), learning disabilities, and Intellectual Disability, as well as for individuals with acquired injuries to the brain. She also maintains a forensic consultation and evaluation practice and has testified as an expert on the federal, state, and local levels on matters including death penalty litigation (*Atkins* cases), juvenile life without parole, competency to stand trial, juvenile waiver/transfer, and general mitigation.

Citations available from author(s) by request.

Chapter

4

Responsibility

Dr. Tianyi Zhang and Dr. Vivek Datta

The general concept of criminal responsibility is probably one of the most misunderstood concepts in the criminal justice system. Contrary to popular belief, an insanity defense is only mounted in a small number of cases, and, of them, only a small number are successful. Part of the reason that the insanity defense is seldom successful may be that the legal definition of insanity does not have a precise medical counterpart. Indeed, the legal definitions are narrow and vary from jurisdiction to jurisdiction. At the same time, the term "insanity" was devised to accommodate criminal defendants who manifest various forms of psychosis and, thus, seems inappropriate for someone with dementia.

This chapter by Dr. Tianyi Zhang and Dr. Vivek Datta explores the intersection between criminal responsibility and dementia. They review the major standards of insanity—McNaughten, Irresistible Impulse, and Model Penal Code—plus Diminished Capacity and Partial Responsibility and analyze how each may or may not accommodate someone with dementia. They conclude that the "Model Penal Code test provides the broadest formulation of legal insanity, and individuals with dementia can more reasonably attempt to claim insanity under this test."

• • •

The concept of criminal responsibility was primarily devised with criminal defendants with psychosis in mind. While psychosis often occurs in the setting of dementia, defendants with dementia are different from those with primary psychiatric disorders such as schizophrenia and bipolar disorder. By definition, dementia is associated with impairment in at least one domain of cognition (e.g., memory, language, executive function, etc.) severe enough to lead to functional impairment. As such, many defendants with dementia who might otherwise be found not criminally responsible, would be adjudicated incompetent to stand trial. Additionally, dementia is frequently, but not always, associated with continued deterioration in functioning. Legal tests of insanity have not kept up with our neuroscientific understanding of dementia as it relates to criminal responsibility. Dementia can impair one's ability to form a culpable mental state and impair a defendant's ability to conform their behavior to the requirements of the law, both of which are relevant to criminal responsibility. However, it is only when the cognitive deficits in dementia are not severe enough to impair competency to stand trial, that criminal responsibility would be relevant. Typically, this would include cases of what is called *mild cognitive impairment, mild behavioral impairment, and mild neurocognitive disorder.*

In mild cognitive impairment (MCI), there is a decline in cognitive function that is not severe enough to impact daily functioning. Mild behavioral impairment is a novel construct that refers to new onset neuropsychiatric symptoms of late life that are suspected to be the harbinger of dementia that occurs in advance or in concert with MCI. Mild neurocognitive disorder is similar to MCI, but is a DSM-5 diagnosis that refers to modest decline in one or more domains in cognitive functioning that could be due to any cause (e.g., vascular, brain injury, Alzheimer's) except for delirium or a primary psychiatric disorder (e.g., schizophrenia, depression). In general, if a defendant is adjudicated not criminally responsible rather than incompetent to stand trial, they will meet criteria for one of these three constructs rather than major neurocognitive disorder (i.e., cognitive decline that substantially impairs functioning).

When to Consider a Neurocognitive Disorder as Impacting Criminal Responsibility:

- New onset psychiatric symptoms first beginning after 50 should raise the suspicion of an underlying neurocognitive disorder or other medical condition as the cause.

- Certain delusional syndromes are more commonly associated with dementia. In Capgras syndrome, the person believes that one or more people have been replaced by an imposter, which can lead to violent behavior toward the imagined imposter. In De Clerambault syndrome, the individual person believes they are romantically involved with someone of higher status such as a celebrity or physician. This leads to stalking behaviors and sometimes violence. In Othello syndrome (morbid jealousy), which occurs in vascular dementia and Alzheimer's disease, the person believes their partner is having an affair, which can lead to violence against the spouse or imagined lover. In delusional parasitosis, the person believes they are infested with bugs or parasites, which may lead to property damage or harm to those believed to have caused the outbreak. Those with dementia are more likely to misplace things and develop delusions that others are stealing from them, which can lead to harm against the perceived abusers.
- Disinhibition, apparent callousness, and loss of sympathy and empathy to others are hallmarks of behavioral variant frontotemporal dementia. This can lead those afflicted to transgress social norms, including indecent exposure, shoplifting, downloading child pornography, or engaging in white collar crime such as fraud or embezzlement.
- Abnormal movements of a writhing, twisting or squirming nature (choreoathetosis) may indicate Huntington's disease, a rare inherited dementia that can begin early in life and is often associated with violence and aggression and in some cases fire-setting.
- Mania can occur in dementia, particularly in those with cerebrovascular disease, behavioral variant frontotemporal dementia, and the behavioral/dysexecutive variant of Alzheimer's disease. Characterized by elation, irritability, disinhibition, risk-taking, and grandiosity, mania can be associated with violence, sexual offending, and white-collar crime.

Expert Qualifications

A forensic neuropsychiatrist or forensic neuropsychologist would be most qualified to assess criminal responsibility in a defendant with suspected dementia. There are very few forensic neuropsychiatrists (i.e., those trained and certified in both forensic psychiatry and neuropsychiatry) and thus several evaluators of different backgrounds may be necessary, such as a behavioral neurologist and neuropsychologist, to confirm the specific type of dementia, and a forensic psychiatrist or psychologist to evaluate whether the defendant meets criteria for legal insanity in the jurisdiction in question. Geriatric psychiatrists and geriatric medicine physicians may also be appropriate to make a diagnosis of dementia in older defendants. In some cases, a neuroradiologist may also be required to opine on brain imaging findings. Brain imaging can be used to support a specific dementia diagnosis (e.g., Alzheimer's disease, vascular dementia, frontotemporal dementia) but cannot itself assess mental state at the time of the offense. (*See* Chapter 6, Neuroimaging, and Chapter 12, Working with the Expert.)

Legal Standards for Insanity

The ongoing availability of an insanity defense in most jurisdictions in the United States reflects enduring concepts around fairness and punishment. At the present moment, the federal system and all but four states (Utah, Montana, Idaho, Kansas) allow criminal defendants to invoke an insanity defense.

The *M'Naghten* rule, established in England in reaction to the acquittal of Daniel M'Naghten of murder charges in 1843, or versions of the rule, form the foundation of the insanity defense standards in around half of the states and the federal government. The standard for insanity formulated by the *M'Naghten* rule requires "that at the time of the committing of the act, the party accused was laboring under such a defect of reason, from disease of the mind, as not to know the nature and quality of the act he was doing; or if he did know it, that he did not know he was doing what was wrong." This standard's sole focus on "knowing" emphasizes the individual's cognitive functioning.

Four states use the irresistible impulse test in addition to the *M'Naghten* rule. Under this test, the defendant may meet the standard for insanity if they acted from an irresistible and uncontrollable impulse due to a mental disorder at the time of the offense (Packer, 2009). The irresistible impulse test takes the individual's ability to maintain volitional control into account, although the concept of an impulse that cannot be resisted has been controversial and difficult to define.

Currently, another 21 states use versions of the standard of insanity formulated by the American Law Institute in 1962 in its Model Penal Code. The Model Penal Code test contains both cognitive and volitional prongs to establish insanity. By this standard, a defendant raising a claim of insanity must show that "as a result of mental disease or mental defect he lacks substantial capacity either to appreciate the criminality of his conduct or to conform his conduct to the requirements of the law" (American Law Institute, 1962).

Dementia and Cognitive Tests for Insanity

The intersection of criminal responsibility and dementia is not well studied. Most policies, research, and case law around criminal responsibility and mental illness focus on psychotic disorders, while overlooking the complex questions around culpability that may arise for individuals with dementia. Historically, dementia has been infrequently represented as a threshold condition for the insanity defense. Psychotic disorders are the most common threshold condition among persons found not guilty by reason of insanity (Callahan et al., 1991; Warren et al., 2004). Also, individuals who had been diagnosed with a psychotic disorder were the most likely to be found not guilty by reason of insanity (Cochrane, Grisso, & Frederick, 2001).

Many cognitive and neuropsychiatric manifestations of dementia could potentially impair a person's ability to know or appreciate the nature and wrongfulness of their actions. Of the various symptoms of dementia, psychotic symptoms such as delusions and hallucinations would likely have the most straightforward application to cognitive tests for insanity. Extensive prior research and case law have explored the relationship between a person's psychotic symptoms, albeit in the context of a psychotic or affective disorder rather than dementia, and their ability to meet the standard for insanity set forth in the cognitive prong (Heck & Vaulter, 2018).

Delusions and other psychotic symptoms commonly appear in various neurocognitive disorders including Alzheimer's disease, Parkinson's disease dementia, dementia with Lewy bodies, and vascular dementia (Cipriani et al., 2014). The delusional beliefs most commonly described in people with dementia have a paranoid or persecutory nature, such as believing that other people are trying to steal their property or mean to cause them bodily harm; these types of delusions have been associated with episodes of physical aggression (Cipirani et al., 2014; Deutsch et al., 1991). Co-occurring symptoms of dementia may contribute to the persistence and intensity of delusional beliefs. For example, increased cognitive rigidity, loss of abstract reasoning, and impairments in working memory may make it more difficult for an individual with delusions to hold and manipulate information that supplies evidence to the contrary.

Many adult defendants, as the result of their significant cognitive impairments in the later stages of dementia, would be considered insane by the *M'Naghten* rule. Individuals with late-stage symptoms of dementia can experience confusion and decreased attentional capacity that can lead to aggression and other behavioral disturbances while rendering them unable to notice and remain aware of their behavior. Individuals with impaired autobiographical memory may forget social norms and laws and engage in behaviors they did not recognize were socially inappropriate or criminal. The preceding examples describe adults with severe, global impairments to the extent that they would also likely be found incompetent to stand trial.

Challenges with Insanity Standards that Only Provide a Cognitive Test

Defendants with dementia in jurisdictions that only provide a cognitive test for establishing insanity face a number of challenges. Some individuals with dementia begin exhibiting socially inappropriate and criminal behaviors while they are in the early stages of their illness and therefore may not appear impaired enough to meet the standard for insanity. A study of patients with dementia who demonstrated physical aggression found that around one-third of patients with vascular or mixed dementia, one-half of the patients with frontotemporal dementia, and one-fifth of the patients with Alzheimer's disease exhibited aggression during the first half of their disease duration (Liljegren, Waldo, & Englund, 2018).

Criminal or socially inappropriate behaviors can be the first manifestation of dementia for many people. One study of individuals with frontotemporal dementia found that 46.2 percent demonstrated behavioral disinhibition and 21.1 percent demonstrated social awkwardness as their first symptom (Lindau et al., 2000). Another study found that 17 percent of patients with Huntington's disease and 14 percent of patients with behavioral variant frontotemporal dementia initially presented with behaviors that could be interpreted as criminal, such as sexual advances, theft, and public urination (Liljegren et al., 2015). Many individuals have relatively preserved cognitive functioning in the prodromal and early stages of dementia and likely would not be considered insane under the *M'Naghten* test.

Defendants with behavioral variant frontotemporal dementia are particularly vulnerable in jurisdictions allowing only for a cognitive prong in their insanity standard. Some people with early-stage behavioral variant frontotemporal dementia can demonstrate severe impairments in their decision-making and judgment, while performing normally on the classical battery of neuropsychological testing (Manes et al., 2011). One study found that patients with frontotemporal dementia were more likely than patients with Alzheimer's disease and normal controls to approve emotional moral violations when presented with moral dilemmas, yet they appeared to have a relatively preserved knowledge of moral values and ability to distinguish right from wrong (Mendez & Shapira, 2009).

Individuals with behavioral variant frontotemporal dementia, who demonstrated nonviolent criminal behaviors, have verbalized an understanding of the criminal nature of their behavior and continued to engage in the behavior (Liljegren et al., 2019). Other adults with frontotemporal dementia, who committed crimes of physical assault, sexual assault, stalking, and child molestation, expressed awareness that their behaviors were wrong and proceeded to act in an unempathetic and disinhibited manner (Mendez et al., 2005; Mendez, 2010). If they were to face criminal charges, they would not be able to use the insanity defense in many jurisdictions.

Dementia and Volitional Tests for Insanity

Structural abnormalities of the brain, particularly those in the frontal and temporal lobes, give rise to a number of symptoms that compromise a person's ability to control impulses or to act freely as a moral agent. Features of frontotemporal dementia and other neurodegenerative disorders involving these brain regions include loss of empathy and remorse, decreased inhibitory control, new compulsive behaviors, impairments in moral and social decision-making, and reward and punishment processing.

The following is an example of impulsive behavior in a person with frontotemporal dementia. A 60-year-old male with two years of personality changes demonstrates an increased appetite and a preference for breads, pastas, desserts, and candy. He starts eating the food off of his children's plates when they sit down for family meals. He develops a pattern of entering the grocery store, walking over to the candy aisle, reaching into the bins of sweets to grab and eat them, and then leaving without paying. When he walks by restaurants with outdoor dining, he grabs leftover food off of the tables and stuffs it into his mouth.

This man with pathological stealing of food would be unlikely to meet the standards for insanity in states that use the irresistible impulse test. The precise nature of the processes in frontotemporal dementia that lead to repeated, impulsive, and often socially inappropriate or criminal behaviors is not fully understood. However, recent literature has compared this feature of frontotemporal dementia to kleptomania and other impulse control disorders, substance use disorders, and obsessive-compulsive disorder (Mendez, 2011), which are generally not accepted as threshold conditions by the irresistible impulse test.

Although impulsivity is a common feature among individuals with dementia, it is unlikely that they would experience an impulse so strong that it could not be resisted. In fact, most manifestations of dementia would not produce an internal coercion strong enough to satisfy the irresistible impulse test. For example, delusions of jealously commonly occur among people with dementia with Lewy bodies, Alzheimer's disease, and vascular dementia and can increase their violence risk (Tsai et al., 1997; Hashimoto, Sakamoto, & Ikeda, 2015), but delusional jealousy would not qualify as an impulse that could not be resisted or controlled.

Many defendants with dementia may find that the Model Penal Code test has better application to their circumstances than the *M'Naghten* rule or the irresistible impulse test. For individuals with early-stage frontotemporal dementia, the volitional prong of the Model Penal Code, which focuses on the lack of substantial capacity to conform behavior to the requirements of the law, may be the only standard under which they could reasonably attempt to establish insanity. The Model Penal Code test does include language that specifically excludes the use of psychopathy

(American Law Institute, 1962), which shares many structural, functional, and behavioral similarities with behavioral variant frontotemporal dementia. However, there currently is no specific language that would exclude people with behavioral variant frontotemporal dementia from using the insanity defense.

The following is an example of a man with frontal lobe dysfunction who raised the insanity defense in a jurisdiction that uses the Model Penal Code test. Andrew Steele was a 39-year-old man living in Wisconsin, who had recently retired as the result of his amyotrophic lateral sclerosis. He was charged with two counts of first-degree intentional homicide after he killed his wife and sister-in-law and then attempted to kill himself. He pled not guilty by reason of mental disease. Prior to killing his wife and sister-in-law, he wrote a semi-incoherent suicide letter, describing a suicide pact between the three of them among other content. The forensic psychiatrist for the defense described the contents of his letter as delusional and consistent with deterioration in his brain. The defense argued that as a result of his amyotrophic lateral sclerosis, Mr. Steele experienced abnormalities in his hippocampus, causing poor impulse control, and in his frontal lobe, causing decreased inhibitory control and changes to his personality, which rendered him unable to conform his conduct to the requirements of the law (Hoag, 2015; Trevelen, 2015).

Mr. Steele was found not guilty by reason of mental disease. He passed away from breathing complications of his amyotrophic lateral sclerosis two years later (Trevelen, 2017). His verdict was controversial within his own community as well as in the legal and medical communities (Louis, 2015). The controversy is unsurprising, as Mr. Steele's verdict occurs at the intersection a number of current trends and challenges in criminal law, including general hostility toward the insanity defense, criticism of the volitional prong of the insanity defense, and ongoing efforts to understand and delineate the legal implications of dementia.

Diminished Capacity: *Mens Rea* Variant

Many jurisdictions permit a diminished capacity defense, or *mens rea* defense, for crimes that require specific intent. Defendants may use a diminished capacity defense to defend against the requisite mental element of the crime charged, which the prosecution must prove in order to convict; this may potentially result in the defendant's conviction on a lesser offense (Packer, 2009). Some defendants, who do not meet their jurisdiction's standards for insanity as a defense, may have experienced a mental impairment at the time of the offense that could arguably have prevented them from forming the required *mens rea* for an offense.

The following are representative examples of individuals with Alzheimer's disease, exhibiting behavior that could be considered criminal, who likely were not capable of forming the specific intent to commit the crimes.

- A 79-year-old woman was diagnosed with Alzheimer's disease two years ago. She recently has become more forgetful and left her house keys in the front door and left the stove on by accident a few times. She and her family felt that it would probably be fine for her to continue shopping on her own in the familiar environment of a nearby grocery store, where she has been a patron for over 30 years. One day, she went to the grocery store, filled her cart with over $300 worth of items, and calmly walked out the store door without paying.
- A 72-year-old woman was recently diagnosed with Alzheimer's disease. She decided to sell her house, where she had been living alone for the two decades, and move in with her daughter, who lives in a different neighborhood. During her first month of living with her daughter, she went on a walk to explore the neighborhood and became disoriented with her new surroundings. Several hours later, her daughter received a call from a disgruntled neighbor, who complained that her mother had just wandered into his backyard and then yelled at him when he asked her to leave.

Criminal behaviors demonstrated by persons with Alzheimer's disease typically involve nonviolent offenses such as shoplifting and trespassing, often inadvertently as the result of the forgetfulness and confusion that develop over the course of the dementia. Most of these incidents likely never come to legal attention. The families, communities, and health care providers supporting an individual with dementia will often problem solve to find a solution without involving the legal system.

However, there are instances in which neighbors and other affected individuals are not tolerant of these nonviolent criminal behaviors. For example, Nancy Daoust, a 58-year-old woman with frontotemporal dementia and a tendency to wander around her neighborhood, was cited for trespassing after her neighbor called law enforcement because she wandered onto his property, rang his doorbell, and then walked away (Low, 2019). More cases similar to Ms. Daoust's may be brought to legal attention in the future, as communities struggle to adjust to certain challenges of living alongside older adults with dementia and as the population of the United States continues to age.

Diminished Capacity: Partial Responsibility Variant

Partial responsibility is the more controversial variant of the diminished capacity defense. Certain forms of a partial responsibility excuse are allowed in a few jurisdictions where it is used as an affirmative defense in criminal homicide prosecutions. Defendants may claim that they were experiencing mental impairments, falling short of the standard for insanity, at the time of the offense and that they are therefore less culpable than someone who killed while in a normal state of mind. Partial responsibility defenses may be used to mitigate the offense from first-degree murder to second-degree murder or from murder to manslaughter (Dressler, 2005).

The doctrine of partial responsibility can be relevant to certain individuals with dementia, who may demonstrate physical aggression and, much more rarely, lethal violence. In adults with dementia, the onset of physical aggression may occur with the emergence of severe behavioral changes, as in the case of frontotemporal dementia. It may also occur as the result of cognitive impairments that make it difficult for people with dementia to accurately interpret their environments, as in the case of vascular dementia or Alzheimer's disease; among this population, the most common triggers for physical aggression are situations such as receiving intimate care that provoke feelings of being intruded upon, threatened, or frightened (Liljegren, Waldo, & Englund, 2018; Keene et al., 1999).

The following is an example of how reactive lethal violence might occur in someone living with dementia. Howard Darst, an 89-year-old man with Alzheimer's disease, was charged with beating his wife to death in August 1996. On the night of the incident, he and his wife slept in their living room to watch the closing ceremony of the summer Olympics rather than keep to their usual routine of sleeping in their bedroom. At some point during the night, Mr. Darst woke up in these unexpected surroundings and then beat his wife to death with a cane (Statement of Donna Cohen, PhD, 2004). The charges against Mr. Darst were ultimately dropped, as he likely was not competent to stand trial. However, his case illustrates how a partial responsibility defense might be relevant to a different individual with milder cognitive impairments, who remains competent to stand trial and had committed reactive lethal violence.

Criminal Responsibility and Parallels in Civil Law

The complex problems around criminal responsibility in adults with dementia have some parallels in the civil law system. One such example is the financial exploitation of older adults, which has important implications to both civil and criminal law. Between 3.5 percent and 20 percent of adults over the age of 65 have experienced some form of financial exploitation such as theft, scams, unauthorized use of their accounts, or coercion or deception into signing documents or engaging in transactions that are misrepresented as legitimate (Wood & Lichtenberg, 2017).

Older adults with dementia experience various impairments that can result in a loss of financial skills, weakening of financial judgment, vulnerability to undue influence, and inability to detect and protect themselves from financial exploitation. Declines in cognitive abilities including memory, arithmetic skills, language, and executive function have been associated with financial incapacity (Wood & Lichtenberg, 2017). Behavioral changes such as apathy, paranoia and suspiciousness toward formerly trusted loved ones, loss of judgment, and impulsivity can make people with dementia more susceptible to undue influence. As adults with dementia experience functional decline and lose their ability to perform the necessary activities of daily living, they may become increasingly dependent on family or caregivers, which further increases their vulnerability to undue influence.

Some older adults may be misled into becoming involved with the fraudulent scheme themselves. The following vignette describes one such example. A 69-year-old male with several years of memory loss, speech difficulties, errors in managing his personal finances, and new beliefs in conspiracy theories, who has never formally received a diagnosis of dementia, was charged with attempting to defraud a government official.

He had been a retired widower, who was living alone, when an acquaintance invited him to join a new business venture. He was excited to participate in this opportunity and eagerly invested a significant portion of his own savings into the new business. He attempted to recruit several of his neighbors and members of his church congregation into the business venture. When his friends and neighbors expressed their misgivings to him, he angrily defended his business partner, who he claimed was a completely trustworthy and reliable man.

Within the civil law system, increased awareness of financial exploitation of adults with dementia has resulted in problem-solving efforts to address this emerging problem. Civil court systems have trialed enhanced service provision, increased referrals for assessments of testamentary capacity and financial capacity, and guardianship as a last resort (Gassoumis, Navarro, & Wilber, 2015; Voskou et al., 2018). Just as the financial and testamentary capacity of older adults is questioned in the civil law system, similar questions around criminal responsibility should be raised for older adults who come into contact with the criminal justice system because of apparent participation in fraud. When working with older clients or clients with dementia facing fraud charges, attorneys should consider whether their client was aware of the fraud or if the client had been misled into participating or had only participated in the fraudulent scheme under undue influence.

Conclusion

Some defendants with dementia, particularly those experiencing psychosis or mania, could be found legally insane under the standards established by the *M'Naghten* rule and the ALI standard. Many more offenders would not be considered legally insane by any cognitive test of insanity. Individuals with frontotemporal dementia and early-stage dementias often have relatively preserved cognitive functions and understanding of social mores and laws yet engage in criminal behaviors after experiencing changes in personality, judgment, decision-making capabilities, and impulsivity. As the impulses featured in dementia typically fall short of being unable to control or resist, most offenders with dementia would not be considered legally insane under the irresistible impulse test. The Model Penal Code test provides the broadest formulation of legal insanity, and individuals with dementia can more reasonably attempt to claim insanity under this test. Other defenses such as diminished capacity can be used by defendants who may have inadvertently engaged in criminal behavior as the result of symptoms of their dementia, but fall short of meeting the legal standard for insanity.

At the time of writing, there are ongoing ambitious endeavors to characterize the precise relationship between dementia and criminal behaviors, expansions in the use of neuroscience in the courtroom, and challenges to the insanity defense, including the recent *Kahler v. Kansas*, 589 U.S. (2020). This chapter offers a preliminary review of the intersection between criminal responsibility and dementia and eagerly anticipates future literature and discussion on this topic.

• • •

Tianyi Zhang is a Forensic Psychiatry Fellow at the University of California, San Francisco (UCSF). She received her B.A. from the University of California, Berkeley, and her MD from UCSF. She completed her adult psychiatry residency at UCSF, where she received awards for her excellence in teaching and in community and public psychiatry. She has provided psychiatric care in correctional, emergency, inpatient, and outpatient settings, and she continues to treat patients at the San Francisco County Jail. She is an active member of the American Academy of Psychiatry and the Law and was a recipient of their Rappeport Fellowship award in 2020. Her areas of interest include trauma-related disorders, elder financial abuse allegations, evaluations related to criminal responsibility, and civil and criminal competencies.

Dr. Zhang's email is tzhang2806@gmail.com.

Vivek Datta is an Assistant Clinical Professor of Psychiatry at the University of California, San Francisco, where he is a Consulting Neuropsychiatrist and Associate Director of Consultation-Liaison Psychiatry for UCSF Health. He received his BSc in psychology from the University of London; his medical degree with distinction from Guy's, King's & St. Thomas' School of Medicine, London; and his master's in public health from Harvard School of Public Health where he was a Frank Knox Memorial Fellow. He completed his psychiatry residency at the

University of Washington Medical Center, Seattle, where he was Chief Resident for Education and Director of the Neuropsychiatric Consultation Service. He then completed his Fellowship in Psychiatry and the Law at UCSF. His research interests are the intersection of neurology, psychiatry, society, and the law.

He has won numerous awards, including the Diversity Leadership Fellowship of the American Psychiatric Association, PRITE and Laughlin Fellowships of the American College of Psychiatrists, and Rappeport Fellowship of the American Academy of Psychiatry and the Law (AAPL). He is an associate editor of the *Journal of Gay and Lesbian Mental Health*, has served as co-chair of AAPL's Forensic Neuropsychiatry Committee, and on the U.S. Medical Licensing Exam Neurology/Neuroscience Test Development Committee. His email is vdatta@mail.harvard.edu and his website is theneuropsychiatrist.com

Citations available from author(s) by request.

Chapter

5

Testing

Margaret S. Russell, Esq., and Dr. Robert Ouauo

Too often, when criminal defense lawyers read forensic evaluations, we skim over the numbers, percentages, and calculations in the testing section, and skip ahead to the bottom-line conclusion. After all, standardized testing involves numbers—the very thing many of us hoped to avoid by going to law school.

Yet testing, as well as other forms of assessments, is vitally important when exploring whether an accused suffers from dementia. This chapter by attorney Margaret Russell and Dr. Robert Ouaou emphasizes that such individuals should not merely be screened for dementia, but also that they should undergo a full clinical evaluation that may include medical testing, neuropsychological testing, brain scans, and genetic testing. The chapter also reviews a variety of tests within each of these categories. The authors conclude the chapter by providing a series of sample direct and cross-examination questions regarding testing instruments.

• • •

Testing

The number of older adults in the United States is rising, as is the incidence of dementia. As a result, older adults are more likely to come into contact with the justice system, and individuals with dementia are appearing in courts at an unprecedented rate. One out of every eight Americans 65 years or older has diminished mental capacity, as well as one out of every four over age 75, and one out of every two over age 85. Recognition and diagnosis of dementia could impact all phases of criminal litigation.

In criminal practice, dementia is raised in conjunction with a defendant's competency or to prove that a defendant is not guilty by reason of mental defect. It may also come into play in the selection of witnesses, the assessment of victims' claims, and sentencing considerations. Due to cost and/or time concerns, dementia is often raised and diagnosed in error after quick screening procedures, rather than a full multifactorial investigation. As a result, legal practitioners must understand the basis of dementia diagnosis and be diligent in probing the methods used to diagnose and establish dementia in a court of law.

Dementia Diagnosis and Its Pitfalls

As our population ages, cognitive screening tools have been used to detect cognitive impairment with increasing frequency. Mental health screening became a reimbursable benefit under the 2010 Patient Protection and Affordable Care Act. As a result, there has been an increase in quick tests for dementia. But attorneys and expert witnesses must be clear about the differences between a cognitive screening test and a full clinical evaluation to diagnose dementia. This especially applies in the context of sentencing proceedings, in which the diagnosis is critical to establishing a downward trajectory in cognitive function. All attorneys should better understand the purpose, strengths, and limitations of cognitive screening tests versus comprehensive evaluations as they impact their practice and their litigation tactics.

A dementia evaluation in the world outside of criminal litigation entails a comprehensive work-up that consists of a multidisciplinary approach. The evaluation can involve professionals with specialties in neurology, psychiatry, neuropsychology, and neuroradiology. A neurologist or other referring physician collects and analyzes data on a patient from mental status examinations, medical history, blood work, prescriptions, and examination of the patient in person. This should be accompanied by data gathered from a full battery of neuropsychological testing, including tests of intelligence, learning, memory, attention, concentration, language, processing speed, executive functions, and mood. (*See* Chapter 3, Restoration.) An evaluation of dementia in the legal context may warrant an assessment of malingering or symptom validity, which has been shown to be difficult to accurately assess in patients with dementia. However, there are studies that have shown that tests of effect can be used effectively but with increased misclassification (Teichner & Wagner, 2004).

Another aspect that is used to assist in diagnosis includes neuroimaging of the brain through an MRI, PET, SPECT, or CAT scan. Genetic studies can confirm the presence of risk factors. This multifactorial method of diagnosis is much less likely to give inaccurate results. It can also serve to inform an attorney of other causes of cognitive and behavioral decline that might mimic dementia but could be curable, such as brain tumors, psychiatric disorders, traumatic brain injuries, over-medication, delirium and temporary memory loss due to illness, infection, or injury. (*See* Chapter 6, Neuroimaging.)

Beware of Cognitive Screening Tests Used in Isolation

Cognitive screening is common in primary care and community settings, but it may be difficult for a lawyer to differentiate between screening instruments and full-scale tests. Some of the most commonly used screening tests include the Mini-Mental State Examination (MMSE) (1975) and the Montreal Cognitive Assessment (MoCA) (2005). Others screening tests that an attorney might encounter include the Cambridge Cognitive Examination (1995), CogState (2001), MiniCog (2000), Neurobehavioral Cognitive Status Examination (1987), NeuroTrax/BrainCare (2003), Six Item Screener (2002), Rapid Cognitive Screen (Malmstrom et al., 2015), St. Louis University Mental Status (Feliciano et al., 2013), and CNS Vital Signs (Gualtieri & Johnson, 2006).

Cognitive screening measures are sometimes used to identify treatable or reversible causes of cognitive impairment, but they are merely screening tools and do not provide definitive answers. There are several advantages for practitioners to using screening tools. Many are in a computerized format that is easy and inexpensive to administer. Cognitive testing contributes to higher rates of detection of dementia in older adults in primary care settings compared to informal observation alone. Screening tests can also establish a baseline measure to determine change in clinical status over time. Increased use of these screening tests is likely related to ease of patient and doctor accessibility, automation of interpretive guidelines and cutoffs, and reduced administration time and cost.

But cognitive screening tests are not in and of themselves diagnostic because they can include vast false-positive and false-negative results and do not include normative data demographic factors like age, ethnicity, race, education, and gender. Important information is routinely omitted when screening tests are administered by support staff or when they are self-administered. Critical non-neurologic factors in performance may not be considered, such as premorbid abilities and reading level, adequate attention and motivation, medication effects, and psychiatric status. Finally, significant limitations exist when screening tools lack adequate classification accuracy. The potential for harm related to false-positive screening test results or over-diagnosis is significant. Psychological distress stemming from false positive screening results is well documented in medicine. False positives and false negatives have no place in the determination of competency to stand trial, testify, or be executed.

Studies comparing the accuracy of the most commonly used cognitive screening tests (i.e., MMSE and MoCA) illustrate that these two screening tests have low sensitivity. *The use of these tests alone will miss a large proportion of individuals with true cognitive impairment.* For example, Chan (2014) found that 78 percent of stroke patients deemed cognitively intact by the MoCA, actually demonstrated cognitive impairment in one or more cognitive domains. Further, a high percentage (59 percent) who scored perfectly on the MoCA was found to be cognitively impaired on comparable neuropsychological assessment. A separate study of patients with brain tumors also found that the MMSE and MoCA were lacking in sensitivity and missed many individuals with true cognitive impairment. The MMSE was particularly low in sensitivity, detecting only 19 percent of individuals with cognitive impairment.

Sensitivity to detect cognitive impairment was better with the MoCA, but it still only reached 62 percent. Although the MMSE was highly specific (94 percent), the MoCA misclassified 44 percent of individuals as impaired when they were not. Misclassification is likely further magnified when relying on individual cognitive domains of the MoCA, that is, scores on individual cognitive domains from the MoCA were poor predictors of actual impairment in corresponding areas on comprehensive neuropsychological testing (Moafmashhadi & Koski, 2012). Inaccurate classification of screening measures is likely due to restricted range of scores, ceiling effects, and failure to measure relevant areas of cognitive functioning, such as intellectual functioning, processing speed, and visual memory. The MMSE and the MoCA are highlighted here as examples of commonly used cognitive screening measures. A systematic review of the many available cognitive screening measures is beyond the scope of this chapter; however, it is likely that similar classification issues arise with other cognitive screening tests. In summary, screening tests provide information about whether a person might have a diagnosis or a condition; they typically are not sufficient to diagnose a condition or determine the clinical status of a patient. The classification accuracy of a screening test will depend on many factors, and there are limitations when using screening tests alone.

A comprehensive multifactorial diagnosis includes the following: evaluation by a medical doctor (neurologist, general practitioner, or psychiatrist), neuropsychological testing, scans, and genetic testing. The next sections will explain each of these kinds of testing. At the end of the chapter, we include sample direct and cross-examination questions you might pose to experts.

Medical Testing

A variety of laboratory tests might be used to help diagnose dementia or rule out other conditions. These tests can include hypertension, cholesterol, blood count, drug and alcohol toxicology screens, cerebrospinal fluid analysis (spinal tap), and analysis of thyroid functions. Other tests that might improve the accuracy of a dementia diagnosis include tests for kidney, liver, or blood glucose problems; B12 level; and tests for HIV and syphilis – infections known to cause dementia. In the context of one's personal and medical history, the overall cognitive profile and pattern of relative strengths and weaknesses can help determine the presence of cognitive dysfunction and which brain systems may be implicated. At a minimum, a mental health evaluation of competence to proceed should include a review of the defendant's history, current functioning, and understanding of the impending execution and the reasons for it.

Neuropsychological Testing

There is considerable clinical as well as biological variability that occurs in different dementing illnesses. Neuropsychological testing can be an important part of the differential diagnostic process in dementia. Standardized tests offer an opportunity to detect subtle cognitive abnormalities and differentiate dementia from normal aging. Neuropsychological examinations can also help differentiate dementia syndromes such as Alzheimer's disease from cognitive impairment associated with psychiatric disorders, such as depression. Additionally, neuropsychological testing is more sensitive to identifying dementia disorders than cognitive screening. Regardless, even with the most sophisticated evaluations, it will not be clear in many individuals' first examination whether a small degree of cognitive impairment represents a change consistent with dementia, so follow-up examinations are commonly needed to track progression.

There is a vast difference between simple cognitive screening tests like the MMSE and MoCA and a brief focused neuropsychological assessment battery, such as the Repeatable Battery for the Assessment of Neuropsychological Status (Randolph, Tierney, Mohr, & Chase, 1998). The use of brief focused neuropsychological batteries is not routine and is determined by patient characteristics and referral questions. Brief neuropsychological assessments may be multidimensional or single-domain, and unlike screening tests may be appropriately used in dementia diagnosis in many cases.

A standardized neuropsychological assessment is the "gold standard" that should be used to assess whether an individual has experienced significant cognitive decline in one or more domains of cognitive functioning as a result of dementia. While there is no "standard" test battery used to evaluate suspected dementia, a neuropsychological test battery should include measures designed to better understand cognitive functioning related to orientation, intelligence, attention, information processing speed, motor speed, executive functions (i.e., reasoning, judgment, mental flexibility, decision-making, and inhibitory control), learning, memory, language expression, language comprehension, and visual-spatial processing. Emotional functioning should also be examined as part of a standard neuropsychological assessment of dementia. These symptoms include depression, anxiety, irritability, agitation, visual and auditory hallucinations, delusional thinking, and apathy.

Performance validity tests (PVTs) are employed to ensure that the derived test results are valid and reliable measurements of the examinee's actual cognitive abilities and that a test subject is not malingering. While PVTs are well studied and widely employed by neuropsychologists in a variety of contexts, they can be problematic in the evaluation of dementia due to unacceptably high false positive rates (i.e., an inaccurate conclusion that test performance is not valid; Dean et al., 2009). Interpretation of PVT failure must be made cautiously, based on measures deemed to be appropriate for use in dementia populations, and within the broader functional context (Slick et al., 1999; Boone, 2007). Because malingering is more problematic in dementia diagnosis than in the diagnosis of other mental health conditions, legal practitioners should proceed with extreme caution when there are allegations that a defendant or witness is "faking" cognitive decline.

Because different dementia-causing syndromes involve dysfunction of specific brain regions, the neuropsychological test results can be used to help determine possible causes of cognitive decline. There are two essential resources for understanding comprehensive information related to appropriate use, validity, and reliability of a major tests in use: a Compendium of Neuropsychological Tests (2006) and Standards for Educational and Psychological Testing (2014). These are excellent resources to consult in concert with an expert in preparing for depositions and trial when testing for dementia is at issue.

Brain Scans

Brain scans may be used to identify strokes, tumors, or other conditions that can cause dementia. Degeneration of the brain's cortex (outer layer) or "cortical atrophy," common in many forms of dementia, can be visible on a brain scan. The brain cortex normally appears wrinkled, with ridges (called gyri) and grooves (called sulci) in brain tissue. In individuals with cortical atrophy, the progressive loss of neurons causes the ridges to become thinner and the grooves to grow wider. As brain cells die, the ventricles (or fluid-filled cavities in the middle of the brain) expand to fill the available space, becoming much larger than normal. Brain scans identify these changes in the brain's structure that suggest Alzheimer's disease and other types of dementia.

The most common types of brain scans are computed tomographic (CT) scans and magnetic resonance imaging (MRI). Doctors frequently request CT or MRI brain scans to assist in dementia diagnosis. CT scans, which use X-rays to detect brain structures, can show evidence of brain atrophy, strokes, changes to the blood vessels, and other problems such as excess fluid or blood in the brain (known as hydrocephalus and subdural hematomas). MRI scans use magnetic fields and focused radio waves to detect hydrogen atoms in tissues within the brain. MRIs can detect the same problems as CT scans, but they are better for identifying certain conditions, such as brain atrophy and damage from small strokes.

Doctors also may use electroencephalograms (EEGs) to detect seizures that occur with some forms of dementia. In an EEG, electrodes are placed on the scalp over several parts of the brain in order to detect and record patterns of electrical activity. These patterns of electrical activity can indicate cognitive dysfunction in the brain. Many patients with moderate to severe dementia have abnormal EEGs. An EEG may also be used to detect seizures, which occur in about 10 percent of Alzheimer's disease patients as well as in patients with many other disorders.

Other types of brain scans allow researchers to watch the brain as it functions. Functional brain scans include functional MRI (fMRI), single photon-emission computed tomography (SPECT), positron emission tomography (PET), and magnetoencephalography (MEG). fMRI uses radio waves and a strong magnetic field to measure the metabolic changes that take place in active parts of the brain. SPECT shows the distribution of blood in the brain, which generally increases with brain activity. PET scans can detect changes in glucose metabolism, presence of amyloid proteins, oxygen metabolism, and blood flow, all of which can reveal abnormalities of brain function. MEG shows the electromagnetic fields produced by the brain's neuronal activity. Abnormalities in brain function revealed by these more novel methods of imaging will be increasingly used in the future. (*See* Chapter 6, Neuroimaging.)

Genetic Testing

Research on genetic predispositions of dementia is rapidly developing. It has been established that there is a link between the APOE allele and its variants and both increased and decreased risk of developing Alzheimer's disease. (*See* Liu et al., Apolipoprotein E and Alzheimer Disease: Risk, Mechanisms, and Therapy (2013)). Genetic testing in dementia diagnosis is both novel and rapidly developing.

Conclusion

As the population of the United States ages, dementia will increasingly become an important variable in competency and insanity determinations, sentencing proceedings, and the criminal justice system. Cost and time concerns favor quick but inaccurate screening procedures that are not precise enough for use in the courtroom. Instead, a full multifactorial diagnosis, including medical, neurological, and neuropsychological evaluation, scans, and even genetic testing, should be used to diagnose and establish dementia in a criminal court of law.

Sample Questions for Direct Exam of an Expert General Practitioner, Psychiatrist, or Neurologist

Start with qualifying the expert witness by education, practice area, board certifications, and number of evaluations done in other cases.

What is your training in dementia?

Do you have a clinical practice that treats/evaluates dementia patients?

If so, how many dementia patients do you see? Or have ever treated/evaluated?

Did you evaluate Client X for cognitive problems or dementia?

What is dementia?

What are the different types of dementia?

How are they different?

Is there a cure for dementia?

What current treatment is available for dementia?

How is it generally diagnosed?

I'm going to ask you some questions about the evaluation of Client X.

What is your medical specialty?

What does a psychiatrist/neurologist/general practitioner do?

What did you do to evaluate client X?

Did you meet with client X?

Where/when/how/how long?

How did client X present?

What symptoms of dementia did you see?

Next, I want to focus on the objective testing that you did on client X.

What testing did you do?

Were any of these tests mere screening tests?

Did you give any tests for symptom validity, or tests that have embedded measures of effort in testing?

Was client X giving full effort in testing?

What other factors contributed to your diagnosis?

Did you interview any collateral sources such as family members or friends?

What did you learn from them?

Did you order any scans, such an MRI or PET scan?

Why or why not?

Next, I'd like to talk about other experts you may have relied on in making your diagnosis.

Were other experts were involved in diagnosing client X?

You reviewed their findings or conferred with them?

What were their specialties?

Did you rely on any of the [neuropsych/radiology/other specialty] testing in reaching your conclusions?

Did you rely on any scans such as MRIs, PET, SPECT, or CAT scans?

Did you review the conclusions of a radiologist or neuroradiologist who reviewed the scans?

What type of dementia does client X have?

What is your diagnosis of client X to a reasonable degree of scientific certainty?

Direct Exam of a Psychologist or Neuropsychologist

Start with qualifying the expert witness by education, practice area, board certifications, and number of evaluations done in other cases.

What is your training in dementia?

Do you have a clinical practice that treats/evaluates dementia patients?

If so, how many dementia patients do you see? Or have ever treated/evaluated?

Did you evaluate client X for cognitive problems or dementia?

What is dementia?

What are the different types of dementia?

How are they different?

Is there a cure for dementia?

How is it generally diagnosed?

I'm going to ask you some questions about the evaluation of client X.

What is your psychological specialty?

What does a psychologist/neuropsychologist do?

What did you do to evaluate client X?

Did you meet with client X?

Where/when/how/how long?

How did client X present?

What symptoms of dementia did you see?

I'd like to ask you questions about the objective testing you did in your diagnosis.

Why is objective testing important in the diagnosis of dementia?

What objective testing did you do?

Were any of these tests mere screening tests?

What full scale test did you do for intelligence?

What did the tests results show?

What testing did you do for learning and memory?

What did the tests results show?

What testing did you do for attention and concentration?

What did the test results show?

What tests of processing speed?

What tests of executive function did you do?

Did you give any tests for symptom validity, or tests that have embedded measures of effort in testing?

Was client X giving full effort in testing?

What other factors contributed to your diagnosis?

Did you interview any collateral sources such as family members or friends?

What did you learn from them?

Did you suggest scans, such an MRI or PET scan?

Why or why not?

Next, I'd like to talk about other experts you may have relied on in making your diagnosis.

Were other experts involved in diagnosing client X?

You reviewed their findings or conferred with them?

What were their specialties?

Did you rely on any of the [psychiatric/neurology/psychiatry/radiology/other specialty] testing in reaching your conclusions?

Did you rely on any scans such as MRIs, PET, SPECT, or CAT scans?

Did you review the conclusions of a radiologist or neuroradiologist who reviewed the scans?

What is your diagnosis of client X to a reasonable degree of scientific certainty?

Sample Cross-Exam Questions for ANY Opining Expert

Let's discuss your method of diagnosis:

Your training in dementia is limited to [insert limitations]?

You do not have a clinical practice that treats/evaluates dementia patients, do you?

[If there is a clinical practice - cross on number of patients with dementia vs. other conditions and how many dementia patients evaluated]

You reviewed client X's medical records in this case, right?

There are other medical causes of cognitive decline, right?

Some of these causes could be reversible?

Such as medications?

Brain tumors?

Thyroid disease?

Liver disease?

Brain injuries?

But you didn't evaluate client X for these conditions?

Let's discuss your examination of client X.

You conducted number of interviews, comprising X amount of time with client X?

You found client X to be cooperative in your exam?

You did no interviews with family and friends?

So what signs of functional impairment did you see?

You didn't have brains scans, like an MRI or CAT scan completed to differentiate problems associated with a stroke or a brain tumor ?

No consultations with other professionals, such as psychiatrists, neuropsychologists, neurologists, or radiologists?

No genetic testing?

No follow-up interviews with client X?

I want to ask you some questions on screening tests for dementia.

You didn't consider the results of the Mini-Mental State Examination test (MMSE) [or the Montreal Cognitive Assessment (MOCA)] in your diagnosis, did you?

It's a screening test, right?

A screening test only reveals if a person MIGHT have a disease or condition, right?

Screening tests aren't made to be used as the ONLY factor in diagnosis?

The MMSE/MOCA is fast and cheap?

It can be administered by support staff?

Or administered without a licensed professional all together?

Which means that used alone, the MMSE and the MOCA screening test can have vast false positive and false negative results?

Both the MMSE and the MOCA are known to lack sensitivity and specificity, and a formal diagnosis of dementia requires a more comprehensive assessment?

Let's discuss the medical testing you did to evaluate client X for dementia.

You didn't do medical testing, including for high blood pressure?

You didn't do testing for HIV?

You didn't test for blood sugar problems?

Thyroid functioning?

You didn't review client X's current prescriptions?

And high blood pressure, HIV, blood sugar variations, and improper prescription medication can all cause cognitive problems that are not related to dementia, right?

You didn't have a psychiatric or psychological evaluation to distinguish Client X's symptoms from depression or bi-polar disorder?

Client X did not complete a standardized neuropsychological assessment?

But you did not seek this important information in finalizing your diagnosis of Client X?

Let's discuss IQ tests of client X.

The Weschler Intelligence Scale, 4th Edition, and the Stanford-Binet, 5th Edition, are the "gold standard" in IQ testing?

But you used a mere screening test for IQ such as the [TONI, KBIT]?

A screening test is not as accurate as a full-scale IQ test, right?

You are not a neuropsychologist?

You have no training in neuropsychological assessment?

You have not done coursework in interpretation of IQ tests?

You are not trained to administer IQ tests?

I want to ask you some questions about medical causes of cognitive decline.

In your diagnosis, it's a standard operating procedure to exclude a medical cause for symptoms before investigating a psychiatric cause?

In short, medical trumps psychiatric, right?

You never evaluated client X for head injury or brain damage?

You never did a psychiatric work up of client X ?

You never consulted with a neuropsychologist or ordered brain scans in your diagnosis?

You never considered other causes of failing memory aside from dementia?

• • •

Robert Ouaou is a psychologist with a specialty in forensic neuropsychology and the president of Naples Neuropsychology in Naples, Florida. Dr. Ouaou received a degree in psychology from Temple University in 1990 and his PhD from Palo Alto University in 1999. He is an esteemed member of the National Academy of Neuropsychology, the International Neuropsychological Society, the American Academy of Clinical Neuropsychology, the American Psychological Association, and the American Association on Intellectual and Developmental Disabilities. From 2009 to 2012, he served as the vice chair of the Board of Directors and Medical Advisory Committee of the Alzheimer's Association of Florida. Dr. Ouaou has published extensively in the areas of substance abuse, neurocognitive impairment, and forensic psychology. He can be reached through the website www.naplesneuro.com.

Margaret S. Russell is an accomplished trial lawyer with experience in complex criminal and death penalty litigation currently employed at the Sixth Circuit Office of the Public Defender in Pinellas County, Florida. Ms. Russell grew up in Cleveland, Ohio, attended Haverford College, and graduated magna cum laude from Case Western Reserve University School of Law in 1993. After clerking for the Honorable Lesley Brooks Wells in the Northern District of Ohio, she worked in private practice at Hahn, Loeser & Parks, then joined Florida's Capital Collateral Regional Counsel, applying her passion to end the death penalty in state and federal post-conviction matters. She can be reached at margaretrussell@co.pinellas.fl.us.

Citations available from author(s) by request.

Chapter

6

Neuroimaging

Dr. Austin Blum and Dr. Vivek Datta

Is a picture worth a thousand words? For someone with dementia accused of a crime, neuroimaging may be worth the price of liberty. The following chapter by Dr. Austin Blum and Dr. Vivek Datta is a good primer on the use of neuroimaging for criminal defense lawyers. (The authors caution that they are not trying to turn attorneys into radiologists!) The chapter surveys the different types of neuroimaging techniques as well as the brain imaging data that those techniques generate. The chapter also discusses the medico-legal questions that neuroimaging can and cannot answer. As the authors note, although neuroimages may be compelling, they must be used in concert with the other assessments discussed in this book such as testing and forensic interviews.

• • •

Neuroscientific evidence is being introduced in the courtroom at an ever-growing pace (Farahany, 2015), posing challenges for judges, juries, and forensic experts alike. In this chapter, we aim to provide guidance for practicing attorneys interested in learning how brain imaging in dementia can be used to support particular legal conclusions.

Brain imaging data may be used in legal proceedings for various reasons. In criminal cases, neuroimaging evidence is sometimes used to support the argument that a defendant is incompetent to stand trial due to a neurocognitive disorder. In *United States v. Gigante*, 892 F. Supp. 140 (E.D.N.Y. 1997), experts testifying on behalf of the defendant Vincent

Gigante—the alleged boss of the Genovese crime family—sought to introduce positron emission tomography (PET) scans (an imaging technique described in detail later) as evidence to show that Mr. Gigante had dementia. However, he was subsequently found competent to stand trial and eventually found guilty of murder and racketeering (Baskin et al., 2007). In *United States v. Kasim*, 2:07-cr-00056, the U.S. District Court for the Northern District of Indiana found that Dr. Kasim, a pediatrician, was incompetent to stand trial for Medicaid fraud based on abnormal neuroimaging findings (Edersheim & Wei, 2017).

Although cases such as *Kasim* may suggest that brain imaging is potentially useful in cases involving neurocognitive disorders, such data (as any other source of evidence) must be approached critically. In some cases, brain images can assist fact finders in answering key legal questions, thereby promoting the administration of justice. However, in other cases, the use of these scans may make the situation ambiguous. By means of this chapter, we hope to explain the different types of neuroimaging techniques and the brain imaging data that they generate, and just as importantly, the types of medicolegal questions these images can be used to answer (and those they cannot).

In the first part of this chapter, we provide a brief survey of the brain imaging techniques that attorneys are most likely to encounter in the course of their legal practice. Some of these techniques (e.g., computed tomography [CT]) are widely known, while others may be more familiar to specialists. We do not expect (or intend) to turn our readers into radiologists; instead, we hope to provide a high-level overview of the working of these imaging tools and their potential use to support a diagnosis of dementia. References are provided for readers wanting to explore the technical aspects in greater detail.

The second part of the chapter focuses on the legal context in which neuroimaging data may be utilized. We hope that by highlighting some of the limitations of these technologies, we can provide attorneys a realistic view of their potential use as well as their drawbacks.

Neuroimaging

We discuss some of the basic principles of the most common modalities of brain imaging, and then discuss their use in the diagnosis of dementia.

The Basics

All of us likely have some familiarity with medical imaging, whether with plain films ("X-rays") or other modalities. Although plain films have a limited role in the diagnosis of dementia, a related technology—CT—is commonly used for this purpose.

In *computed tomography* or computerized axial tomography, X-rays taken from multiple angles around the body are combined to create cross-sectional images (slices) of the head or other anatomic regions. The different colors on a CT scan reflect the varying densities of different tissues in the body: bones absorb the most amount of X-rays and appear white, while soft tissues absorb less and appear in shades of gray (air, through which X-rays pass freely, appears black). CT allows the internal structures of the skull to be visualized in excellent detail, allowing physicians to detect a number of possible diseases and associated processes, including stroke, brain masses (tumors), and atrophy (volume loss in the brain). CT is especially useful in identifying certain structural changes associated with cognitive impairment, including intracranial masses and vascular lesions (Pasi et al., 2011). CT may also be an appropriate imaging tool for patients who are unable to lie in a scanner for a prolonged period (a CT scan takes only a few minutes to do) or who have implanted metal devices, such as a pacemaker, which would make magnetic resonance imaging (MRI) unsafe.

Readers interested in learning about the specific neuroimaging findings seen in CT images of different neurocognitive disorders can refer to LeMay's "CT Changes in Dementing Diseases: A Review" (1986). As a word of caution, many of the anatomical details mentioned by LeMay may be difficult to understand without some medical training.

Magnetic resonance imaging is sometimes confused with CT, but the technology is entirely different. As opposed to CT, which relies on X-rays, MRI uses magnetic fields. As we have learned in high school chemistry or physics, atoms consist of smaller subatomic particles, including electrons, neutrons, and protons. The proton carries a positive electric charge and acts as a tiny magnet. When placed in an external magnetic field, the direction of the proton changes.

This property of the proton allows MRI to produce images. When a patient is placed in a strong magnetic field generated by the MRI scanner, the protons in the patient's body quickly change direction (without moving) to line up with the applied magnetic field. Next, an MRI technologist directs a radio wave at the patient's head (for brain MRI), causing the protons to lose their alignment with the magnetic field. The radio wave is then switched off, allowing the protons to realign with the magnetic field, which causes the protons to release energy. The energy is transformed to produce a detailed image of the brain. (For those interested in learning more, science editor Abi Berger has published a wonderful, jargon-free summary of MRI in the *BMJ* (2002)).

MRI is excellent for visualizing the soft tissue of the brain. Similar to CT, MRI can reveal atrophy of the brain as well as vascular injuries. In legal and forensic settings, MRI may be especially useful in differentiating Alzheimer's disease from vascular dementia (Pantano et al., 1999). MRI is also the preferred imaging tool for the diagnosis of a number of rare causes of dementia, including those caused by central nervous system infections.

Comparable to CT, MRI provides information about the structure of the brain, but it cannot show if particular regions of the brain are functioning normally.

Functional magnetic resonance imaging (fMRI) differs from both CT and conventional MRI in that it provides a measure of brain activity. To do so, fMRI uses the same basic technology as regular MRI, but it uses the technology to detect changes in blood flow. A (brief) overview follows.

When regions of the brain are activated, they consume oxygen, and in turn, fresh, oxygenated blood is supplied to these tissues. Because oxygenated blood has magnetic properties different from those of deoxygenated blood, the magnetic field in these more active neural regions changes, and with it, the MRI signal also changes. Therefore, the ebb and flow of oxygenated blood serves as proxy for the activity of the underlying tissues.

Similar to regular MRI, fMRI has high spatial resolution, allowing changes in brain activity to be detected in areas as small as 1 cubic millimeter. However, fMRI has a notable limitation: it is relatively slow. Blood flow to the brain does not peak until several seconds after a particular neuronal event, meaning that the fMRI signal will always lag behind the underlying activity that it is meant to capture. The technical limitations of fMRI are discussed in more detail by Logothetis (2008).

Although fMRI is primarily a research tool, it has also been used for the clinical diagnosis of Alzheimer's disease.

Positron emission tomography is another functional imaging technique. In PET, a radioactive tracer (called a radionuclide or radiopharmaceutical) is attached to a biologically active molecule, such as glucose. After a small amount of the tracer is injected into the patient, it is taken up by tissues at different rates: more metabolically active regions of the brain take up more of the tracer, while areas with low (or no) metabolic activity take up less (or none) of the tracer. The tracers emit gamma rays (as radioactive substances normally do), which are detected by the PET scanner and translated into a three-dimensional image.

The tissues damaged by neurodegenerative diseases are less metabolically active than are healthy tissues, thus allowing them to be differentiated using PET. PET also allows different types of dementia to be distinguished from one another, since each of these illnesses is associated with a characteristic metabolic "signature." (However, in practice, there may be a significant overlap between the dementia syndromes, making diagnosis using PET less straightforward. (*See* Berti et al., 2013, for a review article).

Although glucose-based tracers (as previously mentioned) are commonly used to diagnose Alzheimer's disease, other tracers have recently been developed to target the proteins amyloid and tau. These proteins are known to accumulate in the brains of individuals with Alzheimer's disease over time, forming the plaques and neurofibrillary "tangles" that are the hallmarks of the disease (Jack et al., 2013). However, amyloid PET data must be interpreted with a certain amount of caution, since high levels of amyloid may be found even in healthy patients (Kolanko et al., 2020). Tau PET may offer certain advantages over amyloid PET in this respect, although this technology is not yet in widespread clinical use (Leuzy et al., 2019).

Single-photon emission computed tomography (SPECT) is a functional neuroimaging technique similar to PET. A particular type of SPECT, called DaTscan, is commonly used to diagnose Parkinson's disease and other Parkinsonian disorders. SPECT is sometimes used to diagnose other types of dementia as well (e.g., Alzheimer's disease).

Neuroimaging and Genetics in the Diagnosis of Dementia

It is important to note that dementia is a functional diagnosis that is made on the basis of a decline in functioning related to the decline in one or more cognitive domains (e.g., language, memory, executive function, complex attention, visuospatial). Thus, findings on brain imaging alone can neither make, nor exclude, a diagnosis of dementia. Instead, imaging findings can support a probable diagnosis of a particular type of dementia (e.g., Alzheimer's, vascular dementia) in addition with the clinical history and neuropsychological testing. Currently, no imaging modality can make a definitive diagnosis of a particular subtype of dementia. Only brain biopsy (seldom performed in living subjects with suspected dementia) and the presence of deterministic genes can make a definitive diagnosis.

Alzheimer's Disease

The classic finding on MRI brain scan in Alzheimer's disease is bilateral medial temporal lobe atrophy. The medial temporal lobe is the site of the hippocampus, the sea-horse shaped structure that is involved in the encoding and retrieval of memories. There are two reasons why this finding cannot make a definitive diagnosis. First, Alzheimer's disease may not lead to this finding (particularly early in the course of the disease). Second, bilateral hippocampal atrophy can occur due to other causes, including head injuries, viral infections, autoimmune disease. Thus, these findings are correlated with the clinical history and performance on neuropsychological testing to support the diagnosis.

FDG-PET imaging uses radioactive glucose to measure metabolic activity in the brain. In Alzheimer's disease, the classic finding is hypometabolism in the parietal and temporal lobes bilaterally.

Amyloid-PET imaging uses a radioactive tracer that binds to beta-amyloid plaques (a pathological hallmark of Alzheimer's), thus allowing the detection of these plaques in living people without cutting into the brain. A positive scan will have abnormally increased uptake in the cortical gray matter, indicating moderate to frequent plaques. While a negative scan is unlikely in someone who has Alzheimer's, a positive scan could result due to causes other than Alzheimer's disease.

Tau-PET imaging uses a radioactive tracer that binds to neurofibrillary tau tangles. Misfolded tau protein aggregation is another hallmark of Alzheimer's disease. Abnormal tau aggregation is also found in some rarer causes of dementia such as progressive supranuclear palsy and corticobasal degeneration.

There are three deterministic genes (i.e., if you have a copy of the gene, you will develop the disease) that cause early onset Alzheimer's. These are Presenilin (PSN), Amyloid Precursor Protein-1 (APP-1), and

Amyloid Precursor Protein-2. The presence of this gene can be used to make a definitive diagnosis of Alzheimer's. There are many other genes that increase the risk of developing Alzheimer's that are not deterministic. The most well-known is APOE-4, as it is also the most common occurring. The presence of APOE-4 is not deterministic, but is a risk factor for the development of Alzheimer's disease.

Vascular Dementia

Vascular dementia refers to cognitive impairment due to processes affecting the large and small blood vessels that supply the brain. This includes cognitive impairment due to the chronic effects of microhemorrhages (small bleeds) and microinfarcts as well as large infarcts (also known as strokes). MRI brain is considered the gold standard imaging technique to evaluate this. This may reveal prior large strokes, as well as white matter hyperintensities of vascular origin (particularly around the ventricles and frontal lobe white matter circuits). There may also be evidence of microhemorrhages and cerebral atrophy.

There is a rare form of inherited severe vascular dementia that typically begins in the sixth decade of life with recurrent strokes, migraines, and cognitive decline called CADASIL (Cerebral Autosomal Dominant Arteriopathy with Sub-cortical Infarcts and Leukoencephalopathy). This disease is caused by a mutation in the *NOTCH-3* gene, which is a deterministic gene.

Dementia with Lewy Bodies

Unlike Alzheimer's and vascular dementia, MRI brain cannot be used in the diagnosis of dementia with Lewy bodies (DLB). MRI brain typically reveals absence of bilateral medial temporal lobe atrophy, though DLB commonly co-occurs with Alzheimer's disease, in which case medial temporal lobe atrophy could be seen.

FDG-PET and SPECT imaging may show diffuse hypometabolism, including hypometabolism in the occipital lobes (thus distinguishing it from Alzheimer's disease).

The Dopamine Transport Scan (DaTScan) is the most useful imaging tool in the diagnosis of DLB. The radioactive isotope *N*-ω-fluoropropyl-2β-carboxymethoxy-3β-(4-iodophenyl) nortropane (FP-CIT) is injected and, in DLB, uptake of FP-CIT is decreased in the basal ganglia, but uptake is normal in Alzheimer's disease. This finding of reduced uptake of FP-CIT in the basal ganglia is not specific to DLB. It is also seen in Parkinson's disease (with or without dementia), and other so-called Parkinson's Plus syndromes, including the less common Progressive Supranuclear Palsy, Corticobasal Degeneration, and Multiple Systems Atrophy. Clinical history, neurological examination, and neuropsychological testing can distinguish between these diagnoses.

Another important non-imaging biomarker that supports the diagnosis of DLB is video polysomnography (also known as a sleep study). REM sleep behavior disorder is common in those with DLB and Parkinson's disease, often preceding the onset of dementia symptoms by 10 to 15 years. Characterized by dream enactment behaviors during REM sleep due to loss of normal atonia (i.e., temporary paralysis of muscles during sleep), this is an important marker, given REM sleep behavior disorder can lead to violence and sexual behavior.

Frontotemporal Lobar Degeneration

Frontotemporal lobar degeneration (FTLD) refers to a variety of disease processes that lead to focal atrophy of the frontal and temporal lobes and the resultant clinical symptoms. FTLD can be classified into three clinical dementia types: as behavioral variant frontotemporal dementia (bvFTD), semantic dementia (SD), and progressive nonfluent aphasia (PNFA). While both bvFTD and semantic dementia have been found to have substantially elevated rates of criminal conduct compared to Alzheimer's disease, given bvFTD is the more common of these rare diseases, and believed to uniquely predispose to criminal behavior, we will focus on bvFTD.

Courtroom Applications

The neuroimaging tools discussed earlier in the chapter have sparked considerable enthusiasm among some scientists and legal commentators (e.g., Greene & Cohen, 2006), while others have urged caution and restraint (e.g., Morse, 2011). Although the methods and goals of law and neuroscience are often oblique at best (Buckholtz & Faigman, 2014), brain images may have a role to play in certain legal contexts (discussed next). We also discuss some technical and conceptual limitations of neuroimaging later in the chapter.

Legal Considerations

Assuming that one (or more) of the tools discussed earlier supports a diagnosis of dementia, it is crucial to consider the specific legal context in which the neuroimaging data is raised. Like any other type of evidence, brain images must be material, probative, and helpful to legal fact finders in order to be admissible (*see* Slobogin, 1998). With that in mind, we offer some key legal questions to consider when evaluating any piece of neuroimaging evidence.

First, is the evidence admissible? Lawyers may wish to introduce neuroimaging in either civil or criminal proceedings to substantiate a diagnosis of dementia or to establish a causal link between a client's mental abnormality and a legally relevant behavior (e.g., rational capacity or self-control). In criminal trials, such evidence may be raised when evaluating a defendant's trial competency, as in *Gigante* and *Kasim*, or during the guilt and sentencing phases. As a general rule, courts appear to be more willing to admit brain imaging evidence at sentencing than when determining culpability (Rushing, 2014).

Second, what is the specific legal question that the neuroimaging is supposed to answer? In criminal cases, neuroimaging evidence of dementia may be relevant to a number of defenses based on cognitive impairment (e.g., lack of *mens rea*, legal insanity, and diminished capacity). In these cases, as previously suggested, courts may treat the same piece of evidence very differently depending on whether it is introduced in the guilt phase (i.e., to argue that a defendant should not be held responsible for a crime) or as a mitigating factor post-conviction. In civil cases, brain imaging of dementia may be potentially relevant to cases involving workers' compensation claims and fitness for duty evaluations, or to prove that a testator lacked testamentary capacity or was vulnerable to undue influence.

Even if a judge determines that a neuroimaging study is admissible, the judge may set restrictions on how the data can be used. For example, in one famous case, *People v. Weinstein* (N.Y. Sup. Ct. 1992), the court allowed a PET scan to be introduced as evidence, but barred defense witnesses from speculating about the link between the defendant's neurological abnormality—a relatively common brain cyst called an arachnoid cyst—and the violent behavior of which he was accused (*see* Jones & Shen, 2012, for further discussion of this case). In other words, simply offering a technically sound neuroimaging study to the court is not enough—the legal relevance of the data must be made clear.

Third, how *well* do the brain images demonstrate what they are supposed to prove? Imaging performed months or years after an event (whether a crime or the execution of a will) may be of limited value when making inferences about a client's past behavior. Brain images, unfortunately, do not speak for themselves—indeed, their interpretation may prove highly contentious.

Finally, lawyers representing clients with dementia should be aware that in rare cases (primarily involving death penalty litigation), the *failure* to introduce some sort of neuroscientific evidence (e.g., neuropsychological data) may constitute ineffective assistance of counsel (Edersheim et al., 2012; Rushing, 2014). If a defendant in a capital case is suspected of having a significant brain abnormality, obtaining confirmatory neuroimaging is likely a prudent strategy.

The Brain–Law Interface

Tens of thousands of scientific articles are published each year on the relationship between the brain and the behavior it produces (*see, e.g.*, Haynes & Rees, 2006 in *Nature Reviews Neuroscience*). Despite this wealth of research, the significance (or nonsignificance) of specific neuroimaging findings to the law is often misunderstood, even by well-meaning specialists. Conceptual traps abound for the unwary. With that said, we believe that even a little knowledge of the brain could help lawyers avoid many of these pitfalls.

The human brain consists of about 85 billion neurons (Herculano-Houzel, 2012), which are organized into "networks" subserving particular cognitive functions. This basic neural architecture, shaped by our genes, environment and development, and millions of years of evolution, gives rise to our whole experience of the world.

In other words, *all* of our behavior is rooted in the physical architecture of the brain. Clearly, then, the fact that behavior is caused by some process in the brain—whether normal or abnormal—is not enough to excuse, justify, or mitigate criminal conduct. Otherwise, all behavior would be excused. Instead, the law's responsibility criteria are based on psychological states and their related actions.

To illustrate this principle, consider two individuals: Mr. A and Mr. B. Both Mr. A and Mr. B are diagnosed with Alzheimer's disease. Both have classic neuropathologic hallmarks of the disease (medial temporal lobe atrophy) on MRI. Yet after being accused of a crime (say, theft), Mr. A is held criminally responsible while Mr. B is not. How could this be so? Such an outcome would be expected if Mr. A retained his capacity for rationality and self-control (to a degree), while Mr. B, perhaps due to the severity of his illness, did not. As the divergent cases of Mr. A and Mr. B show, brain imaging abnormalities may be suggestive, but they do not neatly correlate with symptomatic behavior, and rarely determine the outcome of cases (Morse, 2016). Moreover, because legal responsibility is a normative (rather than empirical or scientific) question, neuroimaging cannot be used to definitively conclude that a defendant should (or should not) be held nonresponsible.

Conclusion

In this chapter, we have provided a brief guide to lawyers who are considering introducing neuroimaging evidence on behalf of clients with dementia. The topic is timely given the high levels of interest it has generated in recent years. Courts have been confronted with difficult questions about whether to admit certain neuroimaging studies, and, if so, how the data should be correctly interpreted.

From the legal system's perspective, nothing has dramatically changed. Neuroimaging is treated the same as any other piece of evidence and must meet the same admissibility criteria, and rightly so. Yet, many participating in the legal system have a sense that neuroimaging is different. It is easy to look at a lesion on a brightly colored fMRI, SPECT, or PET scan and think it *must* have some kind of legal implication.

We encourage our readers to resist this urge. As fascinating as brain images may be, their legal relevance should not be taken for granted. To guard against the fuzzy thinking that neuroscience often invites, both lawyers and the experts they have retained should ask how, precisely, the brain images under consideration help to answer a specific legal question. Upon deliberation, it may become clear that one's initial rhetorical impressions were misleading.

To ensure that neuroscientific findings are communicated as clearly as possible to judges and juries, lawyers and experts should be transparent about the limitations of these technologies. Neuroimaging is often well suited to identify structural abnormalities associated with dementia, but it cannot provide a window into someone's thoughts or motivations. For that reason, neuroimaging should always be presented alongside a rich account of the client's behavior and any available cognitive or psychological data. To use a well-known phrase in the field, actions speak louder than images.

Neuroimaging is likely to play a growing role in the courtroom over the years ahead. By maintaining a healthy skepticism, lawyers should be able to use these technologies to the benefit of both their clients and the legal system as a whole.

• • •

Austin Blum is a fourth-year resident in the Department of Psychiatry and Behavioral Neuroscience at the University of Chicago. He earned a B.A. in history from Cornell University and a J.D. from Cornell Law School before graduating from the University of Chicago Pritzker School of Medicine. He has won several awards during his residency, including the American Psychiatric Association (APA)/APA Foundation Leadership Fellowship and the Rappeport Fellowship of the American Academy of Psychiatry and the Law. His interests include the treatment of paraphilic disorders, legal and ethical issues in consultation-liaison psychiatry, and the role of impulsivity in putative behavioral addictions (e.g., gambling disorder).

Dr. Blum's email address is awb32@cornell.edu.

Vivek Datta is an Assistant Clinical Professor of Psychiatry at the University of California, San Francisco, where he is a Consulting Neuropsychiatrist and Associate Director of Consultation-Liaison Psychiatry for UCSF Health. He received his BSc in Psychology from the University of London, his Medical Degree with Distinction from Guy's, King's & St Thomas' School of Medicine, London, and his Master's in Public Health from Harvard School of Public Health where he was a Frank Knox Memorial Fellow. He completed his Psychiatry Residency at the University of Washington Medical Center, Seattle, where he was Chief Resident for Education and Director of the Neuropsychiatric Consultation Service. He then completed his Fellowship in Psychiatry and the Law at UCSF. His research interests are the intersection of neurology, psychiatry, society and the law.

He has won numerous awards including the Diversity Leadership Fellowship of the American Psychiatric Association, PRITE and Laughlin Fellowships of the American College of Psychiatrists, and Rappeport Fellowship of the American Academy of Psychiatry and the Law (AAPL). He is an Associate Editor of the *Journal of Gay and Lesbian Mental Health*, has served Co-Chair of AAPL's Forensic Neuropsychiatry Committee, and on the US Medical Licensing Exam Neurology/Neuroscience Test Development Committee.

His email is vdatta@mail.harvard.edu and his website is theneuropsychiatrist.com

Citations available from author by request.

Chapter

7

Early Onset Dementia/ Frontotemporal Dementia

Dr. Hal S. Wortzel

When people picture someone with dementia, they picture someone elderly. This chapter by Dr. Hal S. Wortzel describes early onset dementia, otherwise known as frontotemporal dementia or FTD. Indeed, FTD, which can afflict people as young as under age 60, is the third most common type of dementia after Alzheimer's disease and dementia with Lewy bodies. This chapter details the types of FTD and its symptoms. It also discusses the challenges people with FTD face within the criminal justice system, such as meeting the legal standard of competency.

• • •

What Is FTD?

Frontotemporal dementia (FTD) represents a group of neurodegenerative disorders that attack the frontal and temporal aspects of the brain, resulting in progressive decline in functioning, especially as it relates to behavior and language abilities. FTD is the third most common neurodegenerative cause of dementia after Alzheimer's disease (AD) and dementia with Lewy bodies, and a leading cause of young onset dementia (Kerchner and Rosenbloom, 2018). FTD is the most common cause of dementia among persons younger than age 60 (Association for Frontotemporal Degeneration, 2021). FTD frequently presents with prominent behavioral changes, not infrequently leading to violations of both social norms and the law. It also causes impairment in language and higher order cognitive processes, often referred to as executive functions. Executive functions enable us to monitor our environment, come up with a plan to engage that environment, observe the success of that plan in relation to various goals, and make adaptations on the fly to optimize the plan. Stated differently, executive functions enable us to deploy goal-directed behaviors in a manner that comports with societal norms and expectations. Unlike many other dementing illnesses, memory and visuospatial functions are relatively spared in the early stages of illness, a circumstance that often leads to delayed diagnosis, and even diagnostic error. The constellation of impairment seen early on in FTD, with prominent behavioral disturbances frequently accompanied by relatively intact memory, makes FTD particularly salient to forensics, and presents some relatively unique challenges.

Like all neurodegenerative illnesses, FTD's progressive course will eventually compromise various capacities, such as the capacity to draft a will, or to independently manage various rudimentary aspects of life (e.g., treatment decisions, transportation, and eventually basic activities of daily living). However, because memory remains relatively intact early in the course of illness, the nature and magnitude of cognitive and behavior disturbances sufficient to yield various forms of incapacity are prone to being underappreciated by evaluators less familiar with FTD. Stated differently, the individual suffering from FTD may be able to concretely articulate various criteria associated with a specific form of capacity, though is often simultaneously unable to appreciate the more nuanced implications of the decisions being made, or to make rational choices, in a fashion that is consistent with their pre-morbid personality and values.

Behavioral disturbances caused by FTD not infrequently precipitate acts in violation of social norms and legal requirements. The resulting criminal charges often precipitate referral for evaluation by forensic psychiatrists, many of whom may have limited training and/or familiarity with FTD. Alternatively, neurologists more accustomed to diagnosing and treating FTD are often without the requisite forensic training and experience to synthesize the medical science with legal rules and definitions. This vexing state of affairs is further complicated by a persisting general lack of awareness for FTD, among lay persons and medical and legal professionals, with a resulting tendency for such patients to be misdiagnosed. The behaviors and personality changes associated with FTD often result in referral to mental health clinicians, many of whom lack familiarity with FTD, and mistake it for psychiatric disorders like bipolar mood disorder, or even antisocial behavior. This chapter offers an overview of FTD and the medicolegal challenges that frequently accompany it, such that legal professionals may recognize potential cases and more successfully engage with medicolegal consultants to meet the complex legal needs of these individuals and their families.

Clinical Features

FTD actually involves three distinct clinical syndromes: behavioral variant frontotemporal dementia (bvFTD) and two lesser-known language variants, semantic variant primary progressive aphasia (svPPA) and nonfluent-agrammatic variant primary progressive aphasia (nfvPPA). FTD involves strong genetic associations found in 40 percent of patients (Rabinovici & Miller 2010). Patients often report an extensive family history, albeit histories sometimes involving what would seem to represent misdiagnosis of Alzheimer's disease, or psychiatric illness (e.g., bipolar or schizoaffective disorder).

Behavioral Variant Frontotemporal Dementia

Behavioral Variant FTD (bvFTD) is the most common type of FTD, responsible for slightly more than half of cases and more commonly found in men. Revised consensus criteria incorporating clinical symptoms, neuropsychological testing, and neuroimaging were published in 2011, and facilitate accurate diagnosis of bvFTD (Rascovsky et al., 2011). Early onset at ages <65, impaired executive performance on neuropsychological testing, and focal frontal or temporal lobe brain atrophy on neuroimaging are key elements in distinguishing bvFTD from other neurodegenerative conditions. Six major clinical features are associated with bvFTD: early behavioral disinhibition; early apathy or inertia; early loss of sympathy or empathy; early perseverative, stereotyped, or compulsive/ritualistic behavior; hyperorality or dietary changes; and neuropsychological deficits predominantly involving executive functions, with relative sparing of memory and visuospatial function. There is a nearly universal lack of insight on the part of patients in relation to behavioral and cognitive changes that are appreciated by, and distressing to, others.

Behavioral disinhibition is the most widely recognized clinical characteristic of bvFTD, often manifesting with overspending, sexually inappropriate remarks, and socially unacceptable behavior (Rabinovici & Miller, 2010). Apathy often co-occurs with disinhibition early in the course of illness, and is associated with decreased motivation, social isolation, and reduced emotional range. Apathy is often an underappreciated aspect of the illness, and can contribute to diagnostic confusion, especially when apathy predominates during medical encounters, and more episodic behavioral disturbances go unwitnessed or unreported.

Loss of empathy and sympathy is frequently disturbing to caregivers, who are upset by the lack of responsiveness to grief or sadness experienced by loved ones. An increased predilection for sweets occurs often, though it is nonspecific and features in other neurodegenerative disorders as well. Progressive dysfunction can lead to repetitive behaviors, causing compulsive motor symptoms such as throat clearing, rubbing, picking, pacing, or wandering (Rabinovici & Miller, 2010). Compulsive collecting, hoarding, shoplifting, and rummaging may also occur.

Cognitive symptoms include prominent executive dysfunction with relative sparing of memory and visuospatial abilities (Rascovsky et al., 2007). Poor attention can present with distractibility and impulsiveness. Sparing of memory function is common, though exceptions may occur. The cumulative spectrum of cognitive deficits compromises patients' abilities to problem solve or to engage in complex tasks.

Primary Progressive Aphasia

Primary progressive aphasia results in progressive language decline with relative sparing of memory and visuospatial function. PPA comes in two distinct clinical phenotypes: nonfluent-agrammatic variant primary progressive aphasia and semantic dementia variant primary progressive aphasia.

Nonfluent-agrammatic variant primary progressive aphasia (nfvPPA) is a progressive, primary language disorder involving motor speech dysfunction and characterized by effortful, nonfluent speech. Phrase length is shortened, and speech may be slurred and difficult to understand. Agrammatism (i.e., difficulty arranging words to arrive at well-formed, grammatical sentences) also features, with omissions of articles and other syntactic words, leading to telegraphic speech (compressed speech, lacking in conjunctions and articles). Comprehension is relatively spared compared to speech production, though patients may struggle with more syntactically complex sentences. Unlike bvFTD, comportment and behavior is preserved throughout the course of the disease.

Semantic variant primary progressive aphasia (svPPA) spares speech fluency, but instead causes impairments in naming, object knowledge, and single-word comprehension. Patients struggle with word-finding, especially nouns, causing speech that appears empty and impoverished, though more fluent than in nfvPPA. A patient with svPPA not only loses words but also the semantic knowledge surrounding the noun in question. svPPA may involve behavioral symptoms, such as strict routines, food fads, clock watching, and dieting (Rabinovici & Miller, 2010).

Motor Symptoms

FTD may also result in progressive deterioration in motor function. Roughly 10 to 15 percent of patients with bvFTD will go on to develop motor neuron disease (amyotrophic lateral sclerosis, also known as Lou Gehrig's disease), resulting in problems with swallowing, slurring of speech, limb weakness, and/or loss of dexterity (Kerchner & Rosenbloom, 2018). Respiratory weakness and impaired swallowing are frequent sources of mortality. About 20 percent of patients with FTD experience Parkinsonian symptoms, like tremor, rigidity, slowness, or imbalance.

Nomenclature

There has been considerable and rapid evolution in the nosology (i.e., how it is classified as a disease) of the FTD clinical syndromes, reflecting our growing understanding of these diseases and their interrelationships. The DSM-5 includes FTD as a disorder, but it is captured under Frontotemporal Neurocognitive Disorder, designated as mild versus major, and comprising behavioral and language variants. The DSM-5 does not differentiate between svPPA and nfvPPA.

Counseling and Education

Although the present chapter is focused on the forensic aspects of FTD, professionals can greatly assist patients and their families by facilitating the provision of clinical care, to include counseling and education. FTD is a devastating disease that dramatically impacts lifestyle for patients, caregivers, and family. When offering a new diagnosis of FTD, forensic evaluators ought to facilitate appropriate clinical referrals, that in turn will enable formal family meetings where questions related to diagnosis, prognosis, and treatment can be addressed by treating health care professionals. There is evidence that the caregiver burden associated with FTD is greater than that associated with Alzheimer's disease (Wong et al., 2012), and offering information about caregiver support groups is recommended.

FTD and the Law

As previously noted, FTD presents some relatively unique challenges when it comes to legal ramifications of various behavior and issues of capacity. Mendez (2010) describes that while FTD makes individuals prone toward problematic behaviors that violate both social norms and the law, patients with FTD often retain a basic awareness for the nature of their actions and related consequences. Not infrequently, they even demonstrate intact awareness for conventional rules and laws that prohibit the behavior at issue. Mendez (2010) points out that this superficial ability to distinguish right from wrong, combined with the proclivity toward illegal behaviors, presents real challenges to the criminal justice system. In most jurisdictions, legal determinations regarding culpability for otherwise criminal behaviors are anchored to cognitive prongs involving knowledge of wrongfulness, and do not clearly allow for consideration of the degraded moral rationality caused by FTD, or the impaired ability to comport behavior with the requirements of the law. Hence, although FTD clearly causes cognitive and behavior impairments that may directly lead to criminal acts, the law affords relatively limited options to mitigate or nullify culpability when problematic behaviors yield criminal charges.

Liljergren et al. (2015) describe common behavioral manifestations of bvFTD, to include criminal actions such as theft, traffic violations, sexual indiscretions, trespassing, and public urination. Compared to patients experiencing Alzheimer's disease, patients experiencing FTD were more likely to present with criminal behavior, and were more likely to engage in violent behavior. Liljergren offers the compelling argument that forensically evaluating persons with neurodegenerative illness in general, and FTD in particular, may require different criteria than those typically invoked for legally defined insanity. Beyond that, the new onset of criminal behavior in an older adult should prompt the search for FTD, or other neuropsychiatric illnesses implicating frontal and temporal regions of the brain. Unfortunately, the law in most jurisdictions has not adapted to the medical realities of FTD, and most correctional settings are ill-equipped to meet the treatment needs of persons with FTD.

As a consequence, it seems likely that a substantial number of older adults in correctional facilities are suffering from FTD, and in many instances, it's undiagnosed. Dr. Bruce Miller, during an interview about FTD and crime (Shugart, 2015) speculated that many individuals engaging in criminal acts and suffering from FTD, or conditions that similarly compromise behavioral control, are undiagnosed, and lack the support of any physician. "Whether it's infarct, or subtle frontal lobe dysfunction related to AD, or something else, I think this is common, not rare. . . . Our legal system doesn't have clear guidelines of how to deal with frontal lobe dysfunction in the setting of the courts, and this is badly needed." Such persons may wind up facing the full brunt of legal consequences for their actions, especially if they appear to be competent to proceed to trial. That circumstance is then further complicated by placement into a correctional facility that is often ill-equipped to provide for the treatment needs of patients with FTD. Although courts and prosecutors may be open to legal remedies (i.e., dismissal) or alternative placements when physicians or forensic evaluators explain the nature of the illness and its relationship to problematic behaviors, leniency is often lacking when problematic behaviors are violent and/or sexual in nature.

Beyond issues of culpability, FTD also has many implications for various legal capacities pertaining to both criminal and civil matters. Much as the individual suffering from FTD is often able to superficially meet the cognitive prongs for legally defined sanity (i.e., knows the nature and wrongfulness of a particular behavior), similar cognitive requirements for competencies may superficially be met. For example, persons with FTD may be able to demonstrate awareness for the nature and extent of their estate, and their natural heirs, and articulate a plan for dispersing of the estate, thereby appearing competent to execute a will upon cursory assessment. Analogously, persons with FTD may be able to demonstrate an intact knowledge for the charges they face, and rudimentary aspects of criminal court proceedings, presenting as competent to proceed to trial upon more superficial assessment.

Case Example

A defense attorney calls a local forensic psychiatrist seeking consultation regarding his client. The attorney is representing a gentleman with no prior criminal history, but now facing very serious legal charges involving alleged behaviors of a sexual nature, and involving children. The present charges stem from an incident wherein the defendant was apparently viewing pornographic material on the computer, in the presence of young children. Because the defendant had incurred some additional charges of lesser magnitude in the preceding months, and because the present charges involve sentencing enhancers pertaining to both crimes of a sexual nature, and crimes against children, the potential legal consequences are severe. The attorney expresses exasperation with his client, noting that he is minimally cooperative, and seems remarkably disengaged in the process, and expresses concern that the court has been similarly off put by this behavior. The defendant reportedly openly acknowledges his various problematic behaviors, even acknowledging that they are illegal, but otherwise seems entirely unconcerned with his actions, or with the potential consequences. Because of considerable resources stemming from business success prior to his retirement, bail was quickly arranged, and the defendant returned home under his family supervision.

Upon examination, the defendant seems marginally cooperative, offering very little in the way of history. His presentation is generally very flat, albeit punctuated by intervals of irritability and fatuous remarks. His memory is grossly intact, and he is able to acknowledge the behaviors at issue, but offers little in the way of cogent explanation. He offers no complaints, says he is fine, and seems very complacent with his current situation, despite knowing that he is facing some serious charges. His level of disengagement with the examination process makes it difficult to complete neurocognitive screening. Fortunately, an interview of the defendant's wife proves much more useful. She describes her husband retiring approximately two years ago. It seemed that he had lost his spark for the work, and so the family was able to convince him to let his son take over. His retirement initially seemed to be going smoothly enough, but he became increasingly withdrawn, spending much of this time in his basement recreational area. His wife initially thought that he was struggling with the transition into retirement, and maybe was a bit depressed, and so tried to give him some space. But her husband's behavior became increasingly uncharacteristic. Previously fastidious, he soon started attending less and less to his physical appearance and health, putting on weight, and not exercising. She describes one episode in particular that was alarming for her, wherein she confronted him about his weight gain and consumption of Dairy Queen, almost to the exclusion of anything else. In response, he became verbally abusive, and retreated to his basement area.

The defendant's wife describes that his behaviors, and withdrawal from former activities and relationships, became progressively worse. She eventually realized that he was spending inordinate amounts of time viewing pornography, and his withdrawn demeanor was increasingly punctuated with lewd statements, and eventually sexual indiscretions. She relates an event months prior to the behaviors resulting in present charges wherein he came upstairs with his genitals exposed, while their children and grandchildren were visiting. The behavior was only viewed by the adult children and only involved family, such that it was never reported to authorities. Soon thereafter however, a similar episode transpired wherein the defendant exited his home to get the mail similarly exposed, and a neighbor apparently called police. The present charges stem from an incident wherein the defendant had taken his laptop to a nearby park, where he was apparently viewing pornographic websites, and this was witnessed by various children and their parents. The wife denies knowing of any significant history of mental illness experienced by her husband, prior to his difficulties over the past couple of years. When specifically asked, she does indicate a family history of mental illness, reporting that her husband's father had been diagnosed with Alzheimer's and at a relatively early age. She has been unsuccessful in convincing her husband to obtain any sort of medical or psychiatric assessment since all of this started, and he has even avoided seeing his primary care physician. The defendant apparently did have a single encounter with a mental health evaluator while initially (and briefly) incarcerated, during which his prior stature in the business world and "dismissive" behaviors yielded formulations of possible narcissistic personality features.

Recognizing the emergence of various uncharacteristic behaviors so late in life, and a presentation involving prominent apathy, punctuated by irritable and inappropriate outbursts, and in association with a family history suggesting early onset dementia, the evaluator becomes suspicious for frontotemporal dementia. Upon reexamination, a bit more cooperation is elicited with assistance from the defendant's son. Memory and language abilities are largely intact, but assessment of frontally mediated abilities like executive functions (via the Frontal Assessment Battery) indicates severe impairment. The forensic evaluator assists the family in identifying an appropriate neurologist for clinical evaluation, which yields similar findings, and a diagnostic impression of FTD. Neuroimaging completed in that context reveals a pattern of fairly prominent atrophy about the frontal and temporal lobes.

The forensic evaluator, combining data from his own evaluation, as well as clinical data from the treating neurologist, offers diagnostic impressions of FTD, and the medicolegal opinions that the defendant is presently incapable of meaningfully participating in his own defense by virtue of FTD. Acknowledging that the defendant can concretely articulate his charges, and aspects of the judicial process, he lacks the ability to meaningfully and appropriately cooperate in his own defense, by virtue of prominent apathy, and apathy that is punctuated by inappropriate behaviors. Furthermore, despite a superficial awareness for his circumstances, the nature of his neuropsychiatric illness precludes a deeper appreciation for his behaviors, their consequences, and the ability to respond in a rational fashion.

The preceding case example illustrates a number of elements that frequently feature when persons suffering from FTD incur legal charges. Grossly intact memory and language, and a superficial awareness for the nature and wrongfulness for actions, frequently disguise the underlying and causative neuropsychiatric condition in the setting of FTD, particularly among lay persons without medical training, or awareness that illness like FTD exists. Alternatively, erroneous diagnostic formulations may emerge when behaviors and interactions are superficially suggestive of other mental health conditions (e.g., mania, antisocial personality). The evaluator in the case example, recognizing that retained knowledge of wrongfulness might jeopardize claims of insanity or other legal strategies to address culpability, advises that having the defendant declared incompetent to proceed may be the more prudent, expedient, and viable defense strategy.

The forensic psychiatrist receives another call regarding the aforementioned defendant, this time from his spouse. She describes that his supervision at home has been challenging, but had generally been going well with the support of family and some professional assistance. However, it seems that he was able to successfully negotiate a ride to a local attorney's office, who in turn facilitated the drafting of a new will, excluding his wife and family as benefactors. The new will identifies various charities, many of which he has donated to in the past, such that the decision did not seem entirely without precedent. Furthermore, during the process of drafting the new will, he was able to accurately describe his estate, the natural heirs of that estate, and a plan for distribution of the estate. Unfortunately, his rationale for the change was not meaningfully explored.

With the assistance of the family's prior estate attorney, the opportunity for forensic neuropsychiatric examination is afforded. Consistent with circumstances reported in relation to the new will, the evaluee does retain a rather keen awareness for his estate, and is able to name his potential heirs. But with exploring his rationale for the sudden change and his plan for distribution of his estate, it quickly becomes clear that necessary restrictions enforced by family members are the source of disaffection. He complains of not being able to drive, go to Dairy Queen, or use the computer (without supervision). Hence, he has elected to give his fortune to some charities he knows, and not reward his perceived persecutors.

The forensic psychiatrist, recognizing that the evaluee is able to demonstrate the more rudimentary aspects of testamentary capacity (his estate, his potential heirs, and how he wants to distribute his assets), is unable to demonstrate a rational explanation in relation to his new plan for distributing the estate. He instead cites various behaviors by his spouse and children, describing them as harassing and disrespectful, but without any appreciation for the fact their actions are necessary to support him at home and avoid confinement in a locked facility, and in accordance with agreement stemming from his prior criminal proceedings. Notably, the family was very surprised by the change in the will and associated behaviors, describing that apathy remains substantial, albeit punctuated by angry and abusive statements. It seems that the change came in very close temporal proximity to a particularly heated round of rule enforcement around driving restrictions. In the time between completing the new will, and the present examination, he has demonstrated no real investment or interest in the subject.

Once again, grossly intact memory and language abilities oftentimes are superficially suggestive of capacities that are in actuality unrealized. In the setting of FTD, it becomes particularly important to explore not just factual knowledge but also the ability to rationally apply that knowledge to the applicable circumstances. In the aforementioned testamentary capacity dispute, the forensic psychiatrist may allude to a lack of insight, which precludes a rational understanding in relation to the behaviors otherwise perceived as persecutory by the testator. In that context, impulsive and irrational adjustments to the will clearly represents a dramatic departure from clear and cogent values and wishes articulated during his prior state of neuropsychiatric health. (*See* Chapter 15, Guardianships, Conservatorships, and Related Proceedings.)

Conclusion

Representing a client suffering from FTD undoubtedly involves many challenges, starting with the fact that persons with that illness may be undiagnosed at the time of their initial legal encounter. Attorneys enhance their ability to serve such clients by being able to recognize circumstances that might suggest FTD, and arranging for appropriate forensic neuropsychiatric consultation. Though there are very modest treatments available to address this progressive and devastating illness, the provision of a clear diagnosis, prognosis, and professional support can significantly improve quality of life and facilitate appropriate planning for patients and their families. Similarly, recognizing this illness may afford viable defense strategies when behaviors yield criminal charges, or legal remedies when decision-making born of illness runs contrary to well-established principles and values demonstrated throughout their healthy adult life.

• • •

Dr. Hal S. Wortzel is a forensic neuropsychiatrist at the Rocky Mountain MIRECC, where he serves as Director of Neuropsychiatric Consultation Services and Co-director for the National Suicide Risk Management Consultation Program. He is an Associate Professor of Psychiatry, Neurology and Physical Medicine and Rehabilitation at of the University of Colorado and serves as the Michael K. Cooper Professor of Neurocognitive Disease, and as Faculty for the Program in Forensic Psychiatry. Dr. Wortzel maintains a private practice in Forensic Neuropsychiatry and Behavioral Neurology and has consulted on numerous criminal and civil cases. Areas of research/scholarship interest include suicide risk management, aggression and suicide in the context of PTSD and TBI, brain injury litigation, and the application of emerging neuroscientific tools to the legal arena. Dr. Wortzel's email is hal.wortzel@cuanschutz.edu.

Citations available from author by request.

Chapter

8

How Can Lawyers Understand Medicine and Science While Representing People with Dementia?

Cody Miller Pyke, MD, JD, LLM, MSBe

Nothing is more embarrassing (or hilarious, depending on your point of view) than to watch an attorney with no medical background try to go toe-to-toe with an expert during cross-examination. On the one hand, that attorney has a duty of zealous advocacy and competence on behalf of his client. On the other hand, medical, psychological, psychiatric, and scientific concepts and terms may be foreign to attorneys.

This chapter by Dr. Cody Miller Pyke, an attorney and doctor, contains strategies for how attorneys can wade into unfamiliar territory and learn sufficient material to be effective.

• • •

Approaching Complex Medical Issues as a Lawyer

Law is no longer a discrete or autonomous body of knowledge, if ever it was, and the practice of law can no longer be neatly separated from the practice of other disciplines.

—from "Law and Other Disciplines" (Georgetown Law; https://curriculum.law.georgetown.edu/jd/law-other-disciplines/)

The practice of law, by its very nature, requires that lawyers be able to grasp seemingly numerous fields. While this book seeks to prepare attorneys working on cases involving major neurocognitive disorder, more commonly known as "dementia," this short chapter is intended to assist the lawyer tackling a case involving any complex medical issue. The approach is framed around medicine, but its concepts may be applied to any scientific or esoteric discipline a lawyer may encounter.

Medicine is a behemoth of a field, and what's more, it is ever-changing and exponentially growing. Conservative estimates reflect the amalgamated global knowledge of human medicine *doubles* every 12 to 18 months, and some estimate it may double every two to three months. This reality gives rise to a cautionary tale to medical students everywhere—by the time they graduate medical school, much of what they have learned is likely obsolete. Like lawyers, physicians have ethical and professional responsibilities to maintaining their education and keeping up with the latest developments in their field. For lawyers handling cases involving complex medical issues, mastery of both the relevant law and the medical facts can seem intimidating if not impossible. But worry not! Outlined here, three simple points can help make even the most arcane medical cases accessible.

Be Neither Afraid nor Overconfident

As you prepare to represent a person with dementia charged with a criminal offense, it is essential to not be intimidated by the science. No client, colleague, judge, or jury expects you to simply divine personal expertise in medicine. Likewise, it is equally important to give the material due respect—do not assume you will be able to read over the medical facts once and be ready for trial. Like any complex problem, approach a medical case with a strategy in mind, ideally one that breaks the case into smaller components. Such a strategy might look something like:

- **Step One.** Consult the statute of law at issue. Identify and outline the relevant legal elements based on the type of case and/or relief sought by your client.
  - At this stage, secondary legal sources may be a great way to identify what elements you should be keeping an eye out for.
- **Step Two.** Closely read the available medical information.
  - Since you already have the legal elements in mind, take the opportunity to take notes on this first pass as to how the facts do or don't support the legal elements.
- **Step Three.** Identify the following:
  - What you know
  - What you don't know
  - What you need to know
- **Step Four.** Take the items from Step Three and make a list of topic areas where your understanding of the case or underlying science is weak, then tackle them one-by-one. Or, see how the topic areas support, or do not support, the actual elements or legal issues at play.

After applying a strategy like the preceding, you should have a decent understanding of the case from both a legal and medical perspective. At a minimum, you will know exactly where your deficits in understanding are, which brings us to the next essential point of this approach.

Don't Do It Alone

Although the practice of law is inherently adversarial, it is also innately collegial. If your case is novel, either with respect to the applicable law or the particular medical facts at issue, then you should not hesitate to seek out other attorneys with relevant experience. There is no shame in asking for help. The worst that can happen in asking is either you cannot find someone with such experience, or those you do find are not interested in helping you. As you legally and ethically owe a duty of competent counsel to your client, the consequences of "winging it" are much more dire. At the same time, be careful to avoid divulging any information that may be privileged.

If you are unable to reach a comfortable and competent level of understanding within your contacts and personal research, then it may be worth reaching out to a consultant. There is an entire profession of medical-legal consulting dedicated to helping attorneys understand their medical cases and prepare for trial. Although some consultants may also offer serve as expert witnesses, do not confuse the role of the consultant with that of expert witness. The consultant is there to help you better understand the facts and better advocate for the client, whereas witnesses serve an evidentiary role that implicates a host of legal, ethical, and financial questions not necessarily applicable to consultants. (*See* Chapter 12, Working with the Expert.)

Know—and Excel in—Your Role

Speaking of roles, the third and final point of this approach involves recognizing your own. In order to provide competent and effective counsel, it is essential to know your own limits. You should not try to become a medical expert overnight, and you should certainly not hold yourself out as one in court. Whether in an effort to impress a judge or jury, or to undermine the opposition's case, exceeding your own scope of expertise (i.e., knowledge of the law) is inadvisable. Doing so risks embarrassing yourself, irritating the judge, and confusing jurors. Ultimately, trying to show off your newfound knowledge of medicine disservices your client. Instead, focus on the relevant law and how the medical facts interact with the law. The intersection of the medical facts with the law is what wins cases, not the facts alone. Navigating and speaking to that intersection is what lawyers are trained in and what they excel at—it is what you bring to the table that no one else does.

Conclusion

While the preceding approach is not an exhaustive manual, it is an effective starting point for the attorney handling a case involving a complex medical issue, including one like dementia. Other chapters in this book address some of the finer legal and evidentiary points in the context of dementia, but you can always return to this chapter as an initial roadmap. No matter how complex the science in a case may seem at first, you can succeed if you approach it strategically, dutifully, and humbly.

BONAM FORTUNAM ET SCIENTIAM. Good luck and good knowledge.

• • •

Cody Miller Pyke is a transgender and nonbinary human living in Houston, TX. They completed their JD and LLM in Health Law at the University of Houston Law Center and completed their MD at Baylor College of Medicine in spring 2022. They also have a master's in bioethics and bioethics policy from Clarkson University. Cody is a passionate advocate for health care equity across socioeconomic status, race, sex, and gender. Their research focuses on bioethical and policy issues in law and medicine, with special attention to mental health, reproductive justice, and LGBTQIA+ issues.

Citations available from author by request.

Chapter

9

Working with Clients with Dementia

Dr. Eric Y. Drogin

As the following chapter by forensic psychologist and attorney Dr. Eric Y. Drogin notes, if a client with dementia is found competent to proceed, the criminal defense lawyer must soldier on. Dr. Drogin provides practical advice for working with such clients who cannot participate in their defense in the manner of most defendants.

This chapter may very well cause us to reflect upon two issues. First, given that the cognitive abilities of clients with dementia will never improve—in fact, they will probably decline during the course of representation—might it make sense to have additional competency evaluations as the case progresses? Second, given this likely decline, why is the criminal justice system prosecuting someone like this, particularly if the defendant in question is elderly and far beyond the age of recidivism?

• • •

Working with Clients with Dementia

Few lawyers will find themselves in a position to devote the bulk of their criminal defense activities to persons with mental illness, as welcomed as such specialization may be by clients, co-counsel, and the courts. Fewer still—apart from those for whom the balance of their practices is composed of a range of guardianship, conservatorship, probate, and other "elder law" matters (*see* Chapter 15, Guardianships, Conservatorships, and Related Proceedings)—will focus primarily on the needs of clients with dementia. This is not a mode of legal service provision that garners much media attention, and it captures relatively little of the journal and newsletter space afforded to field research or practice tips. There is no national guild that prioritizes the representation of this client population. Clients with dementia may only conclusively be identified as such well after counsel with more general criminal defense practices have committed themselves irretrievably to the case at hand.

As a result, clients with dementia can be expected to come to counsel, rather than the other way around. They usually arrive with little fanfare, but before long may stand out as exceedingly difficult to assist, albeit for reasons that may not readily be apparent. This chapter addresses the needs of counsel when suddenly the need arises to defend someone with this condition. Counsel will learn how to accommodate symptoms typically associated with dementia, and how to obtain additional help in this regard from a variety of sources. This chapter does not concern itself with the retention and employment of expert witnesses (*see* Chapter 12, Working with the Expert) or with crafting a mental health defense (*see*, e.g., Chapter 10, Working a Case of a Client with Dementia).

In addition, when reading this chapter, counsel is likely to wonder (as did the author) how it is that clients who exhibit some of the problems described herein could be considered competent to stand trial (*see* Chapter 2, Competency) in the first place. Certainly, such concerns should be considered as a basis for raising—and continuing to raise—the notion of competency whenever indicated, but when this has occurred and no favorable ruling ensues, counsel will need to soldier on regardless.

Is It Truly Dementia?

Counsel's work with clients typically begins long before counsel has had an opportunity to review documents, commission evaluations, and conference with collateral sources of information. It may be apparent at the point of retention—or court appointment—that clients are experiencing some form of potentially disabling mental condition. What might this be? Clients themselves may not know. If they do know, they may not necessarily want to admit it to counsel or to anyone else. Clients may have been misinformed, receiving several inaccurate diagnoses in the past, and perhaps some accurate ones as well.

Representation of persons who appear to have disabilities cannot come screeching to a halt just because experts funds have yet to flow and medical determinations are yet to be made. With this in mind, counsel should at least be in a position from the outset to consider what *might* be the root cause of such readily observable problems as confusion, inattention, contradictory assertions, deficits in recall, or even a seeming inability to communicate with counsel at all. There are a number of diagnoses that have symptoms in common with dementia.

Depressive disorders, for example, involve much more than just being sad. Severe cases can literally be immobilizing, and are associated with deficits in memory. Clients may be suffering from a form of delirium—perhaps due to excessively prescribed medications, and perhaps due to an ill-advised combination of prescribed medications—that renders them acutely incapable of rational decision-making. Long-standing rather than acute addictive processes involving prescribed medication, illicit substances, or alcohol can have an effect on mental functioning that persists for weeks or even months after incarceration, and may in some cases occasion permanent brain damage. Intellectual Disability (formerly termed Mental Retardation) is manifested by an array of cognitive limitations and is registered across the lifespan.

Perhaps clients are just displaying the natural effects of old age, possibly exacerbated in some instances by medical conditions that are not usually associated with psychiatric problems. It is worth observing in this regard that dementia is not an inevitable consequence of aging, and also that the mere presence of dementia does not automatically lead to problems with legal representation any more than it necessarily translates into incompetency to stand trial (*see* Chapter 2, Competency) or a lack of criminal responsibility (*see* Chapter 4, Responsibility).

Should dementia wind up being the diagnosis to which client problems can be attributed, then counsel's approach to criminal representation will need to be tailored to the symptoms that make up that specific condition. Counsel will quickly determine that mere common sense will not be enough to navigate this situation. Just as some symptoms of dementia exist in common with the disorders that counsel is more used to encountering, others are virtually unique. Patience and empathy, while surely among the most significant attributes of successful criminal attorneys, will not suffice in and of themselves.

Accommodating Specific Symptoms of Dementia

The fifth edition of the *Diagnostic and Statistical Manual of Mental Disorders* (DSM-5) renamed what were once "Dementia, Delirium, Amnestic, and other Cognitive Disorders" as simply "Neurocognitive Disorders." This does not mean that mental health professionals suddenly realized that for the better part of a century they had gotten it all wrong, and that there never really was any such thing as dementia, or any meaningful distinction between dementia and other problems with how patients process information and express themselves. Rather, this essentially involved a reshuffling of categorical groupings and an updated analysis of how much certain disorders were either different or alike. (For a broad clinical overview of such matters, *see* Chapter 1, What Is Dementia?) However long counsel may have been practicing, familiar terms inevitably resurface, and fortunately the new scheme makes these matters a lot easier to understand.

Following is a collection of symptoms that the DSM-5 associates with what is still commonly called "dementia," along with a practice-oriented look at what each of these symptoms can mean for counsel's attempts to work with clients with dementia. American Psychiatric Association, Diagnostic and Statistical Manual of Mental Disorders 591–643 (5th ed. 2013).

Declines in Complex Attention

This symptom refers to the ability of clients to keep information in their minds and then process that information. An example that is often used for this skill is mental arithmetic. Let's say that the client is facing a charge that normally carries a penalty of 20 years, but the prosecutors are offering a deal that instead would involve a sentence of only ten years, with the possibility of parole after serving 50 percent of the prison sentence rather than the 85 percent normally associated with this particular offense. To be fair, counsel themselves may stumble a bit at the end of a long day when attempting to grapple with these numbers, but the point of this example isn't "if clients can't work these sums on their own, that means they have dementia." Rather, the attempt here is to illustrate that demands for mental arithmetic and other forms of complex attention can make themselves known at any time in the course of representation, and that clients with dementia can find themselves unduly challenged when this occurs.

In this situation, counsel might fixate on the inability of clients to compare the penalties associated with these two options, and then—choking back their visible frustration to the extent possible—simply convey which outcome counsel considers more favorable and then move on to other matters. Of course, the very way in which this approach is being worded suggests that there are better ways to address such problems. Whenever clients are experiencing difficulty understanding something, it's best to ally with their sense of the difficulty of the task and to normalize the potential embarrassment that may accompany an inability to find the best solution with ease.

Here, counsel can acknowledge that math isn't everyone's cup of tea. Out comes the pocket calculator. "I know we're dealing with two different calculations here, as if one wouldn't be hard enough. If there's anything I don't miss about school, it's math. Let's see if we can run a few numbers here and figure out together what the best outcome might be." As clients are led through this determination step by step, with counsel modeling perseverance along the way, the bottom line can be presented in terms of five years one way and 17 the other, followed by a renewed discussion of the factor that really counts: risk.

Declines in Executive Function

Here, counsel runs up against an issue that inevitably surfaces whenever the time comes to wade into psychiatry's DSM-5 or any other discipline's form of Holy Writ: the obscurity of technical terms, made even more confusing by their substantial overlap in meaning. One way to cope with this is to picture how much fun the doctors are having when they find themselves having to distinguish between cause, cause in fact, factual cause, actual cause, but-for cause, proximate cause, superseding cause, and sole cause. In any event, executive function refers to the ability to manage combined tasks that *include* the sorts of processing associated with complex attention. Counsel's going to be just fine with this. If executive functioning difficulties are expressed in a combination of challenges, counsel can come the aid of clients with a combination of helpful solutions.

Much is made of the inability of clients to understand things. With deficits in executive functioning, the stakes are raised for those situations in which we are now asking clients to *do* things. For example, counsel may need to convey instructions that amount to the following: "Please give your daughter another call. My investigator will come by tomorrow with what we believe is her new number. It would be great if you could ask her if she's willing to look over your medical bills and find the name of the hospital where they performed that brain scan for you a year or two ago. Please write down the name of that hospital and we'll bring you another release to sign. We'd contact your daughter ourselves, but frankly I don't think she trusts us yet, and we need to get those records for you in a hurry."

There are a few different steps embedded in this request. In these scenarios, clients would need to wait for information, act on it, make a request, obtain more information, and convey it to counsel. Presented with what may seem like a barrage of contingent instructions, clients with dementia may well doubt their ability to follow through, and complicate things still further by becoming flustered, defensive, and perhaps even uncooperative. Counsel can help to defuse this state of affairs by breaking down such requests step by step, and by rehearsing with clients how each stage might play out. Perhaps the contacts in question could be the focus of a roleplay with counsel as the daughter. Counsel may also wish to consider limiting the task to fewer steps, leaving other steps for later. Offering too much instruction at once may lead to cognitive overload that contributes to forgetting, costing even more valuable time and delaying the implementation of counsel's complex litigation plans still further.

Declines in Learning and Memory

Beyond juggling and comparing different potential outcomes on the one hand, and following through on multistage tasks to make counsel's goals more attainable on the other, clients may be facing a more basic barrier to successful participation in pretrial proceedings. They may essentially be incapable, to some extent, of encoding and retrieving counsel's requests and instructions at all. Of course, this won't be a unique experience for counsel, who has encountered similar difficulties when interacting with clients who suffer from psychotic disorders, or with clients who are still in the process of detoxifying from polysubstance abuse or dependence. The difference here is that counsel cannot count upon eventually being rescued when the effects of psychiatric medication kick in, or when intoxication and withdrawal symptoms have run their course. Dementia is a permanent condition, the effects of which will only worsen over time.

Faced with neurologically determined, inflexible limitations on the ability of clients to grasp what counsel is saying, and perhaps also to recall at some later date whatever information was eventually internalized, counsel will need to find some way to revisit key points and then to move forward to other issues as time passes and new practical issues surface. Clients who lack the capacity to learn and memorize must still find a way to participate in their representation, in one fashion or another.

In this situation, counsel can employ one strategy typically utilized to good effect at a much later stage in legal proceedings. Successful trial attorneys inevitably become skilled at "looping," which involves adding a witness's prior answer to the next question on direct or cross-examination. When consulting with clients with dementia, counsel can find a way to build old information into new avenues of exploration. This promotes rehearsal, builds a narrative that is easier to follow, and keeps older (and perhaps now forgotten) information fresh. Another strategy is the development of a log that addresses—in a straightforward, client-friendly, and accessibility-worded fashion—what was discussed during every prior meeting. Counsel can then refer to this material on the spot, directing clients back to what was proposed, discovered, and settled in the course of previous encounters. Sometimes this material can even be left with clients for their own review between visits, with an understanding that this may be a far more dubious enterprise regarding clients who are currently incarcerated, and for whom document security is thus more questionable.

Declines in Language Abilities

Just as counsel has discovered when crafting direct and cross-examination questions, or when conducting voir dire in high-stakes legal matters, there are more- and decidedly less-effective ways to elicit information and make one's point when participating in a client conference.

Here's one approach:

I'd like to take up what could be quite a bit of time here, but in a way that I think may ultimately serve to benefit your representation substantially. I don't mind sharing that this is an approach that has stood the test of time, and that has led to gratifying outcomes in cases both similar to and dissimilar from your own. Please follow me the best you can. At this juncture, I'd like to ask you to share your answers to a series of questions. At what point in time did you initially encounter the entity we'll refer to as the alleged victim, under what particular circumstances this is deemed to have occurred, and what sorts of assertions were made to you by the other party, and vice versa?

Here's another:

Can I ask you some things that could be helpful?

When did you first meet Chris?

Where was this?

What did you say to Chris?

What did Chris say to you?

Counsel will not have much difficulty ascertaining which of these approaches is more likely to have the desired effect. Indeed, the same can be said of attempts to communicate with clients who are *not* afflicted with dementia. At issue here are two distinct concerns: the potential obscurity of the specific words in question, and the convoluted way in which those words may be arranged, in terms of such factors as excessive length, dense structure, distracting commentary, and so on. How can counsel get all the necessary information from clients who are even more likely than others to have difficulty understanding language?

The most effective approach in this regard is one that focuses on brevity, simplicity, and a willingness to break down ideas into their most basic elements. Counsel can practice such methods by jotting down potential inquiries and then reducing them to the simplest, bit-by-bit inquiries possible. No evidentiary standards must be met. No record for appeal is being made. No jury is watching and expecting to be impressed. Counsel and clients just need to figure out what happened and what needs to happen next.

Some problems with oral language can be addressed by the simple expedient of communicating in writing—and vice versa. If counsel can introduce a computer tablet or suitably large-screened smartphone into the consultation space, writing things out for clients will be far less arduous than doing so by hand, as in decades past. Similarly, when the difficulties that clients with dementia are experiencing are specifically those involving grasping written language, essential passages from legally relevant documents can be cut and pasted into readily available, free-of-charge oral translation applications.

Declines in Perceptual-Motor Ability

More than any other concern, this is one that is not confined to clients with dementia. Counsel will have encountered clients with perceptual-motor deficits (involving the ability to make sense of what one sees) throughout a career of any significant duration. This having been noted, the host of other potential dementia-related symptoms may make it exceptionally difficult for counsel to discern if this particular problem is present. More than with perhaps any other concern, this is one in which obtaining and perusing relevant medical records—and obtaining, when possible, a contemporaneous dementia workup—can be a critically important step in establishing a positive working relationship with affected clients.

When successfully distinguished from language problems, and also from more straightforward visual problems that may amount to clients having been legally blind before the onset of dementia, perceptual-motor deficits most directly impact the ability to perceive and process visual information. This can become particularly relevant when reviewing with clients such materials as crime scene photographs, witness identification composites, and various charts and graphs that may form some portion of discovery or perhaps attachments to the pleadings proffered from either side of the case in question.

Counsel should make it a point to demystify and otherwise normalize the effects of these hurdles when working with clients with dementia. Like every other barrier in criminal proceedings, this one can be called out for what it is, without undue drama or implicit blame. Materials that cannot successfully be incorporated by traditional visual means can always be described by counsel in detail. Similar to when the physical challenges faced by clients may require some form of accommodation, counsel may need to consider making perceptual-motor deficits an acknowledged factor in how evidence is presented in the courtroom, particularly in the event that a decision is made for clients to take the stand and undergo direct or cross-examination that involves the presentation of visual exhibits.

Declines in Social Cognition

This symptom refers to the inability of clients to explain their behavior—and that of other persons—with reference to commonly accepted norms for human interaction. Do clients appear to grasp that their actions on the date in question would typically be perceived as unusual? If so, do clients seem to understand that the response to such actions might range from idle curiosity to outright hostility and perhaps the use of violence in response? Similarly, is it possible that clients have overinterpreted the comments, gestures, or facial expressions of the alleged victim in a given criminal matter? Sometimes, people reach into their jacket pockets in order to produce a weapon, while at other times their purpose is instead to retrieve a stick of chewing gum.

Interpersonal misunderstandings associated with dementia are not necessarily confined to the source of criminal charges. They may actually pertain to the ways in which clients perceive counsel's own actions and attendant motivations. Misperceptions of this nature can inspire a degree of suspiciousness that in some instances will evolve into full-blown paranoia. Legal representation is a complex undertaking under the best of circumstances, but clients who find counsel's behavior questionable and even deliberately injurious may of course disrupt and delay pretrial duties to a considerable and ultimately even intolerable extent.

When it comes to addressing the arguably actionable prior behavior of clients with dementia, counsel is best advised to review these in as matter-of-fact a fashion as feasible, checking in periodically as to how clients figure their actions would have been viewed by others, and the extent to which such considerations really matter. There may be quite a bit at stake here, since what counsel may be seeking to attribute to dementia is often what the prosecution is seeking to characterize as the manifestation of life-long antisocial attitudes and other long-standing criminal proclivities. The implications of a failure to understand the implications of the behavior of others may be central to eventual determinations of criminal responsibility (*see* Chapter 4, Responsibility). Problematic views of counsel's own behavior may be mitigated to some extent by the enlistment of other persons who still enjoy the trust of clients, and also by modest reference, where appropriate, to gains made and bonds formed in the course of representation to date.

Sources of Support

In addition to counsel's access to the aforementioned medical records and contemporaneous workups, the DSM-5 appropriately emphasizes the value of "a knowledgeable informant" when seeking to determine the existence, extent, and ramifications of dementia-related symptoms. Time is precious in the course of any form of legal representation, and this becomes all the more salient when clients are saddled with a condition that, by definition, involves some combination of complex attention, executive function, learning, memory, language, perceptual-motor, and social cognition deficits. To whom can counsel turn for support when seeking to obtain just outcomes for clients with dementia?

Family Members

Although clients with dementia are typically older persons, it is still entirely possible that the family members in question may include parents, aunts, uncles, and older siblings who can directly describe the lives of clients from birth. This is particularly useful when seeking to develop a full developmental profile, but may also have very direct value in supplementing counsel's working relationship with clients, due to the natural authority that such persons may still carry. Family members may also have direct knowledge of significant life events worth exploring, as well as subjects that counsel would be better off avoiding if a truly collaborative relationship can be expected to continue. To engage one family member is potentially to engage many others—which is well worth considering since clients with dementia may themselves have little or no valid information to share concerning the identities and contact information of even first-degree relatives. Family members may possess long-term medical records, personal correspondence, and other sources of information that can lend to counsel's insight when seeking to determine the most effective methods for moving a case forward.

Corrections Personnel

Counsel may be committing a very serious and ultimately consequential error by assuming that corrections personnel are, by the nature of their jobs, irrevocably aligned with the prosecution and negatively inclined toward clients. On the contrary, it is at least as important a function of corrections personnel to keep clients alive and otherwise healthy than it is merely to prevent them from being discharged prematurely into the community at large. Should counsel take the time to discuss with corrections personnel the personal situations of clients with dementia, the result may be a very pleasant surprise. Corrections personnel—virtually all of whom have older relatives and who are very likely to have encountered dementia amongst the ranks of their own family members—are typically more willing to adopt a more understanding perspective toward persons whose alleged transgressions and current circumstances are more attributable to an underlying medical condition than to ingrained antisocial personality characteristics. On a more practical level, clients with dementia can be very expensive, providing all the incentive necessary to support efforts for alternative placement. Much can be learned from corrections personnel about current moods and worsening conditions of counsel's more cognitively fragile clients, as well as those clients' receptivity to guidance.

Treating Clinicians

These persons can become useful fact witnesses in time, but they also have much to offer when it comes to assisting counsel in developing successful attorney–client relationships. Treating clinicians have themselves been able to overcome many of the barriers with which counsel is now seeking assistance. They are also likely to have determined which of the many symptoms and types of dementia (*see* Chapter 1, What Is Dementia?) are present for particular clients, since these conditions are by no means uniform in their medical presentation. A desire to be helpful is deeply ingrained in the training and professional indoctrination of treating clinicians, who are in a position—once their trust has been legitimately obtained—to be invaluable reinforcers of counsel's ongoing efforts to support clients with dementia. Clinical cases, like legal cases, evolve in real time, and treating clinicians who maintain an active role with counsel's clients can provide crucial advance warning about further cognitive decline, shifting attitudes, deteriorating perceptions, and erroneous observations with respect to the course of current legal proceedings. It is a good idea to make it clear very earlier on whether helpful treating clinicians might be expected to take the stand in the future.

Examining Experts

This is a relatively complex avenue of professional consultation, but it is by no means one that counsel should reflexively seek to avoid. It is true that examining experts—be they retained by either side, or be they managed exclusively in some instances by the court—are supposed to adopt an unbiased role that focuses on a forensic determination devoid of treatment or independent advocacy. This having been noted, there is certainly nothing wrong from counsel's view in asking pointed questions, not just about such matters as trial competency, criminal responsibility, competency to waive *Miranda* rights, and mitigation, but also about recently assessed cognitive abilities, memory functioning, the ability to track conversations, and the capacity to follow instructions. It is not a partisan act on the part of examining experts to provide such assistance, and considerable weight can be placed on the role that their clinical training plays in qualifying them to make relevant observations. Examinations experts are, of course, also well-attuned to what it is that counsel would find essential for clients to be functioning rationally in their own defense. Examining experts receive the same foundational training and acculturation as treating clinicians do, and as such should not be blind to the reasonableness of requests that fall short of soliciting advice on *how* to represent clients with dementia.

Trial Consultants

Unlike examining experts, trial consultants do not find themselves bound by a need to be pointedly, transparently, and verifiably unbiased. By contrast, trial consultants arrive on the scene with an acknowledged purpose to help counsel win. Barring the commission of actions such as misrepresentation and dual agency that run afoul of codified ethical principles, trial consultants are unconcerned about how their contributions will play on the witness stand, because they have no expectations of testifying in the first place. Trial consultants are simply there to assist counsel. If counsel has (or can procure) the funding to engage mental professionals with specialized expertise in dementia as trial consultants, then a variety of functions can be performed. Trial consultants can sit in on meetings with clients and offer candid assessments after the fact concerning cognitive abilities and deficits. They can assist in translating the statements and behaviors of clients with dementia in light of current research studies and other aspects of the relevant scientific literature. Trial consultants can also opine on the likelihood that specific clients are likely to fare well when clients are sitting next to counsel or testifying on their own behalf. If clients with dementia subsequently convey to trial consultants that counsel's inquiries and directions are confusing, trial consultants can come back to counsel with a summary of these concerns and suggestions for how communications can be improved.

Advocacy Groups

These groups provide a very different sort of advocacy than that performed by counsel, but they are nonetheless in a position to offer highly useful support to those tasked with conducting legal representation. As a general matter, advocacy groups that focus upon persons with dementia are a gateway to a vast trove of instructional materials on this topic. In some ways better still, these materials are almost invariably designed to be accessible to such entities as community assistance providers, law enforcement personnel, legislators, and family members. Counsel already has more dense medical information to wade through; something that actually makes objective sense, gets right to the point, and is readily digestible will make for very welcome fare indeed. Advocacy groups are not hindered by the objectivity requirements of, say, counsel or examining experts. Counsel's difficulty in accessing this resource may actually be more one of gently persuading advocacy groups *not* to get involved, as targeted institutional contacts and public pronouncements might undercut certain strategies of legal representation. In addition to their own well-developed and highly focused contributions, advocacy groups are often willing and able to share contacts that can result in the recruitment of examining experts and trial consultants.

Conclusion

When representing clients with dementia, counsel should be prepared to accommodate the symptoms associated with that diagnosis in a fashion that, to the extent possible, enables clear communication, respect for client wishes, and favorable legal outcomes. Counsel should not be forced to go this alone. Even in the absence of funding for expert witnesses and trial consultants, accessible resources will typically exist that can uncover vital background information, provide ongoing monitoring of cognitive status, and establish conduits to additional support. Clients with dementia are not considered incapable of self-determination by virtue of the mere presence of this condition. Much can be done to assist them when the court has determined that a finding of incompetency is not an option and that criminal proceedings must go forward.

• • •

Eric Y. Drogin is a fellow of the American Psychological Association, a fellow of the American Academy of Forensic Psychology, a diplomate of the American Board of Professional Psychology, and a diplomate and former president of the American Board of Forensic Psychology. Dr. Drogin teaches on the faculty of Harvard Medical School, where he serves as the Affiliated Lead of Psycholegal Studies for the Psychiatry, Law, and Society Program at Brigham and Women's Hospital and participates in the Program in Psychiatry and the Law at the Massachusetts Mental Health Center and the Forensic Psychiatry Service at Beth Israel Deaconess Medical Center. Dr. Drogin received PhD in clinical psychology from Hahnemann University.

Dr. Drogin is a life fellow of the American Bar Foundation. He currently serves as immediate past chair of the ABA's Science & Technology Law Section. Dr. Drogin teaches as an adjunct professor of law and mental health for the University of New Hampshire's Franklin Pierce School of Law, as an instructor for the Harvard Law School Trial Advocacy Workshop, and as an honorary professor of law for the *Prifysgol Aberystwyth* (formerly "University of Wales") Department of Law and Criminology. He received his JD from the Villanova University School of Law.

Currently serving as associate editor of the *International Journal of Law and Psychiatry*, and formerly serving as editor in chief of the *Journal of Psychiatry & Law* and as co-editor in chief of *Psychological Injury and*

Law, Dr. Drogin has authored or co-authored over 300 legal and scientific publications to date. His multidisciplinary practice encompasses mental health law, expert witness testimony, and trial consultation. Dr. Drogin describes himself as an avid musician, while conceding that "avid" is not synonymous with either "accomplished" or "well-received."

Dr. Drogin can be reached at eyd@drogin.net, and his website is www.drogin.net.

Citations available from author by request.

Chapter

10

Working a Case of a Client with Dementia

Allison Matthis, Esq.

There's a saying among trial lawyers that we learn more from the trials we lost than the trials we won. In this chapter, public defender Allison Matthis extends that theme to learning more from a case in which, in hindsight, she believes she could have done more. (In truth, Ms. Matthis is a fearless and creative attorney, so her personal standard of zealous advocacy is a high one.) She charts out all the key junctures of the case of an elderly man and explains what she wished she had done.

Most criminal defense lawyers, new or experienced, when dealing with clients with dementia, must deal with the reality of limited resources, whether it be mental health experts who do not readily recognize dementia to a lack of proper care options in the community.

• • •

The first time I dealt with a client with dementia was when I was an inexperienced, overconfident public defender, working in a small island nation in the South Pacific. My client, Rubak (not his real name), was a very gifted baseball player in his youth, and now, at 73, a well-regarded elder in the community. He was charged with aggravated assault for hitting his wife over the head with a cast-iron frying pan in the middle of an argument. Neighbors were used to hearing the couple fight, but when it escalated to the wife's loud screams for help, they called the police. Somewhat amazingly, the wife did not suffer serious permanent injuries, but she was righteously angry and asked police for a restraining order.

That Monday morning, sitting in my office, Rubak was quiet and seemed embarrassed. He answered most of my questions with "yes" or "no," but provided no elaboration. "Have you been diagnosed with any medical problems lately?" I asked. He shook his head. "What about medication? Are you taking any medication?" No. "Well, it's just kind of strange that all of a sudden you got arrested—is everything ok? Did something exceptional happen?" He shrugged. "I hit her with a frying pan because she wouldn't stop talking. That's all. Can I go?" He said, through a translator.

I had him evaluated for mental health concerns by the local (and only) psychiatrist on the island, a specialist trained in the Philippines whose credentials I was always a little suspect of. But she generally did what she could; she seemed kind and compassionate, and there weren't any other options, really. "He's just an alcoholic," she told me. "There's nothing wrong with him other than that."

Dear friends, trust your instincts. Alcoholism is a terrible disease, and a mean drunk can do an awful lot of damage. But usually mean drunks have gotten into trouble before they're 75 if they're going to get into trouble. Out on bond, Rubak reconciled with his wife and almost immediately assaulted her again. The prosecutor agreed to dismiss the second assault for a plea on the first one. No jail time, just probation and a no-contact provision. It was a good deal. We took it. And then he assaulted her again, and again.

Four assaults resulting in charges in less than a year. Frustrated, I asked the psychiatrist to evaluate him again. She took him into the single secured room at the tiny hospital facility and performed another evaluation, this time observing him and interviewing him over the course of a couple of days. This time, she diagnosed him with alcohol-related dementia.

At yet another bond setting hearing, the wife spoke out for the first time. She told the judge that she was constantly angry at him because he was cheating on her with the vice-president of a local bank—a woman the judge knew personally and who had been dead for 20 years. It started to become apparent that not only did Rubak have significant cognitive decline, but his wife did, too. Both of them had been on a downward slope for some time. She believed that it was 1980 and he was having an affair, and he had no idea what she was talking about, and sometimes no idea who she was—just some strange woman standing in the kitchen yelling at him about nonsense until he got so frustrated he'd hit her.

This led to one of the worst situations of my entire legal career. I had him plead to a felony assault with a domestic violence finding prior to his diagnosis. The island had no elder-care facilities, with most elders being cared for by their children, but Rubak and his wife had just one daughter who lived in the United States. She was willing to take in either of her parents, but the wife did not want to leave her life-long home, and Rubak now had a conviction for a violent felony on his record, preventing him from being able to enter the U.S.

I called the State Department. They told me that were I to get a habeas writ granted on the grounds that he was incompetent at the time of his plea, or even a presidential pardon issued, the U.S. would deny entry. "Yeah, well, we don't really want violent people with dementia coming over to the U.S., either, even if they're not technically criminally responsible," they told me.

I talked to other legal services providers and family members. I concocted involved schemes where the daughter could somehow take guardianship over her mother and coerce her to get on a plane. The guilt and horror of this situation were terrible.

In the meantime, Rubak was stuck living in a holding cell at a Department of Fish and Wildlife outpost since the jail was overcrowded and understaffed, incapable of providing the serious attention and care that he needed—and there were no behavioral health or eldercare facilities. The rangers would call me and say, "He pees on the floor, and we don't like having him here. He complains all day. It's not my job to care for an old man."

And they were right, of course. It wasn't their job. But every time I convinced a judge to let him out of custody, he went home and assaulted his wife again, and even though everyone now knew he wasn't competent, there were no resources available to handle this situation.

Eventually, to my great relief, the daughter quit her job in the U.S. and came home. We created a plan where Rubak would be released, and a neighboring social worker would check in with him daily to make sure he was taking his medication and not drinking. The daughter stayed with them, took care of them, and cooled them off amazingly well when her mom started going on about the affair. There were no more assaults.

I think about that story frequently—mostly because of how wildly unfair it seems to both Rubak and his wife that they had to spend the last few years of their lives confused, miserable, and fighting, and that I played a role in making his life just that much more miserable because I failed to advocate for my client when my instincts told me something was wrong.

Investigating a Hunch

There are specific symptoms of dementia that you may be able to spot in cases where your suspicions are aroused. One of the major and most notable symptoms is an increase in aggression and agitation. Even if we don't see the agitation during our consultations with our clients, things like picking up assault charges for the first time could be indicative of a change in mood!

PRACTICE TIP: Symptoms of dementia are often more pronounced at the end of the day. If you have only met with your client early in the day (like before court), consider setting up a brief appointment in the late afternoon or early evening to determine if your client's affect is different or if your client appears more confused than she has previously.

Age is definitely the largest risk factor for dementia, and being attuned to this in clients over 60 is a good idea. But there are other factors as well, including genetic predisposition, heart disease, alcohol abuse, and head trauma, that increase dementia risk even in the young.

Screening tools for general medical practitioners are helpful here. Though not all of the questions are things one could easily work into a typical attorney consult ("Hey, sir, could you please draw a clock really quick? Why? No reason . . ."), there are several things that are easy to incorporate and may help you determine if there is more need to investigate potential cognitive disorders.

For example, asking a client as you're filling out paperwork together, "Oh, by the way, what's the date today?" as if you've forgotten it yourself, could fit into the conversation quite naturally. Additionally, a lawyer can and should build rapport with the client through conversation about things unrelated to the case, and could easily work in a breezy but fairly specific conversation about current events or weather patterns (avoiding contentious political issues, of course).

An attorney should be careful not to only engage about issues personal to the client. If a client tells you confidently that her husband cheated on her recently and that has led to a world of problems, you as the attorney will not likely know that the affair was actually in 1980, whereas if you engage with the client about discrete contemporary happenings, such as reported on the local news, you have a better chance of being able to suss out whether the references are actually recent. Circling back around to a similar question several minutes into the conversation ("I'm so sorry, what high school did you say you graduated from?") is a good strategy to determine if the client is able to maintain orientation for longer periods of time.

As an attorney, you are in a position to ask a series of questions as part of a file intake process, which may be telling. One of those questions should absolutely be, "Have you ever suspected you are experiencing symptoms of dementia, Alzheimer's disease, or any other kind of cognitive decline?" Another question might have to do with history of traumatic brain injury or even family history of cognitive issues ("Did either of your parents have dementia/Alzheimer's/cognitive decline?").

As defense practitioners, we cannot be embarrassed to ask questions that may have sensitive answers. As a practical matter, acting like you are asking the question not because the client prompted it, but because it is part of the generic intake paperwork you are required to complete (even if it's not), can help sidestep awkwardness many times. Additionally, getting a client to allow you to talk to a family member or friend that they've known for several years may also help guide you in your investigation. Most specifically, what you want to ask is whether they have noticed a behavioral change in the past years, or whether, as is the case with this author, perhaps they are just absentminded and a bit quirky.

Diagnosis and Evaluation

Above all, if there is a whisper of a doubt about a client's competency, sanity, or cognitive ability, you should get them evaluated by a psychiatrist. In my situation with Rubak, I had very few options (actually, only one), because there was only one psychiatrist in the country and the internet was not strong enough to support sustained overseas video conferencing. Now, even in rural areas, Zoom has given us some additional options as far as expert evaluations are concerned.

If resources are limited, contacting a nearby jurisdiction's public defender's office or criminal defense bar association and asking for their list of approved experts might be a place to start. Otherwise, I would probably recommend calling a local medical school and asking for referrals. Unless, of course, you have a practitioner in mind whom you think might be a good resource. I have asked for referrals from my own personal providers whom I trust and think are good at what they do, and have gotten some great experts that way.

If your client has insurance, there is no reason why you can't send them to one of their own doctors for an initial screening and diagnosis, but an evaluation with an eye toward the legal consequences of diagnosis is a separate and requisite thing. If your client does see a doctor other than a forensic psychiatrist, make sure that the client signs a waiver allowing you to discuss the case with that doctor, or at least have access to the client's medical records at that medical office. If your client starts taking medication prior to being evaluated by the forensic expert, not disclosing that medication may have an impact on the evaluation's results.

Prior to the evaluation, your client should sign a confidentiality waiver allowing you and the psychiatrist to speak to each other. It is absolutely necessary and appropriate for you to express your concerns about possible cognitive decline to the psychiatrist so they can be alerted about what to look for.

Additionally, you should discuss expectations for what the psychiatrist will produce as an end-product with them prior to engaging their services. By this, I mean that in jurisdictions with reciprocal discovery statutes that may require expert reports be turned over to the state, ethical defense lawyers will talk to the psychiatrist about whether they will necessarily produce written reports or whether they are free to disclose the findings to you verbally first, and then ask whether the defense team wishes a written report to be issued. In states with less-draconian discovery laws, you should still discuss with the psychiatrist what the written report will cover, including whether or not you want the psychiatrist to discuss the specifics of the charges with the client, or whether you are hoping to leave that out if possible.

In cases involving assaults of children/elderly, and especially sexual assaults, if you suspect there may be additional victims, be aware that the psychiatrist is almost certainly a mandated reporter and ask them how they have handled that situation in the past. Some psychiatrists are more comfortable than others in admitting that they are able to avoid asking specific questions about uncharged offenses, and those are the psychiatrists you should be trying to retain.

One of the most difficult aspects of handling a criminal case where the client is suffering from a cognitive decline is that it is really difficult to assess how bad the cognitive decline was at the time of the incident. Clarity and judgment can change daily and even hourly, so being able to accurately assess what a person's state of mind was several months prior to the evaluation is quite literally educated guess work. This is a big deal to us here in mens rea land, and you should discuss this with the expert you retain and ask them what their experience is in similar situations. Talking to them about this will also help you be able to explain to the prosecutor and, eventually, the fact finder, why sanity at the time of the offense is such a difficult thing to confidently assess, and how that plays into your jurisdiction's standards.

Mitigation Efforts

Once your client has an actual diagnosis and a forensic psychiatric report, what do you do? The answer to that question largely depends on what the report says, of course, but in general you need to start working up mitigation. In situations where your client is unable to help you reliably construct their past because of memory impairments, start pushing family members and friends to step up.

Personally, I think letters of support that appear formulaic are worth very little, but personalized, meaningful letters, even (and sometimes especially) if they are handwritten and a little overly emotional, are a thing of great beauty and power. Of course, I specifically said I dislike letters that "appear" formulaic, because the savvy defense lawyer will provide specific instructions for the support letters, along with a sample letter that the attorney knows will likely be borrowed from heavily. It doesn't matter if it is formulaic, as long as it doesn't *look* formulaic. A sample letter of support and instructions are included at the end of this chapter.

Obtaining a client's records from one agency can also help you figure out where to obtain further records. For example, a medical records request from a private hospital is returned and shows that a client has been previously treated at a veteran's hospital for hearing loss. The attorney could then request military records, which, in addition to their own wealth of mitigating information (combat duties, awards, and honorable discharge being some of the most frequently cited mitigating factors for military service) often also disclose what academic institutions the client attended. Workforce commission searches, if available to you, can also help determine previous employers, who could be sources for more support letters or information to help support your theory of the case as far as who this person was before they developed dementia.

If your client has previous arrests, you may be able to get contact information for close friends or family who posted bond, or previous addresses where the client lived. Additionally, contact previous attorneys who represented the client and, with a waiver signed by the client, ask them their impressions about the client's mental state at the time of their representation and whether they can think of any friends or family members they believe would provide good support letters.

A key part of mitigation is making the state feel like justice will not be done by punishing this person. There are two elements, in my opinion, that a successful mitigation packet should focus on in cases like this. First, they should tell the state why the punishment would be unjustified, and second, they should tell the state why this type of thing won't happen again.

As far as the first prong of this equation is concerned, that the punishment would be unjustified, I think is satisfied in almost any case by talking about what dementia actually means. This person is unable to appreciate that the punishment is the consequence of their actions. This person was, at the time of the offense, likely unaware of what they were doing. This person is suffering in a peculiar and cruel hell that will only get worse before they die. Prison, or even the requirements of probation, are things that are uniquely torturous to a person who can't reliably remember what day of the week it is, or how to use a telephone, toilet, or spoon. All of these things can be presented in a letter from a physician detailing the diagnosis of dementia, the estimated prognosis (what will happen in the future), and a general discussion about dementia patients and how they fare in prison.

Too often, defense attorneys fail to evaluate the evidence against their client effectively and fall trap to the knee-jerk reaction of "I can't admit my client did anything ever." In some cases, of course, that's the right response, but in many cases, it's not and can actually harm your client when it defies credulity. Mitigation packets that prefer vague language and legalese over remorse and specificity are really just file-padding and churning at its worst. Mitigation packets are generally considered part of plea negotiations, and as such, are not admissible at trial. I put a statement to this effect at the beginning of my introduction to the packet and have never had an issue with this. At the same time, I would also suggest to you that if a mitigation packet is well done, candid, and strong, it should not contain letters that are untruthful or statements by folks who the defense wouldn't want to testify at trial.

In the case of Rubak, for example, there was no issue that they got the wrong guy or that the injury came from something else. Having letters from neighbors saying that they had never seen him lose his temper to the point of violence toward his wife before that night is an appropriate and credible sentiment for a mitigation packet. Having letters that say, "He told me he didn't do it, and I believe him, he's the best guy ever and never has a drop of alcohol or wakes up on the wrong side of the bed," is at best worthless.

Rubak himself was horrified by what he had done to his wife, and his heartbreaking sobs in the courtroom as the situation became more and more hopeless were what kept convincing the judge to let him out of custody, even though we all feared that he was just going to have another episode and assault his wife again.

That's the difficult prong, and the one that I failed at the most in Rubak's case—trying to make sure this doesn't happen again. In your case, it may require a considerable amount of holistic practice. I have found that I am a better lawyer than I am a social worker, and for that reason I discourage other lawyers from pretending to be social workers. We all have a niche, and mine is the law. Social workers are better able to address housing and government assistance needs and know of more programs and resources than I ever will, so I bring them in on cases as early and often as I can.

Being able to show a prosecutor or judge that your client has been diagnosed and is receiving treatment since their arrest is a big deal, and I suggest, probably as close as you will be able to come to making a showing that things have changed and this won't happen again. Adding that they are in an assisted-living or memory-care facility, along with some information about the facility and whether or not that facility would allow the client to stay there should he be adjudicated guilty would also be beneficial.

Should your case proceed to trial in spite of these efforts, my heart is with you and your client, but unfortunately that scenario is outside the realm of this chapter and my experience. Suffice it to say that a person with dementia will need extra support and/or accommodations for attending hearings in court. The trial may take much longer. The person may need a family member or trusted person to assist counsel. They may need lots of breaks. Or because of attention span and rest cycles, they may require that proceedings only be conducted in the mornings.

Best of luck.

A sample support letter and instructions for writing it follow.

ALLISON MATHIS
ASSISTANT PUBLIC DEFENDER
1201 FRANKLIN ST., 13TH FLOOR
HOUSTON, TEXAS 77002
713-274-6700
ALLISON.MATHIS@PDO.HCTX.NET

Support Letter Instructions:

Thank you for helping write a letter to support John Doe.

Your letter can be very important in helping to decide what happens in the case.

Your letter should be typed on a computer or typewriter if possible. If not, neatly handwritten is ok. Either way, the letter should be signed by you.

Your letter should start by introducing yourself. You should say your name and what you do for a living. You should also say how you know John and how long you've known them. It would be great if you could think of a short story or memory involving John.

Next, you **should** mention that you know about the charges.

In this case, John is charged with **Assault of a Family Member.**

Do you think John is the kind of person who would ever do that again? Do you think John is sorry? Why do you think that? Include reasons, if you know any, why it would be hard for John and his family for John to stay in jail. What do you think you will be able to do to help John if he gets released? Some ideas might be: check on them regularly, help them find a job, listen to their problems, bring them to church with you, and so on. Be as specific as you can be.

Make sure to put in your contact information in case the someone wants to call and make sure you really believe the things in the letter.

The whole idea of the letter is to give the judge or prosecutor a chance to get to know John, aside from just the pieces of paper they have in front of them.

On the next page is an example of a letter. Be sure that yours is in your own words and tells your own story about John!

And please sign and scan the letter so the court knows that this is an original letter.

We are trying to get the letters together by May 15th. You can send the letters through regular mail to my office, drop them off with my receptionist, or email them to me. The sooner you can get them to me, the better, so I can have a chance to review them before court.

Thank you again for your help!

/s/Allison Mathis
Allison Mathis

• • •

January 25, 2022
To Whom It May Concern:

My name is Deborah Jones and I am an administrative assistant for CompEval USA. I have worked there for eight years. I have known Mark Smith for the past 15 years, because he is a member of my church, Holy Light.

Mark has always been the kind of guy you could call if you got into trouble. He's a nice person, and has always been good at giving advice. I will never forget how Mark showed up at my baby shower at the church ten years ago with a big box of diapers and pages and pages of parenting advice he had written down. He is funny and kind.

I know that he has struggled in the last few years with increasing confusion. At first everyone just thought it was Mark being his usual funny self, but it has started to become clear that there is more going on than that. I know that he has been seeing doctors and taking medication for dementia recently.

I also know that he was charged with a crime for stealing a car. I truly don't think this is something Mark would do at a normal time in his life. He is not the kind of person to take things that aren't his—he is the kind of person who is always giving things away. Though I wasn't there, I have to tell you I really believe this was a misunderstanding, and you would too if you spent time with Mark.

Please let me know if you have any questions, or if I can tell you anything else about Mark. You can call me at 779-5555.

Thank you,

Deborah Jones

• • •

Allison Mathis is a criminal defense attorney in the post-conviction writs division of the Harris County Public Defender's Office in Houston, Texas. She has worked as a public defender in various different jurisdictions, including Tribal Advocate for the Swinomish Indian Tribal Community in Washington State; as an assistant public defender in Aztec, New Mexico (where she lived in a yurt—that's right—a yurt!) and as the chief public defender of the Republic of Palau. She lives in Houston with her big, bearded husband and two adorable children. Before she was a lawyer, she was a superlative late-night diner waitress. You can reach her at tallisonmathis@gmail.com.

Citations available from author by request.

Chapter

11

Representing People on Death Row with Dementia

Vicki Werneke, Esq.

If the concept of executing another human being is repulsive, the concept of executing someone with dementia is even more so. Veteran federal public defender Vicki Werneke has represented clients on death row for more than 30 years. In this chapter, she tells the story of two clients who, despite their profound cognitive deficits, were deemed competent to be executed. Attorney Werneke gives practical advice about how to communicate with as well as best serve clients who have little if any understanding of their legal situations and are in no way capable of assisting their counsel.

• • •

My Client Does Not Remember

I have been representing men and women on death row for almost three decades in their post-conviction and final habeas appeals, first in Oklahoma and now in Ohio. I often get asked how I can do this work for so many years. It is because I find humanity in my clients and have developed positive relationships with most. I have even become friends with some clients who were released from death row and prison. Sadly, I have witnessed nine clients murdered by the State.

In my years of representing many clients though, I have found the most challenging are those who have developed dementia, or cognitive decline, in some form or other and who cannot remember my name, let alone anything about their case. Those clients are difficult to connect with on any intellectual level. I do not know if I have any answers for other practitioners, but maybe I can give some insight about how best to assist the client who probably does not even remember they have been convicted of murder and sentenced to death. Prison populations, especially death row, are aging. How to treat and house elderly inmates has become a significant concern for prisons throughout the country.

"I know you are my lawyer because . . ."

Life in prison for any individual is driven by routine, with rules and set times when tasks and events occur. Meals are served at the same time and usually the same food every day. In some prisons, a person can tell what day of the week it is by the meal on their tray, like Wednesdays are always meatloaf (or what they pretend is meatloaf). When a person is on death row, it is even more routine, as most people are served their meals in their cells and they spend most of the day in that small, confined place. Showers are on certain days of the week and the person is escorted by a guard to go to the shower, to a medical appointment, or the rare occasion of a visit. Any recreation opportunities are also on certain days. Visits occur in certain areas of the prison depending on whether it is a legal or nonlegal visit. These events and tasks take place when a guard appears at the person's cell door and tells them either it is time for a shower, time for a meal, time for recreation, or time for a visit.

A legal visit is usually (hopefully) in a private room where there is a table and chairs for the person and the lawyer. The guard escorts the person and the lawyer to the room separately. Any person who has been on death row for any length of time knows the room where the lawyers get to visit. The guards also tell the person "You have a legal visit today." Following is a typical conversation to open a visit with a client who may have dementia:

Me: Do you know who I am?

Client: You are my lawyer. And the guard told me I have a legal visit today.

Me: How do you know that I am your lawyer?

Client: 'Cause we are in the lawyer room.

Me: Do you remember my name?

Client: Ummm well, don't you know your name?

It is significant that this same conversation happens with the investigator who may come to visit the client by themselves. The client believes the investigator is the lawyer because they are meeting in the lawyer room. That is not a problem, if that investigator is from the defense team and I directed them to go visit the client. The concern is whether someone not on the defense team can visit with the client in the "lawyer room," someone who may not have their best interest at heart.

Gathering information from the client is like trying to assemble a jigsaw puzzle with most pieces forever lost and extra pieces there from other puzzles.

Dementia is not a mental illness, but a collection of symptoms that can be related to a medical condition, mental illness, or chronic drug addiction. When an attorney encounters a client with dementia at any stage of a legal proceeding (trial, appeal, post-conviction, execution), counsel should always investigate and question whether the client is competent during that proceeding, meaning are they able to rationally assist counsel and to comprehend the proceedings. Statutes that govern trial competency reflect a perception that the defendant must have a mental illness to meet the stringent standards. Until a recent Supreme Court decision, standards for competency to be executed applied only if an inmate's severe mental illness was not in remission and made them unable to appreciate that they were about to be executed and for what reason. In *Madison v. Alabama*, 139 S. Ct. 718, 728 (2019), the Court recognized for the first time that the execution of a prisoner with significant dementia may violate the Eighth Amendment if that person's memory loss prevents them from being able to "rationally understand the reasons for [the] death sentence."

Collecting records is even more critical for older clients. A client who cannot remember that I am their lawyer, or that they have been charged with a capital offense, cannot assist with gathering records. They may not be able to sign their names on a release. Before a client's brain becomes eaten away from disease, obtain as many records as possible.

Trying to gather information from the person is difficult if not impossible when their memory has been affected by dementia, stroke, or seizures.

They will typically repeat information known already, or they will tell an off-color joke they learned decades ago and repeat at every visit. They will revert to a previous time, sometimes decades ago. They will give accounts of something they think recently happened, but you know that would be impossible since they have been incarcerated for years. The doctors will tell you this is "normal" for someone whose brain has become like Swiss cheese, but it makes it difficult to effectively represent the person.

I had a client with dementia in Ohio. I will call him Bob, although that was not his name. Bob was 65 years old when he was convicted of murder and sentenced to death. Bob was borderline intellectually disabled. Had I been able to establish the "prior to 18" prong of the ID test, he would have qualified for relief under *Atkins v. Virginia*, 536 U.S. 304 (2002). Bob was also profoundly deaf. By the time my office was appointed to represent him, all of Bob's appeals had been exhausted. For about three years, my office investigated and researched Bob's case hoping to find a claim to challenge his conviction and death sentence, as there were serious questions about his culpability for the murder for which he was convicted and sentenced to death.

After being on death row about 15 years, Bob had a stroke; he was found on the floor of his cell unresponsive in his own urine and feces. He was taken to a local hospital, then transferred to the prison hospital about an hour away. Bob never returned to his cell on death row.

When I visited him at the prison hospital, Bob was convinced that his nephew was on the eighth floor of the building he was in (but there were only five floors) and that the nephew was setting him up for a murder. Bob did not remember that he had been convicted of murder and sentenced to death. He thought he was waiting for trial. When asked why he was in the hospital, he said "cause my legs don't work right now." He also felt the guards were out to get him because they put a sign outside his hospital room that read "DEATH ROW." Bob could not assist us any longer with his case.

Competency to Assist with Proceedings

The legal standard for determining whether someone is competent to stand trial is "whether [they] have sufficient present ability to consult with [their] lawyer with a reasonable degree of rational understanding and whether [they] have a rational as well as factual understanding of the proceedings against [them]." *Dusky v. United States*, 362 U.S. 402 (1960). The test for competency to be executed is similar, although the question is framed more as to whether the inmate is aware of why the State intends to execute them. *Ford v. Wainwright*, 477 U.S. 399 (1986); *Panetti v. Quarterman*, 551 U.S. 930 (2007).

But between conviction and execution, the courts are less concerned about whether the client can "rationally assist" their attorney; therefore, the client need not be competent to proceed in habeas proceedings. The Supreme Court decided a habeas proceeding cannot be stayed when the petitioner is incompetent and not able to assist appointed counsel. *Ryan v. Gonzales*, 568 U.S. 57 (2013). Although the Court found a client at trial needs to be able to rationally assist counsel, the Court failed to recognize the same benefit for a habeas petitioner. "Given the backward-looking, record-based nature of most federal habeas proceedings, counsel can generally provide effective representation to a habeas petition regardless of the petitioner's competence." *Id.* at 68. The reason the Court gave for the decision was habeas proceedings do not necessitate new investigation and issue development. Since the Antiterrorism and Effective Death Penalty Act (AEDPA) places onerous procedural barriers to the federal court's ability to grant habeas relief, the petitioner need not be able to assist habeas counsel. Clearly, Justice Thomas and the other justices in the majority have never represented someone in a habeas proceeding, let alone a person with significant health issues that affect their ability to rationally assist counsel.

"But she can remember what happened decades ago . . ."

A client with diminished capacity may remember parts of their life, but those memories are not reliable, often taken out context, and not verifiable. The psychologist who evaluated Bob before the stroke and after told us that because he was at least borderline intellectually disabled, his cognitive reserves were already subpar. The dementia made the situation far worse.

I offer the reader this example of how this phenomenon works in a nonclient context. My mother, Ruth Adams, passed away in January 2014.

She was only 75 years old. She had a progressive form of Parkinson's disease first diagnosed in 2010, but the symptoms were present for a couple of years prior. Although her official cause of death was a massive stroke, her brain had atrophied from the Parkinson's. The doctor warned us that as the disease progressed, she would become irrational and demented. She did not have a formal diagnosis of dementia, but her symptoms were very similar.

She was in the hospital on Christmas Day 2013. My father, husband, and I went to visit her. Christmas had always been her favorite holiday, but she had no clue that day. She knew it was December 25, 2013, because there was a marker board in her room where the nurse had written the date in blue dry-erase marker. But Mom had no understanding it was her favorite holiday. We brought her a few gifts, like a photo blanket that one of her granddaughters had made for her. We were all stunned. (My father is a retired minister, so Christmas was always a special holiday in our home.)

When we got to her hospital room, her nurse was in Mom's room getting vitals and giving her some medication. The very attentive woman asked my father if he had a blue wedding band. He said "No" and showed her his gold wedding band that matched Mom's wedding band they had for decades; Dad never had a blue one. The nurse then shared with us that about an hour before we got there, Mom demanded the nurse go out to the parking lot and search the pile of hay for her husband's blue wedding band. The nurse did not do that, and not just because there was no haystack in the parking lot. Dad asked, "Ruth, what blue wedding band are you talking about?" Mom insisted there was a haystack in the parking lot. She finally just said "you don't understand." And she was correct that we did not.

Mom knew who we were. She knew that I had just turned 50 the month before. She knew my brothers' names and their birthdays. But she forgot most names of her many grandchildren, whom she loved immensely. She was coherent and talkative with us. Her mind though kept taking her back to events that happened 20 to 30 years before. She insisted that Dad needed to get tickets to an art exhibit at the Museum of Art in Tulsa, Oklahoma. I asked her how Dad was to get to Tulsa to get the tickets by 5:00 p.m. when it was 7:00 p.m. and we were in Cleveland, Ohio. She did not understand why that was impossible. She kept insisting. The conversation was very unnerving. We told the nurse this was not Mom's normal.

In the month that followed until Mom's passing, there were similar conversations where she would talk about an event that happened decades before that we needed to get to without realizing she was 1,200 miles from that place. After she passed, when going through pictures and family memories, I discovered that in 1982 Mom organized a political fundraiser at the Tulsa Museum of Art. She was remembering that event in 2013 as if it were current.

I share that personal story with you as an illustration of what happens to our clients. Just as my mother would not have been competent to make any personal decisions about her care, a client whose mind is fading away will also not be competent.

Competency to Be Executed

After Bob's stroke, the State set his execution date as we anticipated would happen. My colleagues and I had begun developing and preparing a petition challenging Bob's competency to be executed as we knew his condition would continue to deteriorate.

The prison records revealed that the correctional officers on death row had been concerned about Bob's cognitive functioning for some time. There were notes in his prison records where he was found urinating in the trash can in the common room. There were other behaviors the officers noted, and they wrote that they were concerned he had dementia. However, the medical staff did not address the situation.

The petition we filed was supported with psychological and medical reports and the prison records, both before the stroke and the medical records after. Shortly after we filed though, Bob caught COVID-19 and passed away.

I represented another man in Oklahoma whose severe seizure disorder left him in a demented state for years. I will call him Joe, although not his real name. Joe probably had the seizure disorder most of his life, but it manifested most dramatically when he was shot in the eye by a police officer when the two struggled over the officer's gun. Joe had just shot his ex-wife on the steps of the day care center where she was dropping off their two sons. The center staff called the police when Joe showed up at the day care because they knew there was a restraining order against him. After he shot his ex-wife, Joe took off running with an officer in hot pursuit.

Joe survived the gun shot and was left with a deformed face that made him look frightful and an eye that leaked cerebral fluid constantly. He stuffed tissues in the open eye socket and wore an eye patch.

Psychological testing done on Joe before he was shot in the face revealed his IQ was 110; after he was shot his IQ was 75. He pled guilty to the murder and was sentenced to death by the trial court. When his appeals ran their course and an execution date was set, his habeas attorney made a compelling plea for mercy to the Oklahoma Parole Board and the governor because Joe was incompetent to be executed.

The habeas attorney had been representing Joe for almost ten years, but Joe could not remember his name. Joe still had regular seizures, some that were obvious and some that were not. A neurologist testified at the clemency hearing that these seizures left Joe in a fugue state for a few minutes up to possibly an hour, where he was not aware of where he was, who he was, or what happened to him. During those fugue states, Joe was not competent. The Parole Board recommended clemency, but without deciding the clemency question, the governor insisted the State commence competency to be executed proceedings. In Oklahoma, the inmate's attorney cannot initiate proceedings; only the State can.

I was appointed to represent Joe in state court at a jury trial where the issue was whether he was competent to be executed. As far as I know, Oklahoma is the only state that requires a jury trial on this issue.

John Echols, a more seasoned trial attorney, was lead counsel and I was second chair with him. I was grateful for John's experience, and I learned a great deal from him, as I am not a trial attorney. The first day of the trial, I sat close to Joe at counsel table while John sat across from me. I would reach over to lightly touch Joe on the arm and talk to him quietly throughout the day. Joe would sometimes flinch, but he did not seem afraid of me or even concerned about the proceedings. Joe was clearly not with us. I suspect the jurors were disturbed by Joe's appearance with his thick, black, curly hair speckled with gray and unkept, his black eye-patch, and in his prisoner blues. The trial was held in the same county courthouse where the Oklahoma State Penitentiary was located. Most people in the small town knew someone who worked at the prison since it was the largest employer in the community.

During the first break, co-counsel suggested I not engage with Joe as he was concerned the jury might think he was assisting us with the trial.

I understood why John was concerned, as we must be ever mindful that our interactions with the client are not to be taken out of context or misconstrued. I told John it was important the jury see I was not afraid of Joe. After some discussion, John agreed that it was appropriate. It also helped that John's paralegal, also at counsel table with us, agreed with me.

The State offered no counter medical evidence to suggest that Joe was malingering or did not have seizures. Instead, the State argued that it did not matter as the test for competency to be executed was whether the inmate was "insane." We needed to convince four jurors to prevail. Despite Joe's well-documented medical condition and its impact on his cognitive functioning, the 12-person jury found 9–3 that he was competent to be executed. The three jurors we did convince reported they believed our neurologist and that Joe was not aware. However, the other nine were more concerned about a death row inmate "winning" something.

Had Joe been found incompetent to be executed, he would not have been removed from death row, as it would not have vacated his death sentence. He would have been hospitalized, or left to spend out the rest of his life in his tiny concrete cell on death row. Instead, the state executed him. The only consolation is that he probably was not aware of what was happening to him during the lethal injection.

The Client Still Needs You Even If They Forgot Who You Are

Although the Supreme Court has failed to recognize that competency is important at all stages of a case, as practitioners we know that is just not true. As the prison population ages, especially people who have been on incarcerated for 20, 30, and yes even 45 years, as attorneys we need to be prepared for the possibility that the cognitive functioning of some of our clients may decline to a significant degree. How that decline impacts their case will depend on the stage of the proceedings. The most important suggestion I can offer is to continue to have regular contact with the client, even if they forget you. And two or three people on the defense team should have regular contact. For example, with Bob, one attorney on the case lived in the same town as the prison hospital. She visited him more often than the rest of the team. That regular interaction helped inform us and the experts when it came time to prepare the final petition. Had we been able to have a hearing on the competency to be executed petition, those interactions would have been important. Do not fear the client. And do not take it personally when they forget you. Finally, document and memorize the interactions with the client.

• • •

Vicki Werneke is an assistant federal public defender with the Capital Habeas Unit of the Federal Public Defender Office for the Northern District of Ohio. Vicki moved to Cleveland in June 2008 from Oklahoma where she had represented Oklahoma death row inmates for about 15 years. Vicki has represented clients in state post-conviction and federal habeas proceedings. Her most recent position in Oklahoma was chief of the Capital Post Conviction Division of the Oklahoma Indigent Defense System, which is the statewide public defender in Oklahoma, where she had been for six years. Before that, she was an assistant federal public defender with the Capital Habeas Unit for the FPD office in Oklahoma. In March 2018, Vicki was named Outstanding Assistant Federal Public Defender at the national Capital Habeas Unit Conference. She can be reached at vicki_werneke@fd.org.

Citations available from author by request.

Chapter

12

Working with the Expert

Dr. Jonathan DeRight and Dr. Elizabeth Vartkessian

Selecting the right expert or team of experts is key to effectively representing the accused in a criminal matter. Selecting the right expert or team in a matter involving someone with dementia carries unique challenges and requirements.

This chapter by Dr. Jonathan DeRight and Dr. Elizabeth Vartkessian is a valuable guide for selecting and working with an expert. The co-authors explain the difference between a neurologist, neuropsychiatrist, neuropsychologist, and social worker; the differences between a consulting and testifying expert; and the strengths and weaknesses of various assessment tools.

An important note in regard to selecting and working with experts as the criminal justice system struggles to come back after COVID-related closures: experts are at a premium. Make sure potential experts have the time to devote to your case, that they are accessible, and they can make themselves available as required. Do this before giving them a retainer. Replacing an expert is costly in terms of time as well as money.

• • •

Mental health issues are pervasive among inmate populations and, as such, many defense teams are familiar with the warning signs of certain types of illnesses related to bipolar disorder, depression, schizophrenia, and others. Yet dementia and other degenerative brain diseases are not as easy to differentiate, which results in a higher probability that these serious mental health syndromes could be missed. The consequences of defense teams failing to recognize the warning signs are significant, as these degenerative brain syndromes can lead to behaviors that cause problems for the working relationship, lead the client to act out in ways that may be harmful to themselves or others, and affect the client's mood. Identifying the correct mental health issue is essential to facilitating the best representation for the client and for determining how best to house and support them during any incarceration. This chapter provides an overview for behaviors and interactions with the client that may signal the need for further investigation into the existence of a degenerative brain disease, the types of experts used in dementia cases, how best to select and effectively work with experts, often-used terminology, and what the defense can do with the information provided by expert assessment, including planning for proper management.

Warning Signs

Incarcerated persons with dementia frequently do not have a diagnosis of the condition prior to becoming justice involved. The incarcerated person might also have limited insight into their loss of functioning and fail to accurately report critical information to medical staff. They may also have comorbid conditions that obscure the dementia disease or syndrome. Thus, the client's legal team is often the first to suspect neurological or psychiatric conditions that warrant further analysis.

The legal team often has the benefit of observing a client on numerous occasions, at different times of day, for extended lengths of time, with another member of the team, and in various settings including one-on-one in a prison or jail and in court. For these reasons it is critical that defense team members approach client contact with an eye toward understanding the client's behavior. Counsel, investigators, paralegals, and any other members of the defense team that have contact with the client must memorialize that contact in a way that enables the team to track the client's symptoms. Counsel and others on the defense team should note the client's physical appearance—whether the client looks rested, has adequate hygiene, shakes, twitches, or shows other involuntary movements throughout the visit, maintains eye contact, fatigues after a short period of time, has difficulty regulating the volume of their voice, and other observations that can only come with in-person contact. Likewise, the post-visit notes should also include descriptions of the client's ability to track conversation, follow and engage in a substantive discussion with counsel about the charges, legal strategy, and facts of the case; ability to accurately recall information including names, dates, and places; whether the client utilizes words that do not make sense for the context or creates words in an effort to mask their impairments, and so on.

From a clinical perspective, commonly known signs of dementia include drastic memory loss; confusion about date, time, and location; word-finding problems; and significant difficulty multitasking. In regular meetings with a client, an attorney may recognize these signs as seemingly no recall about what was discussed at the last visit or court date (or, often, being adamant that they had never been informed of something despite being provided the information several times), relative sense of time being off, noticeable gaps in conversation or filling in incorrect words while speaking, and inability to think about more than one aspect of something at a time. Counsel may also notice that the client does not provide details when asked or that the details provided are not in line with the information counsel has about the facts of the case.

Lesser-known symptoms that can stem from dementia include broad personality changes, paranoia, difficulty concentrating, social withdrawal, new obsessions (such as a sudden focus on foods or dieting, workout routines, and other daily tasks or topics that occupy an inordinate amount of your client's time), and changes in balance.

There are also many conditions that can mimic aspects of dementia, including hearing loss, depression, other neurological disorders, and even illiteracy where the client is presented something in writing and does not indicate that they cannot read the material due to shame. In order to parse out what is going on with the client, investigation is essential. Witness interviews with those who have known the client at various points in their life may reveal long-term patterns and confirm or refute alternative explanations. The types of records that counsel should prioritize obtaining include all medical records for the client and the client's immediate and extended family, mental health, education, employment, incarceration, social service including any disability records, and vital statistic records including death certificates, which often list the cause of death. This is especially important given that dementia and other degenerative brain diseases have a hereditary component that may help an expert narrow the type of disease the client has. Records should be collected using a signed medical authorization rather than a subpoena since the contents of those materials should not be disclosed to the prosecutor unless the defense determines it necessary. Publicly available records such as criminal and civil court records may also reveal patterns of behavior that speak to dementia-type disorders such as frequent calls to the police about missing items that are not in fact missing, odd behaviors leading to a court-ordered mental health evaluation, civil records that show frequent lawsuits, to name a few. Taking these investigative steps will help counsel determine whether and what type of expert is needed, and the resulting information will assist in the expert's evaluation.

Selecting and Working with Experts

There are various types of experts in dementia that can be utilized depending on the perspective and expertise needed. A breakdown of commonly used experts is provided in the following table. They are often used in conjunction with each other. Briefly, neurologists and neuropsychiatrists are particularly helpful in determining the medical basis for a given disease or syndrome through specific testing, such as neurological examination conducted by a neuropsychiatrist or neuroimaging and laboratory results ordered by a neurologist. Both neuropsychiatrists and neuropsychologists are adept at characterizing the client's behaviors as a function of their dementia syndrome, and social workers are often utilized for determining potential living needs and resources. Each type of expert is capable of providing insight into the specific symptoms, severity, and prognosis to some degree.

As can be seen in the table, a neurologist, neuropsychiatrist, and neuropsychologist are each able to diagnose dementia. Appropriate use of each type of diagnostic expert will be determined by the types of symptoms the defense team observes. For instance, a neurologist may be the more appropriate expert where the defense team observes that excess neurological symptoms, such as uncontrollable movements of limbs, muscle spasms or twitches, or incontinence, are present. A neuropsychiatrist may be more appropriate where the defense team observes that excessive psychiatric symptoms such as pronounced mood swings, paranoid behaviors, or delusional thoughts are present. A neuropsychologist can be helpful in providing objective test results to underscore a diagnosis and comprehensively characterize specific strengths and weaknesses. Social workers can be especially helpful in finding sources of information and real-world opportunities for treatment or management of symptoms. Combinations of these experts are routinely used in legal cases involving dementia as well. In addition, experts in related fields such as radiology are helpful in choosing and interpreting diagnostic imaging data.

	Neurologist	Neuro-psychiatrist	Neuro-psychologist	Social Worker
Degree	MD or DO	MD or DO	PhD or PsyD	Master's degree
Specialty Training	Residency, Fellowship	Residency, Fellowship	Postdoctoral Fellowship	Licensing requirements for clinical practice determined by state, dependent on experience and setting
Board Certification	American Board of Psychiatry and Neurology	American Board of Psychiatry and Neurology	American Board of Professional Psychology or American Board of Professional Neuropsychology	None per se, but various specialty trainings are available
Primary Function	Assessment, diagnosis, and treatment of neurological diseases	Assessment, diagnosis, and treatment of neurological diseases	Assessment, diagnosis, and prognosis of neurological diseases	Prognosis, coordination of care, and resource options

Choosing the Right Expert

Not all mental health experts are the same and, indeed, the observations of the client by the defense team will be the most critical part of selecting the right mental health expert to assist the team and/or evaluate the client.

The first question to consider is whether this expert will act as a consultant to the team or as a testing/testifying expert. It is important to note that all information that a testifying expert relies on to form an opinion will be available to the prosecutor. So, if you are unsure that your expert will eventually be in this role, it may be best to provide only the most pertinent information needed for the expert to conduct the evaluation until you make your informed decision. Consulting mental health experts operate as members of the defense team and, thus, counsel can and typically should share the entire confidential case file with the expert. The purpose of having a consulting expert is to assist counsel in understanding the materials collected about the client, identify the appropriate testing expert, assist in drafting referral questions, assist in helping counsel understand the advantages and potential disadvantages of administering specific types of tests, and generally be a resource counsel is able to go to who understands the specific issues in the case. A testifying expert will be someone for whom counsel makes strategic decisions about disclosures. Anything a testifying expert relies on to form an opinion will be available to the prosecutor, so counsel will need to be careful not to provide information to the testifying that is both unnecessary for the determination of their medical opinion and harmful to the client. To be clear, it is possible that counsel will need both a consulting expert and a testifying expert, especially if counsel is unfamiliar with dementia. In instances where counsel is familiar with dementia, it is possible that counsel is able to determine the most appropriate testing expert.

Once counsel determines the role the expert will play in the case, a thorough review of potential candidates should be conducted, including collecting and reviewing transcripts from previous testimony, reports where the expert has been retained to render an opinion in court, research or general audience publications, public-speaking events, and a curriculum vita. Counsel should also run the expert's name through criminal and civil court databases to ensure there is nothing in the expert's history that would call their judgment into question.

While seeking references from colleagues is a good starting point, experts are not one-size-fits-all. This is especially critical when considering the need to select an expert who is culturally competent and therefore more effectively able to work with the client in order to obtain a diagnosis. This might mean working with a new expert who has not often been used in court. This approach can militate against the expert being viewed as a hired gun and therefore lend strength to the ultimate opinion of the expert.

Preference should also typically be given to experts who are engaged in a clinical practice. This is due to the subtly of symptom presentation in many cases. A clinician who is engaged in the daily treatment of people with dementia will be far more capable of picking up on nuance than a purely forensic evaluator is.

The Referral Question

Counsel should have a referral question drafted and use that as the starting point for outreach to an expert. A referral question is the reason for the evaluation or assessment. It is critical for framing the evaluation for the potential expert.

A referral question does not need to be more specific than communicating some of the observations counsel has had that makes them think something is "off" about the client and that counsel have concerns about a possible psychiatric or neurological condition. In instances in which a disease or disorder has been previously identified, a referral question may be to evaluate accuracy of the previous diagnosis and to opine as to how much those symptoms have and continue to affect the client. At other times, a referral question is necessarily more limited in scope. For example, dementia experts are frequently consulted to perform evaluations for various competency hearings due to the nature of dementia and its ability to affect decision-making. Experts familiar with dementia are preferable in these cases because questions about competency are inherently different amongst those with dementia as opposed to a psychotic or otherwise psychiatrically mediated disorder.

After reaching out to potential experts with a referral question, counsel should interview potential experts and take up references. Part of the interview should include a discussion about the types of information that the expert would need to review, the testing the expert would usually conduct, and an opportunity to hear how the expert, if counsel is planning to use the person to testify, is able to explain complicated medical results to people with little knowledge of the disorder.

Do's and Don'ts of Engaging an Expert

DO	DON'T
• Have a referral question, even if it's broad • Conduct collateral investigation including records collection and interviews with those who have known your client at various points throughout their life • Write memos including observations from each client interaction, taking note of the client's mood, physical presentation, language use/misuse, reasoning, and memory • Tell the expert all of your observations, big or small, that seem "off" • Work with experts who are comfortable giving you null results • Organize records and provide all relevant materials to the expert, including any that the prosecutor will have access to • Give the expert all relevant records, including any materials that the prosecutor will have access to. • Know the level of certainty necessary for a particular legal situation (e.g., is it enough for the expert to be reasonably certain that the behavior is due to a dementia syndrome in general or a specific etiology?) • Ask the expert for recommendations for other types of providers that can better address certain aspects of a condition • Communicate with the expert frequently; set deadlines and/or firm dates to reconvene • Make sure the expert knows the audience for a report/testimony • Ensure that the expert uses generally accepted procedures and measures	• Worry about trying to diagnose the client before seeking an expert • Rely on the client for all the information related to their functioning • Force a diagnosis or mental health defense • Expect the expert to have "the answer" after meeting with the client once; follow-up or additional information is often required • Provide the expert only with summaries of records • Worry if you think there is conflicting evidence that does not help your case; you and the expert are better off knowing all aspects of the evidence • Ask the expert to opine on something that is beyond the scope of their practice • Forget that dementia syndromes can impair a client's ability to attain competency to stand trial • Hire or exclude an expert solely on experience in a particular type of case or situation

After counsel has decided which expert to hire, counsel should create an index that details the materials provided to the expert with the date it was given and the method used to furnish the materials. This will ensure that there is a record of what the expert relied on in reaching an opinion.

Common Procedures

Depending on the type of dementia being assessed, a combination of procedures is often warranted. Each of these procedures has its own strengths and weaknesses, and while there is typically not a hard-and-fast rule about using one method over another, there are common procedures involved in most evaluations.

Magnetic Resonance Imaging (MRI). MRI is a neuroimaging technique best for analyzing structural features of the brain, including degeneration of certain key structures. Volumetric analyses of certain areas, such as the region largely responsible for memory, can be undertaken to describe the extent of degeneration.

Computerized Tomography (CT). CT is a neuroimaging technique best for assessing acute neurological emergencies such as tumor or stroke. It offers less detail than an MRI but is more cost effective, is more easily obtained, and is captured more quickly.

Positron Emission Topography (PET). PET is a neuroimaging technique that, combined with MRI, provides insight into the function of a brain to provide clarification related to tumors and areas of increased/decreased activity.

Electroencephalogram (EEG). EEG is a measure used to detect electrical activity in the brain. It is the method of choice for detecting seizures and can also be used to assess aspects of brain damage from other conditions. (*See* Chapter 6, Neuroimaging.)

Neurological exam. A neurological exam involves examination of a patient's mental status (e.g., orientation, language, speech, cognition), cranial nerve examination, motor examination, sensory examination, coordination, reflexes, and gait.

Neurobehavioral status exam. A neurobehavioral status exam is a type of mental status exam employed by a psychiatrist or psychologist. It focuses on the assessment of a patient's appearance, behavior, and knowledge, especially as it relates to various cognitive abilities such as language, spatial abilities, memory, and reasoning.

Screening measures of cognition. Screening measures are often used by various medical personnel to obtain a broad assessment of a patient's cognitive abilities/weaknesses. These can be helpful in order to document decline using medical records due to their ubiquitous use but have weaknesses due being relatively simplistic and lacking a comprehensive analysis.

Neuropsychological tests. Neuropsychological testing is the gold standard for objective classification of various cognitive, emotional, and behavioral symptoms. It involves administering a group of tests that tap all aspects of someone's thinking and comparing their scores to a peer group in order to determine a pattern of strengths and weaknesses and inform diagnosis. Assessment of the validity or accuracy of a patient's test performances is essential to any neuropsychological evaluation, though care must be taken in choosing the correct measures for the population being assessed (e.g., measures of performance validity that are known to be effective in a population with dementia). Common tests used to diagnose dementia include assessment of premorbid (i.e., baseline) abilities, current IQ, motor speed, simple and complex attention, working memory, processing speed, language memory (learning, recall, retention, and recognition), executive functioning (e.g., organization, problem solving, judgment), and spatial abilities.

Treatments. Medications that help to control behaviors associated with dementia and potentially slow disease progression are available, but there are no curative treatments for irreversible dementia syndromes. There are certain reversible conditions, such as Vitamin B12 deficiency or normal pressure hydrocephalus, that are known "reversible" causes of dementia such that treatments are available that will be expected to completely alleviate the dementia syndrome.

Terminology

As the expert works, counsel should become familiar with the medical terminology for various types and symptoms of dementia, which is often used interchangeably, but have clear differences and are important for accuracy in legal pleadings. Following is a list of terms to help defense teams navigate through technical medical language and often incorrect colloquialisms of terms associated with dementia.

Syndrome, disorder, and disease. These terms are often used interchangeably but carry specific meanings with increasing levels of certitude and appropriateness. A syndrome refers to a constellation of symptoms that are expressed by the individual. A disorder typically refers to a diagnosis made using specified criteria (e.g., ICD-10 or DSM-5). Finally, a disease refers to a condition with a known physiological origin. The attorney or expert can refer to any one of these as is necessary when communicating the client's symptoms. For example, a client's "dementia syndrome" may be more helpful to describe a group of behaviors associated with their deficits, while the diagnosis of "Major Neurocognitive Disorder due to Alzheimer's disease" may be better used as the basis for an expert opinion. References to the actual disease (e.g., "Alzheimer's disease") may be more appropriate when discussing disease progression or prognosis or to provide a medical explanation for the client's behaviors.

Dementia. Broadly, dementia is a condition in which a person's mental faculties have deteriorated to an extent that their thinking, judgment, emotions, and/or behaviors are affected on a regular basis. There are varying degrees of severity though the inability to care for oneself and need supervision are common as the disorder becomes more extreme. It is important to note that when defense teams are working with incarcerated clients, the structured environment in which the client lives may obscure the full nature of deficits.

Neurocognitive disorder (major or mild). In the DSM-5, the term "neurocognitive disorder" is used instead of "dementia" (e.g., "Major Neurocognitive Disorder Due to Alzheimer's disease"). Functional impairment, meaning the ways in which daily living skills become limited, is often the line between "major" and "mild." DSM-5 criteria separate the syndromes into "probable" and "possible," though this terminology can be confusing to the trier of fact, as a "possible" diagnosis does not ostensibly carry the weight that corresponds to the seriousness of the syndrome.

Alzheimer's disease. A degenerative brain disease that most notably affects memory, orientation, and language. Examples here would be individuals who require the same information presented repeatedly, difficulty with accurately recalling events, limitations in locating words or in using words appropriately. Deficits in judgment, complex attention, and spatial abilities are also common, especially as the disease progresses. Symptoms can start out relatively mild (e.g., "Amnestic Mild Cognitive Impairment" or someone with significant memory deficits and relatively normal functioning otherwise) and can become increasingly severe as the disease progresses (e.g., Major Neurocognitive Disorder Due to Alzheimer's disease, severe, with behavioral disturbance).

Other Types of Dementia. Dementia can be caused by various events or medical issues, including frontotemporal lobar degeneration, Lewy body disease, vascular disease (including stroke), traumatic brain injury, substance or medication side effects, infection, Parkinson's disease, and many other medical diseases. It is also possible and common for multiple medical issues to be present within an individual. Understanding the client's medical history through the collection of records and collateral witness interviews will greatly aid the defense team in determining the potential etiology. (*See* Chapter 1, What Is Dementia?)

What to Do with What You Learn

After the assessment of the client is complete, counsel should communicate verbally with the expert to receive a summary of the client's performance and initial impressions of the exam. Depending on this, counsel will need to decide whether to obtain a report from the expert or utilize the results in other ways. For instance, it might be the case that a report is not needed, but the expert has provided information about supports for helping the client better communicate with counsel. For instance, it is possible that the expert might suggest that counsel needs to put everything in writing so the client is able to have accessible information about the case due to memory problems. Counsel might also learn about some of the impairments impacting the client's behavior and consider sharing that information with prison staff. Deciding on what to do with the information obtained can also be something that the consulting mental health expert is able to discuss with counsel.

In addition to determining the final product required from the expert, the results provided to counsel may speak to the appropriateness of a particular detention facility for the client. As the prison population continues to age, many facilities are not equipped to handle the medical, behavioral, and psychiatric needs of clients with progressive dementia syndromes (*see* Cipriani et al., 2017). Notably, a Bureau of Prisons facility (Federal Medical Center (FMC) Devens in Massachusetts) recently opened a memory disorder prison unit specifically to address the unique needs of this population.

Conclusion

In conclusion, it is important for defense teams to consider the possibility of dementia when working with older clients or individuals with developmental disabilities. This will enable the team to select the appropriate expert, if necessary, and to appropriately and effectively monitor for potentially concerning signs. In addition to commonly known characteristics of dementia such as significant memory loss, less well-known features such as personality changes, paranoia, and social withdrawal are also important signs to watch out for. Choosing the expert or multiple experts in the correct field and for the correct role (e.g., testing, testifying, etc.) is essential in properly representing individuals with dementia. Defense teams who correctly utilize this knowledge can help with case-specific issues that may arise, such as various adjudicative competencies, and practical issues such as improved ways to communicate with a client.

• • •

Dr. Jonathan DeRight is a board certified clinical neuropsychologist. His practice—Precision Neuropsychology, PLLC—is based in the Washington, D.C. metro area, and he performs evaluations around the country. Dr. DeRight routinely sees patients in the clinical and forensic settings, including evaluations for criminal cases, civil cases, disability, worker's compensation, fitness for duty, and independent medical examinations. In the criminal setting, Dr. DeRight frequently performs competency to stand trial, sanity, and mitigation evaluations for individuals with cognitive impairment. Dr. DeRight earned his bachelor's degree in neuroscience from the University of Rochester and his master's and PhD degrees in clinical psychology from Syracuse University. He completed his postdoctoral residency in clinical neuropsychology at the Johns Hopkins University School of Medicine. He may be reached at jderightphd@gmail.com.

Elizabeth Vartkessian is a mitigation specialist and the founding executive director of Advancing Real Change, Inc., a national nonprofit with locations in Baltimore, Maryland, and Jacksonville, Florida, dedicated to conducting high-quality life history investigations in criminal cases. She may be reached at either www.advancechange.org or esv@advancechange.org.

Citations available from author(s) by request.

Chapter

13

Jail and Prison Conditions

Dr. Marc Blatstein and Fay F. Spence Esq.

Prison is grim for any inmate. But for a person with dementia, it is like trying to survive in a foreign country where they don't know the language or the customs and everything is completely baffling. This chapter and the one that follows—Jail and Prison Conditions, by Dr. Marc Blatstein and attorney Fay Spence, and The Reality of Daily Life for Someone with Dementia in Jail or Prison, by Dr. Phillip Wise—can arm the criminal defense lawyer with powerful information to advocate on behalf of a client with dementia in order to dismiss charges against them or to mitigate penalty.

This chapter outlines the many challenges for people with dementia in state and federal jails and prisons. The chapter shows that institutions are ill-equipped to house people with dementia, whether because of institutional rules that are impossible for them to understand or follow, personnel who do not understand dementia, lack of access to proper medication, or institutional programming that may be completely inappropriate. This chapter underscores that if jails and prisons were incapable of dealing with COVID-19, they are certainly incapable of dealing with the projected explosion in the number of older inmates with cognitive impairments.

Chapter 14, by Dr. Phillip Wise, weaves the story of a fictional inmate, Ray, who suffers from dementia with an analysis of how the organization and structure of the prison environment can impact people with dementia. This chapter moves beyond facts and figures and shows the tragic descent of a person with dementia within an institution that was never designed to care for someone like him.

• • •

The graying of America is affecting all aspects of society, including those who are incarcerated. Over the last 20 years, the inmate population over age 55, as a percentage of all inmates, has quadrupled (Ferri, 2013, p. 200; Ollove, 2016). Reasons for the increase include the imposition of much longer sentences due to "tough-on-crime" policies adopted in the 1980s and 1990s (mandatory sentences and three-strikes laws) and the aging of prisoners, plus the increased number of people over 55 being convicted and incarcerated (Ferri, 2013, p. 201).

By 2030, those over 55 will account for more than a third of those imprisoned, amounting to approximately 400,000 older prisoners (Lopez, 2020). Most of these older prisoners will have special medical needs. Just as prisons and jails on the state and federal levels lacked the medical, and nonmedical, resources to handle COVID-19, the tsunami of incarcerated seniors will stress the ability of the institutions to provide medical care. The burden of attempting to provide this care will financially impact entire states and the federal system. For example, the Federal Bureau of Prisons (BOP) spends approximately $881 million per year caring for the elderly (many of whom have dementia), with much of that money spent on medication, medical care, and the peripherals of caring for this age group (Lopez, 2020).

Keeping a person with severe dementia incarcerated debases their personal human dignity for no penologically justifiable reason (Lopez, 2020). The normally recognized purposes of punishment are retribution, rehabilitation, and deterrence. When a person no longer understands that they are in prison, much less why, due to advanced dementia, then imprisonment fails to accomplish these purposes. As the Supreme Court recognized in *Madison v. Alabama*, executing prisoners with dementia serves no retributive purpose when prisoners cannot rationally understand their sentences (Lopez, 2020). This reasoning applies to continued imprisonment as well. Nor does prison rehabilitate one with dementia. Because dementia is a progressive disease with no known cure, there can be no rehabilitation. Moreover, prison conditions can, and do, exacerbate the disease (Lopez, 2020).

Prison Activities of Daily Living (PADL)

As discussed at the beginning of this book all forms of dementia involve degenerative changes in the brain that cause loss of memory and other mental abilities that can be severe enough to interfere with the activities of daily living (ADL). The normal ADL affected include toilet hygiene (including remembering that one is supposed to use the toilet for elimination functions) and getting dressed, for example. Those living in prisons have additional routines that are normal to prison life, called prison activities of daily living (PADL) (Williams et al., 2006). These PADL routines include standing for head counts, walking to the dining hall for meals, dropping to the floor for alarms, hearing and obeying orders from staff, and, for some, climbing up or down from the top bunk. Dementia affects an inmate's ability to perform these PADLs as well (Williams et al., 2006).

One readily understands how physical ailments impact an inmate's ability to stand for a head count, but many laypeople, including prison guards, do not realize that dementia affects an inmate's ability to remember what he is supposed to do during a head count, or why. He may fail to stay where he is told during the head count, which correctional officers without training on dementia may perceive as insubordination, leading to disciplinary consequences (Maschi et al., 2012).

Likewise, an impaired inmate walking to the dining hall may forget where he is going or why, leading him to wander around in confusion rather than remaining in line. Breaking in line or grabbing food from another inmate's tray could result in confrontations with fellow inmates (Belluck, 2012). This creates greater risk of victimization and physical injury to the cognitively impaired inmate, as well as increased risk of punitive disciplinary sanctions.

Sounding alarms and officers shouting orders are likely to leave an inmate with dementia disoriented, fearful, and not knowing what to do. At best, the inmate will be noncompliant; at worst, the impaired inmate may become combative with staff or other inmates (Belluck, 2012). Once again, if corrections officers do not recognize the behavior as a sign of dementia, they will perceive the behavior as a disciplinary infraction. The normal penal response to disciplinary problems is punitive, ranging from loss of privileges to more restrictive housing units or even placement in solitary confinement, which only exacerbates the mental condition of an inmate with dementia (Maschi et al., 2012).

Additionally, while brain function includes memory and cognitive skills, the brain also controls voluntary and involuntary movement and coordination. An inmate with dementia may have trouble remembering how to climb to the top bunk. Upon awakening, the inmate may not realize where he is and can fall off the bunk when he starts to step out of bed.

For the inmate with dementia, assignment to a top bunk increases the risk of physical injury.

Prison can be a dangerous place for a person with dementia for other reasons. With limited space and overcrowded conditions, prisoners are territorial about "their turf" (Belluck, 2012). Wandering into the wrong cell or area, as an inmate with dementia is apt to do, can result in the inmate being assaulted. Impaired inmates are also more vulnerable to predatory inmates because they lack the awareness and ability to protect themselves (Belluck, 2012; Ollove, 2016).

Dementia and Care in Federal Prisons

Currently, prisons are taking the place of mental health care providers and hospitals, but some diagnoses may not be best suited for incarceration. Imprisoned persons with dementia stand a greater chance of being victimized, sexually assaulted, and bullied by other prisoners (Bollinger et al., 2019; Lopez, 2020). The subsections that follow discuss some of the programs and policies adopted by the federal Bureau of Prisons (BOP) to deal with inmates with dementia.

The BOP's Memory Disorder Unit (MDU)

Until recently, the federal BOP had no specialized resources for dealing with dementia in their Care Level classification and placement structure. Inmates in the early stages of dementia who were becoming involved in conflicts with corrections staff and/or having trouble taking care of themselves were often not recognized as having a medical problem. They were treated as having disciplinary problems and subjected to punitive sanctions, including placement in the special housing unit (SHU).

In 2019, Federal Medical Center (FMC) Devens, a federal prison in Massachusetts, opened its Memory Disorder Unit (MDU), the first of its kind (Bollinger et al., 2019). Modeled after memory care units in nursing homes, the MDU is the first correctional unit in the country to have staff certified in dementia care. The National Council of Certified Dementia Practitioners (NCCDP) developed a specialized training program, the Alzheimer's Disease and Dementia Care (ADDC) curriculum, along with certification requirements for nurse educators and correctional officers. Correctional officers working in the MDU are required to be

Certified Dementia Trained Correctional Personnel (CDPDT), and educators working there are required to be Certified Correctional Personnel Dementia Trainers (CCPDT). Inmate volunteers who wish to work as companions for inmates in the unit may do so after completing training to become certified nurse's aides (CNAs).

The MDU is designed to house 36 inmates diagnosed with dementia who are in the middle stages of the disease (Bollinger et al., 2019). This is not nearly enough to deal with the number of incarcerated inmates with dementia, however, nor with the estimated more than 70,000 prisoners expected to be in state and federal prisons by 2030 (Lopez, 2020). Further, unless appropriate training is provided to corrections staff in all prisons, inmates in the early stages of dementia are likely to continue to be viewed as disciplinary problems rather than patients.

Mental Healthcare (MH) in the BOP—Classification

The federal BOP uses a Care Level classification system for placing prisoners in facilities capable of addressing medical and mental health needs of inmates (Federal Bureau of Prisons, 2019). The Designation and Sentence Computation Center places inmates into Care Level 1 or 2 upon entry into the BOP. The Office of Medical Designations and Transportation places inmates in Care Level 3 or 4.

If the inmate has had two or more psychiatric hospitalizations within three years or takes three or more psychotropic medications (antipsychotics, antianxiety medications, antidepressants, stimulants, or mood stabilizers) for a single mental illness or five or more psychotropic medications for multiple diagnoses (e.g., psychosis, schizophrenia, bipolar disorder, depression) or requires contact with a prescribing health care provider more frequently than monthly, he will be classified as Care Level 3-MH (BOP, 2019).

An inmate will be classified as Care Level 2-MH if he has had a psychiatric hospitalization within five years (not related to substance abuse) or is regularly prescribed more than two psychotropic medications or requires contact with a prescribing health care provider more often than every six months. This fails to consider whether an inmate companion is needed and is available.

Progressive neurological conditions, including dementia, are also classified in the Care Level system. If an inmate has been diagnosed with a progressive neurological condition, he can be classified at Care Level 2 if he is controlled with medication and is still able to perform ADLs independently. If the inmate requires assistance from an inmate companion to perform ADLs but does not require 24-hour skilled nursing care, he will qualify for Care Level 3. This is the stage for which the MDU at FMC Devens is designed. If the dementia patient requires 24-hour skilled nursing care, he will be classified at Care Level 4.

Medication Availability

There are good medications that doctors can prescribe to treat persons suffering from dementia. Unfortunately, BOP at this time does not carry those as formulary medications. Like with most insurance companies, the BOP has established formularies for which drugs are available, based on cost-containment measures. Where available, generic drugs are provided. Many generic prescriptions look different from one another, and the brand names associated with them differ too, so an inmate being treated with a specific generic medication before entering the BOP may receive the same medication even though its generic form differs in color, size, and shape once incarcerated. Informing your client about how the same medications may differ before they're incarcerated can go a long way to allaying their fears.

Among medical doctors, the current medications of choice for treating dementia are cholinesterase inhibitors and memantine (Melinosky, 2020). Cholinesterase inhibitors help prevent the breakdown of acetylcholine, a neurotransmitter in the brain. Acetylcholine is important to learning, memory, and mood stability. By preventing the breakdown of acetylcholine, cholinesterase inhibitors delay the worsening of Alzheimer's symptoms and symptoms of other dementias, allowing patients to experience less anxiety, improved memory, better concentration, and improved motivation. Unfortunately, the benefit is limited; usually, the improvements last for only six months to one year. For moderate to severe Alzheimer's disease, doctors may prescribe memantine (brand name Namenda), with or without a cholinesterase inhibitor. Memantine helps improve memory, attention, reasoning, and language, as well as reduce delusions, hallucinations, agitation, aggression, and irritability. Cholinesterase inhibitors include donepezil (Aricept), galantamine (Razadyne, Razadyne ER, and Reminyl), and rivastigmine (Exelon) (Melinosky, 2020). *None of these medications are available in the BOP, either as a formulary medication or as a nonformulary requiring preauthorization* (BOPHS, 2020b).

Other (older) medications used to treat dementia symptoms include antidepressants, especially serotonin receptor antagonists such as trazodone and selective serotonin reuptake inhibitors (SSRIs), such as fluoxetine (Prozac), sertraline (Zoloft), and paroxetine (Paxil); antianxiety medications such as lorazepam (Ativan) or oxazepam (Serax); and antipsychotics, such as aripiprazole (Abilify), haloperidol (Haldol), olanzapine (Zyprexa), and risperidone (Risperdal) (Bhandari, 2020). Of these, the antipsychotics—except for aripiprazole—are on the formulary, but they must be dispensed daily by a qualified BOP employee who observes the consumption of the pill when it is dispensed (BOPHS, 2020a; BOPHS, 2020b). Aripiprazole is a nonformulary drug, requiring preauthorization and justification for not using one of the other antipsychotic medications. Trazodone is formulary but must be administered crushed. Prozac is the only formulary antidepressant available; Zoloft is the first-choice nonformulary, followed by Paxil. Both Zoloft and Paxil require preauthorization. None of the antianxiety medications are available for prescription, although all facilities are required to have injectable lorazepam available for psychiatric emergencies (BOPHS, 2020b).

The BOP updates the formulary regularly, with the formulary drug list available online. If a client's generic medication is not on the formulary, the attorney should connect with the client's physician, preferably well before sentencing, to discuss whether an alternative medication on the formulary list is suitable for the patient, in the doctor's opinion. If not, the lawyer representing the client must take whatever steps available to try to get preapproval of the nonformulary medication before the client is admitted to BOP custody. This process takes considerable time. At a minimum, the lawyer should provide the probation officer preparing the presentence report and the BOP MDU with the client's medical records and documentation by the treating physician of specific reasons that a particular medication is necessary rather than a formulary medication. If necessary, counsel may schedule a hearing and attempt to have the sentencing court order the medication. Unfortunately, courts are reluctant to tell the BOP in advance how to treat a particular inmate, but if the treating physician has documented that the formulary medication may cause physical damage or death to the inmate, that is an expert opinion the court might consider sufficiently strong to overcome the deference normally accorded to the BOP's policies. While the BOP usually will do what they want, at minimum the defense attorney is obligated to document and formally request the most effective medication for the client, even though the likelihood of success is low.

Compassionate Release

Compassionate release is intended to shorten a prisoner's sentence when circumstances such as imminent death or significant illness lessen the need for, and morality of, continued imprisonment. In 2018, Mary Price, on behalf of Families Against Mandatory Minimums (FAMM), prepared an extensive report that describes the compassionate release laws and policies in the 50 states plus the District of Columbia, each of which has its own individual regulations. The jurisdictions have varying categories of release, eligibility criteria, and reporting requirements. The report also highlights a troubling number of barriers faced by prisoners and their families when applying for release under these policies (Price, 2018). Compassionate release may be a viable alternative for people with dementia. Counsel could explore this option and document the ways a given institution is not providing appropriate care.

People with dementia usually don't recognize their condition, although their family does. Thus, counsel should tell family to let them know when the client is showing signs of dementia. At that point, counsel can pursue compassionate release (or whatever might be their state equivalent) and/or request medical assistance from the BOP or Department of Corrections. Counsel should also request that the court appoint him or her to file compassionate release motion because the client is incapable of filing pro se.

The main problem that impairs an inmate's ability to seek compassionate release for dementia, whether in a state court or in federal court, is lack of awareness. The inmate may not know that he is impaired or may not be able to communicate the problem. Even if an inmate recognizes that she is impaired, her memory, concentration, and other cognitive skills may leave her unable to follow the procedures to request early release. As discussed previously, many corrections officers lack adequate training to recognize early signs of dementia (Ferri, 2020). This may lead to disciplinary sanctions for misbehavior rather than proper medical treatment.

Attorneys representing an older client going to prison—or a client who will become elderly while serving his sentence—should advise the client's family members about symptoms of dementia to be aware of, especially if there is any family history of dementia or personal history of closed head injury. Family members will be in the best position to observe noticeable changes in behavior of their loved one between visitations. If the family believes that the client has become disoriented, more vulnerable to threats of other inmates, or less capable of taking care of himself, then they can retain an attorney to consider filing a compassionate release motion, or they can ask the court to appoint an attorney for the inmate.

Federal Compassionate Release—Background

In the federal system, compassionate release changed significantly because of the First Step Act, enacted in December 2018. Previously, only the director of the BOP could file a motion asking a sentencing federal judge to grant early release, with a term of probation or supervised release that did not exceed the remaining unserved portion of the defendant's sentence (Ellis & Allenbaugh, 2020). The statutory criteria for courts to consider, in addition to the sentencing factors of 28 U.S.C. § 3553(a), in deciding whether to grant compassionate release have remained unchanged since 1984; the court may grant such a motion if the court finds:

> (i) extraordinary and compelling reasons warrant such a reduction; or
>
> (ii) the defendant is at least 70 years of age, has served at least 30 years in prison . . . for the offense or offenses for which the defendant is currently imprisoned, and a determination has been made by the Director of the Bureau of Prisons that the defendant is not a danger to the safety of any other person or the community . . .
>
> and that such a reduction is consistent with applicable policy statements issued by the Sentencing Commission. 18 U.S.C. § 3582(c)(1).

The Sentencing Commission's policy statements are incorporated into the application notes to U.S.S.G. § 1B1.13. In those notes, the Commission identifies the following as a nonexhaustive list of "extraordinary and compelling reasons" for the court to grant compassionate release: (1) inmate medical conditions, such as terminal illness of the inmate (no prediction of life expectancy is required); inmate suffering from a serious physical or medical condition, or suffering functional or cognitive impairment, or experiencing deteriorating physical or mental health because of the aging process, if any of these substantially diminish the ability of the defendant to provide self-care within a correctional environment and the condition is not expected to improve; (2) Age of inmate—if an inmate is over age 65 with declining physical or mental health because of aging and has served the lesser of 10 years or 75% of his or her sentence; (3) Family Circumstances—death of inmate's primary caregiver for minor children or incapacitation of inmate's spouse or domestic partner if inmate is the only person who would be available as a caregiver for the spouse; (4) Other reasons as determined on a case-by-case basis. *Id.* at App. Note 1. Clearly, the problem of dementia, whether early onset or due to aging, falls within this list of extraordinary and compelling reasons.

Despite the legislature's intent and the Sentencing Commission's advisory notes, the director of the BOP has rarely filed motions for compassionate release of inmates. Between 2002 and 2008, for example, only 22 inmates per year, on average, received compassionate release from federal prisons across the entire nation (Ferri, 2013). In 2018, before the First Step Act was signed on December 21, 2018, only 34 people received compassionate release sentence reductions (Eagles et al., 2021). Compared to the number of elderly inmates with physical, mental, and cognitive difficulties, this is extremely low. The Sentencing Commission held hearings on compassionate release in 2016 and concluded that the BOP was not seeking such release as often as appropriate (Ellis & Allenbaugh, 2020). The U.S. Department of Justice, Office of the Inspector General, also issued reports critical of the BOP's (lack of) implementation of the compassionate release program (2013 & 2015).

Because inmates aged 55 and older are the fastest growing segment of the prison population, with medical expenses three to eight times higher than those of younger inmates, and Congress faced the ever-increasing cost of federal prisons, Congress looked to alternative procedures for implementing compassionate release. The First Step Act amended code § 3582 to allow inmates or their attorneys to file motions for compassionate release directly with the sentencing judge, either 30 days after the inmate's warden received the request from or on behalf of the inmate or after the inmate exhausted his administrative appeals from the BOP's failure to file a compassionate release, whichever is earlier (18 U.S.C. § 3582, eff. 12/20/18). Between passage of the amendment and February 22, 2021, federal courts granted 2,950 motions for compassionate release, roughly 6,000 percent more than the BOP ever requested during the preceding years (Eagles et al., 2021). The COVID pandemic accounted for much of the increase. Of course, courts have denied large numbers of compassionate release requests as well (Zalubowski, 2021). Some judges are less inclined to grant compassionate release because of their personal philosophies, but some inmates file motions seeking release for conditions that are substantially less than extraordinary and compelling (Hamilton et al., 2021; Zalubowski, 2021).

Federal Compassionate Release and Dementia—Recent Cases

Few published decisions address dementia or Alzheimer's disease as grounds for compassionate release, but the cases discussing dementia and compassionate release were all filed directly by inmates after enactment of the First Step Act and after denial of release by the BOP or failure of the BOP to act timely. In three cases, the court granted compassionate release, over the government's objection. In *United States v. Montgomery*, 481 F. Supp. 3d 1179 (E.D. Wash. 2020), the court granted release to an 82-year-old prisoner with dementia, diabetes, hypertension, and cataracts. The court did not expound on the reasons for the decision.

In a more fulsome opinion, a district court judge in Colorado granted release to a man with dementia. *United States v. Lochmiller*, 473 F. Supp. 3d 1245 (D. Colo. 2020). Institutional records documented that he was often confused about where he was, could not recognize himself in the mirror, and had lost much of his ability to communicate. He experienced occasional episodes of delirium and hallucinations and believed that staff members in the prison were people from his past. On one occasion, he tore up pictures of himself and his wife; when staff asked why, he said he didn't know who the lady was, and he denied that he was in the pictures. In granting release, the court noted that "Continued incarceration of Mr. Lochmiller does not serve a punitive purpose if he does not know that he is being punished or why," nor does it promote respect for the law. *Id.* at 1249.

A district court considered compassionate release under procedurally unusual circumstances in *United States v. Thrower*, 495 F. Supp. 3d 132 (E.D.N.Y. 2020). Initially, Thrower had been sentenced to serve 180 months based on an Armed Career Criminal Act (ACCA) enhancement. After exhausting his direct appeals, Thrower filed a habeas petition, challenging the enhancement. The district court granted the petition, reduced the sentence to 120 months (time served) and released him from prison. The government appealed, and the Second Circuit Court of Appeals reversed the district court's decision. Thrower filed a motion for compassionate release before he was required to report back to the BOP to serve the remainder of his sentence. This district court held that this was proper, under the unusual circumstances of the case. At the time of the motion, Thrower had made substantial steps toward successful reintegration into society, obtaining a place to live and finding gainful employment. He was also 56 years old and suffering from dementia and a major neurocognitive disorder due to traumatic brain injury in the past. Finally, he had been diagnosed with both diabetes and hypertension, which would increase his vulnerability to COVID. For all these reasons combined, the court found extraordinary and compelling circumstances. *Id.* at 141–42.

The authors found only one case denying compassionate release based on dementia, *United States v. Rodriguez-Gonzales*, 492 F. Supp. 741, 746 (N.D. Oh. 2020). Mr. Rodriguez-Gonzales had mild dementia, but he remained able to care for himself in the correctional environment. Because his capacity for self-care was not impaired, and he failed to establish that the BOP was not adequately managing his condition, the court denied release.

Practical Implications for Requesting Compassionate Release

Dementia is a progressive and degenerative condition. As such, the illness is grounds for compassionate release. However, having an eligible extraordinary and compelling medical condition, by itself, is not enough. The court still must balance the sentencing factors set forth in 18 U.S.C. § 3553(a) to determine if a prisoner's extraordinary circumstances outweigh other interests. Relevant factors that influence court decisions include:

- Severity of the inmate's condition
- Interaction of multiple conditions
- Seriousness of the offense for which he is serving time
- Length of sentence already served

- Adequate documentation of the claimed medical condition
- Specific examples of how activities of daily life are affected for this inmate
- Adequacy of care provided by the BOP for the condition

For the attorney representing a client seeking compassionate release, whether for dementia or another medical condition, thorough preparation is essential to address as many of these factors as possible. Severity of the inmate's condition was the primary distinguishing factor between *Lochmiller* (release granted) and *Rodriguez-Gonzales* (release denied for mild dementia). The introduction of concrete evidence of specific events, such as tearing up marital photos because he did not know who was in the pictures, was highly persuasive in *Lochmiller*. In both *Montgomery* and *Thrower*, the dementia was not as severe as that in *Lochmiller*, but several other conditions combined with dementia were enough to persuade the judge that release was appropriate. All the opinions relied upon medical and other documentation to determine the inmate's condition, not the claims of the inmate himself. In one case, the infamous crime boss Peter Gotti added early-stage dementia and possible lung cancer to his list of complaints; no records mentioned dementia, and the BOP medical records affirmatively denied that Gotti had any lung cancer. *United States v. Gotti*, 433 F. Supp. 3d 613 (S.D.N.Y. 2020). The court quickly pointed out the lack of proof.

Gotti is instructive for other reasons, too. Convicted of racketeering in 2002, with a release date of 2032, Gotti was 79 years old at the time he filed his motion. Medical records confirmed a history of low thyroid, high cholesterol, gout, glaucoma, left eye blindness, hypertension, ischemic cardiomyopathy, chronic atrial fibrillation, heart failure, chronic obstructive pulmonary disease (COPD), and esophageal reflux. Although he had a pacemaker and used a wheelchair, he was able to care for himself and perform activities of daily living independently, according to the medical records from the BOP. Acknowledging that some of Gotti's illnesses were serious and progressive, the court noted that Gotti nevertheless failed to show that his condition had deteriorated sufficiently to qualify as an extraordinary and compelling reason for release. *Id.* Had this been a different inmate, those medical conditions may well have been enough. One cannot help but think that the court's perception of Gotti's crimes influenced its view of how serious Gotti's medical problems really were, especially since Gotti remained able and willing to be deceitful in efforts to exaggerate his medical condition.

Considering the § 3553(a) sentencing factors, as required, the court denied Gotti's request for compassionate release, finding both that a sentence reduction would undermine the retributive and deterrent goals of sentencing and that Gotti remained a threat to the community. Dispensing with counsel's argument that Gotti, nearly an octogenarian, was too feeble to engage in violent conduct, the court responded that "The danger posed by a Gambino family leader like Gotti is not that he will personally engage in acts of violence, but that he can command others to do so." *Id.* at 620. The court also made the following statement, an important reminder for attorneys:

> A court is not required to reduce a sentence on compassionate release grounds, even if a prisoner qualifies for such reduction because of his medical condition (and it bears repeating, Gotti does not so qualify). The First Step Act was drafted using the word "may," not "must." In the end, whether to reduce a sentence is a matter that rests in the discretion of the court.

Id. at 619. On appeal, courts apply de novo review of whether an inmate is *eligible* for compassionate release, but the decision to grant release is discretionary, and will only be reversed for abuse of discretion. *United States v. Rodd*, 966 F.3d 740, 746 (8th Cir. 2020). Accordingly, an attorney must acquaint herself with the court's thought process to know which evidence and arguments will be most persuasive to that judge.

Conclusion

Dementia is a symptom with multiple causes and devastating effects on a person's memory, mood, rational thought, moral reasoning, impulse control, and ADL. Tragically, many in the criminal justice system are unaware of the intricacies of this illness.

• • •

Dr. Marc Blatstein had a successful foot and ankle practice for 30 years, providing quality patient care. Over a decade ago he received a felony conviction of 1 year–1 day due to insurance coding, for which he took full responsibility. There was never any question regarding the quality of patient care he delivered, and his medical license has been current for over 30 years. This has provided him with an extensive health care background that allowed him to experience firsthand how the system at times failed defendants. His firsthand experience and medical knowledge have provided him a clear understanding of the medical and mental health care issues, along with security requirements, that defendants face and the BOP requires. This comprehensive understanding provides him the skills necessary to help mitigate the sentences while suggesting appropriate prison placement options that would be acceptable to all parties.

He maintains an active medical license and is the founder of Physician Presentence Report Service, LLC. Dr. Blatstein can be contacted at info@PPRSUS.com, (240) 888-7778, or through his website: https://pprsus.com/federal-sentencing/.

Fay F. Spence Esq. is an attorney with more than 30 years of experience in criminal law, including 13 years with the Federal Public Defenders Office for the Western District of Virginia as First Assistant Public Defender and then as Senior Litigator. She currently serves as a pro se law clerk for the U.S. District Court for the Western District of Virginia. She can be reached at fayspenceatty@msn.com.

Citations available from author(s) by request.

Chapter

14

The Reality of Daily Life for Someone with Dementia in Jail or Prison

Dr. Phillip Wise

Whether there is good reason to confine anyone who has been diagnosed with dementia in jail or prison is a discussion that can be addressed elsewhere, but it is certain that there are increasing numbers of jail detainees and prison inmates who are elderly. Because prison inmates are typically 15 years older medically than they are chronologically, for that population, "elderly" is generally defined as over the age of 50. The total number of sentenced prisoners under the jurisdiction of state or federal correctional authorities has been slowly declining from 2015 through 2019. However, from 2015 to 2019, the percentage of those inmates in state or federal custody who were over the age of 60 increased from 5.2 percent to 6.8 percent (Table 14.1).

It is estimated that about 8 percent of individuals in the community over the age of 65 suffer from some form of dementia (Koller and Bynum), and it is likely that the rate is as high or higher for prison inmates who either arrive at the facility with some level of dementia or develop dementia during their confinement. With the increasing average age of prison inmates, due in part to long mandatory minimum sentences, elimination of parole at the federal level, and terms of life in prison, an increase in the incidence of dementia in an aging population is inevitable. Defense

Table 14.1 Total number and percent of sentenced prisoners under the jurisdiction of state or federal correctional authorities

	Total number of prisoners under jurisdiction of state or federal correctional authorities	Percentage of inmates 60 years old or older under jurisdiction of state or federal correctional authorities
2015	1,526,603	5.2%
2016	1,508,129	5.6%
2017	1,489,189	6.0%
2018	1,464,385	6.4%
2019	1,430,805	6.8%

Source: Bureau of Justice Statistics, Prisoners 2015, 2016, 2017, 2018 and 2019.

attorneys, the courts, and sometimes prosecutors question whether a correctional agency can manage an individual with dementia, and without fail, the response from the jail or prison system is: Yes. The question, then, is not whether, but how, these inmates and detainees are managed, and how the significant challenges they encounter during confinement and that they present to correctional administrators are addressed. Compassionate release or parole can often be considered for those who develop dementia in custody; the Federal Bureau of Prisons (BOP) acknowledges that "Those with moderately severe or severe dementia should be considered for a reduction in sentence/compassionate release" (Bureau of Prisons Program Statement 6340.04, Psychiatric Services, January 15, 2005).

However, like other authorities, the BOP is extremely reluctant to move forward with compassionate release for an inmate with dementia who has a significant history of violence or is committed for a sex offense. They determine that early return to the community presents a risk too great, particularly as dementia does not necessarily decrease the probability of re-offense, but also, the anger issues, mood swings, paranoia and confusion often associated with dementia may increase the probability of unacceptable behavior. It is inevitable, then, with the current structure of the criminal justice system that there will be those in prisons and jails with varying levels of dementia who will remain there until they complete their sentences or they die.

Ray (not his real name)

My name is Ray, I'm 73 years old, and I'm going to tell you my story. One afternoon 12 years ago, I was in a bar, got a little drunk, and got into an argument with a big guy who was a little drunk, too. He started swinging, and, not being a big guy or much of a fighter, I pulled out my knife. I always have one around. I cut him a couple of times, not trying to kill him, just back him off and teach him some respect. Well, they took him to the hospital and me to jail. He got some kind of infection and died, I got 30 years. Not my first time doing time, but it's getting harder . . . things aren't like they used to be.

Chaos Behind the Order

At first pass, it might seem that a regimented environment with monotonously repetitive daily routines, as are common in a correctional setting, would be a pretty good place for someone with significant cognitive impairments, memory loss, and confusion. There is no need to navigate the outside world, manage finances, shop for food, or prepare meals. Basic health care is available, inmates have few possessions to maintain, and few family responsibilities. They don't need to plan activities in advance or manage complex logistics to get essential services or things accomplished.

Upon closer examination, however, an apparently stable, structured setting is replete with challenges that are overwhelming to those with significant cognitive impairment. Staff in housing units change not daily, but three times a day, making it difficult for those with dementia, who may not recognize their own family members, to recognize or remember the officer in charge of a housing unit or which staff member to approach for assistance or information. Without warning, a cellmate may be re-assigned and replaced by another stranger who may not be sympathetic to an individual's struggle with memory and confusion. Most necessary activities require navigating the institution compound, usually from one building to another, finding the right building that is available for limited, often changing hours. The dining room is huge, loud, and confusing, with its own set of rules for dress and behavior; commissary shopping is limited to specific times and items and may mean waiting in line for a while; phone systems are complex and require advanced planning and resources. Movement around the facility may be limited to short intervals each hour and, during that time, the whole population is in motion.

Unknown people can stop an inmate anytime and require a search for any or no reason. Inmates are responsible for knowing where to be at every moment and are expected to be in that place or else face disciplinary action. A visit means finding the visiting room and having a strip search before entering what is a crowded, loud, busy, and confusing space with activity going on everywhere, with rules of behavior that are not intuitive. Then there's a strip search when leaving. At night, the housing units are full, and until lights out, inmates are moving about, there is noise everywhere, and gathering points, such as TV rooms, are crowded and active. Bathrooms and showers are shared with other inmates in the unit, and often full, or remote and difficult to get to for an inmate with urgency, memory issues, or confusion.

Beneath the apparent order and regimentation, life in a correctional setting is constantly changing with little or no control by an inmate, requiring attention, adaptability, and adjustment constantly—three very real challenges for those with dementia.

Ray

Got up this morning when the guy in uniform came by shouting, dressed and headed to the dining room for breakfast. Walked in, and knew right away it wasn't the dining room, but I wasn't sure where I was. A guy in uniform asked me what I was doing there, I told him, I was looking for breakfast, and he told me it was the commissary, they are not open now, that I am out of bounds and need to leave, and that the dining room is in the next building. Left feeling stupid and flustered, but found the dining room and got in line. It was so loud and crowded . . . just wanted my Raisin Bran and a banana. At the cereal counter, there was no Raisin Bran, only Corn Flakes and Coco Puffs; I don't even know what those are. Couldn't decide what to do, and the guy behind me starts making noise about there are only two choices, pick one and move on . . . picked the Corn Flakes; they at least sound familiar.

Written and Unwritten Rules

Because custody and security are the ultimate focus for any correctional or detention facility, a host of rules, many nonintuitive, are required and enforced. The written rules are generally presented in writing at admission and orientation, and it is expected from that time that an inmate knows, understands, and is responsible for following those rules. In the Federal Bureau of Prisons, for example, there are 92 prohibited acts, some as straightforward as "killing," others such as "insolence" are much more subtle and nuanced. Complying with many of these prohibited acts often requires knowing other rules, such as when "conduct which disrupts or interferes with the security or orderly running of the institution" means an inmate has to be standing by his bunk for the 4 p.m. count, or that certain spaces are out of bounds at certain times. Similarly, to avoid "being unsanitary or untidy; failing to keep one's person or quarters in accordance with posted standards" requires an inmate to know and remember what those posted standards are and when they change.

For an inmate with impaired memory or confusion, knowing, remembering, and avoiding these prohibited acts and all the accompanying rules is challenging. When the rules are violated, it is assumed the transgression is volitional, not due to any impairment, and typically disciplinary procedures follow, potentially resulting in loss of privileges or even placement in disciplinary segregation for some time. The disciplinary process itself is typically complex, with multiple levels of hearings and reviews and varying levels of assistance for inmates to negotiate the proceedings. Appeals of the outcome require knowledge and understanding of the required administrative remedy process and the ability to remember and coherently present information accurately. Many inmates are daunted by the complexity of the process and seek the assistance of "jail house lawyers" to help negotiate the various levels.

The written rules and posted requirements are not the only rules an inmate has to understand and respect to exist without conflict. Each prison or jail population comprises a unique subculture with its own rules of conduct, which can be different in each population. The unwritten rules govern interaction with other inmates and staff and are not intuitive. An inmate who has grown older in prison and had the opportunity to learn those unwritten rules has a better chance of avoiding conflict than does a newly committed inmate who has even mild dementia.

However, even for an individual who has grown older in prison, a transfer to a different institution means a different set of rules that have to be discovered and committed to memory. Included among these rules can be where an individual can sit in the dining room. In some institutions, the dining room is self-segregated by race or ethnic origin. Those whose offenses are particularly not well accepted, such as sex offenders, may be required to eat in a completely separate area or avoid the dining room at all. Which parts of the recreation yard he has access to and when may be controlled by unwritten but well-enforced rules, allowing some individuals to take advantage of recreational equipment and space while prohibiting it for others during certain times. Any area with concentrated, in-demand recreation equipment is more likely to have rules governing its use.

Unwritten rules may dictate with whom an inmate can share a cell or cubicle without harassment. It is not uncommon for those who willingly share a cell or cubicle with a known sex offender, particularly one whose offense involved children, to receive pressure to obtain assignment to different housing, even to the point of "checking in" with the institution's special housing unit to avoid such a housing assignment. How and where an individual can speak to staff may also be governed by unwritten rules requiring that interaction occur in an open area with at least one other inmate within hearing distance.

There are rules that govern how an individual is required to maintain personal space and hygiene, and consequences from both other inmates and institution staff for violations that can result in removal from the general population and placement into the more restrictive special housing unit.

Certain jobs within the institution may be reserved by the inmate population for members of a particular race, ethnic group, or religion, and an inmate seeking one of those assignments without the required characteristics can expect to be pressured to look elsewhere. Even the religious programs in which an individual can participate may be governed by unwritten rules, with pressure to avoid some religious services and practices or to actively participate in others. The rules regarding religious activity may be substantially unique for different racial and ethnic groups.

As the unwritten rules govern the interaction between inmates, they can include prohibitions against asking about an individual's offense or criminal history, or conversely can require an inmate to divulge, even by producing court documents, the details of their offense.

The definition of personal space and how personal property is to be respected, as well as the consequences for violation of those rules, may not be explicit. It may be particularly difficult to discern by an individual who has memory deficits and is easily confused. The individuals with whom he can and cannot spend time may be well defined and this list may be governed by unwritten rules. Again, those rules governing interaction with other inmates can vary based on racial or ethnic characteristics, religious affiliation, or offense types.

Institution subcultures can be complex and vary according to population, and they may have rules and sub-rules that vary based on a variety of factors, including race, ethnicity, offense characteristics, and age. For an individual with memory deficits and confusion, or those with some pronounced level of paranoia or anger issues, discerning those rules can be extremely difficult, and committing them to memory and acting within their permitted boundaries consistently is difficult even for those new to the environment who have full cognitive abilities. For those with dementia, some nonvolitional actions are particularly troubling, both to staff and other inmates. When an individual enters a large dormitory with hundreds of cubicles, he may have difficulty remembering which one he is assigned to and exactly where it is located. If he inadvertently enters the wrong cubicle, the consequences can be serious. Similarly, if he violates another's space by nearing their bunk, even by putting some object on it, it will likely not be well tolerated. The touching or handling of the personal property of another inmate without permission is a serious offense, and can lead to significant consequences. Inmates with dementia may find themselves inadvertently in areas that are prohibited either by institution regulations or unwritten inmate rules, again, with substantial consequences. Inmates with dementia may not understand the difference between rules governing interaction with other inmates or with staff, and may unknowingly violate boundaries.

While a prison setting may, on the surface, appear to be a controlled, stable environment with monotonous daily regimens, it is, in fact a dynamic, complex environment with hundreds of written and unwritten rules. Those rules vary by any number of factors or characteristics, are not at all intuitive, and are challenging even for those with intact cognitive functioning to discern and function successfully within.

Ray

Woke up in the middle of the night, had to pee. Headed for the bathroom while my cube mate grumbled for me to be quiet, but in the dim light, had trouble finding it. Finally found it, but not before I peed myself, so finished up and cleaned up best I could and headed back to the cubicle. In the dark, they all look the same, and even at night there's all this noise, guys snoring and farting. . . . Officer wanted to know what I was doing, told him I was looking for my cubicle, and he showed me where it was. So confusing, took a long time to get back to sleep.

Security

Inmates, by far, outnumber staff in almost every correctional facility, and general compliance with established rules coupled with vigorous monitoring and enforcement are the only ways these facilities can operate with any degree of safety and security. Aberrant behavior, whether volitional or the result of mental illness, drugs, or cognitive dysfunction from trauma or illness, creates a threat to the security of staff and inmates, and has to be managed quickly and effectively. Failure to control these events quickly leaves inmates involved, even peripherally, uncertain of their own safety and security and can lead to extraordinary efforts to restore that equilibrium. Those who are in the continuous presence of an individual who repeatedly acts in an unpredictable manner, disrupts the normal flow of life, or creates conflict with staff or other inmates may take measures, such as procuring or manufacturing a weapon of some sort for self-protection. They may individually or collectively create an event or circumstance that will result in that individual's removal from the general population, either through threats or overt activity. An unstable individual, such as one who frequently, aggressively, and publicly accuses another inmate of theft or some other transgression, can be highly disruptive and create an environment that is dangerous to that inmate, other inmates around him, and staff. When an inmate, even one known to have dementia, commits a rule infraction or becomes disruptive, staff have to quickly decide how best to manage that situation, whether to proceed with the disciplinary process, refer to medical for a mental health evaluation, or attempt to informally resolve the situation, and every inmate in the area is watching to see how it proceeds.

Specific behaviors often associated with various levels of dementia can be very disruptive in a closed setting: wandering, paranoia, anger, mood swings, poor personal hygiene, confusion, confrontation, and sleep disturbances. The classic "sundowners" syndrome in which an individual becomes more confused in early evening, happens exactly when most inmates are in the housing unit, the activity and noise levels are high, and before everybody settles down to sleep. The probability of a confused or paranoid inmate lashing out in that setting is increased, and with a large number of inmates and a small number of staff, can be volatile.

Vulnerability

Advanced age alone increases vulnerability for prison and jail inmates (see the National Institute of Corrections' website, nicic.gov). Less physically able to defend or assert themselves, elderly inmates are often seen as fairly easy targets for manipulation or abuse. For those who are confused or suffer memory impairment, the vulnerability increases. Inmates with dementia, particularly in the disease's earlier stages, may be undiagnosed. However, it is likely that those inmates who live in proximity or are assigned to the same work detail with one who is in the earlier stages of Alzheimer's disease recognize when that an elderly inmate does not think as quickly or clearly as they used to, repeats a particularly dysfunctional action, or exhibits behaviors that indicate he is unsure of his surroundings. While not all inmates will take advantage of an inmate with dementia, there are always those who will, even in the lowest security setting.

Inmates with dementia may be recruited for illicit activity. Elderly inmates are often seen as lower security risks, and may be allowed to move about an institution relatively unchallenged by staff so long as the movement occurs during allowed times and appears to be appropriate, such as returning to the housing unit after work or a medical appointment. Coupled with confusion or difficulty understanding complex activities, elderly inmates may be recruited to move contraband around the facility or to serve as "lookouts" while illicit activity is underway. If taking advantage of an individual's limited cognitive reasoning to recruit them to such activity doesn't work, veiled or overt threats may be used, and without the physical ability to defend or assert themselves, elderly inmates with cognitive impairment may recognize no alternative but to comply.

Elderly inmates with cognitive impairment may be abused more simply and directly, by having portions of their food taken in the dining room, their commissary purchases or property stolen, or being told they have to "pay" for basic activities, like taking showers or using the toilet. If an individual with dementia is known by other inmates to have resources in the outside community, he may receive pressure for his family to provide money either directly to an inmate or to that inmate's family in the community. Individuals who have grown older and developed dementia, particularly the earlier stages, in custody, may be less vulnerable to abuse. However, those newly arriving with some level of dementia likely will have more difficulty developing strategies on how to deal with potential abuse by other more aggressive inmates.

Some activities common to dementia make those with moderate to severe impairment even more vulnerable. Wandering or getting up at night and moving about, particularly if it includes entering another inmate's space (cell or cubicle), can have very severe consequences. Getting up in the middle of the night to use the toilet—not an uncommon need for elderly men—and getting confused in the dim lighting, trying to return to the correct cubicle, can be a real challenge for an individual with only mild dementia. Agitation, the need to move or walk about, the tendency to hold or handle objects, or mood swings—all common in those with dementia—can all increase the frequency of confrontation with other inmates, and, in the wrong circumstances, with staff, as well. Anger, paranoia, and belligerence expressed with staff is generally seen as a volitional act, and can result in disciplinary action and loss of privileges or activities. Failure to maintain adequate personal hygiene is often not well tolerated by other inmates and can result in efforts to have the offending individual removed from the general population. Staff may be warned, "If you don't take care of it, we will."

The difficulty that an elderly individual has in negotiating the correctional environment without conflict with either other inmates or staff may cause them to simply withdraw. It is not uncommon for elderly inmates, even those with intact cognitive and memory capabilities, to withdraw and limit activities and interactions to those that are necessary. As an elderly member of a younger, louder, more aggressive population, the confusion, risks, and aggravation make interaction just too expensive. In the extreme, these individuals, known to staff as "cave dwellers," leave their assigned housing only when essential; avoid any program or recreational activity; eat most of their meals from purchased commissary, avoiding the dining room; and decline to seek essential services, such as medical care, for chronic, age-related conditions. They may miss important medications or medical appointments and, as stated, fail to seek medical care, even when it is needed. They may avoid shower facilities altogether, or try to use them at very odd hours; they may fail to exchange their bedding or clothes for clean replacements; and they may avoid using telephones or visits from family. The environment just becomes too overwhelming, confusing, and dangerous to venture out of the relative safety and security of their assigned living space.

Ray

I'm done with the dining room. Went to dinner, didn't know what most of the stuff they were serving was, and didn't know what I wanted, so I just said yes to everything. It was so loud and crowded I couldn't even think. Took my tray, found an empty seat and started eating. Noticed that everybody around me was giving me the number three hard stare and realized I was sitting in the middle of a Latin gang . . . guy across the table leaned over and told me I needed to find somewhere else to eat, so I did. Don't know what I was thinking, been here 12 years and know better; I just couldn't think with all the noise and crowd. Too dangerous, staying in my cubicle from now on, eating commissary.

Diagnosis and Treatment

In the outside community, those who first notice the signs and symptoms of dementia are usually family or caregivers who have frequent and extended interaction with an individual. They may notice the individual has increasing difficulty with memory or finding the words to express what they want to say. They also may be confused with previously familiar activities or be disoriented. Even subtle changes are apparent to those who interact on a daily basis and are familiar with an individual's typical behavior and routines, and they can usually get an individual to a health care provider for evaluation relatively early in the process. In a correctional setting, that kind of close, regular monitoring does not exist, so it is far less likely that dementia will be diagnosed in an early, timely manner.

Staff assigned to housing units may know who the inmate is, where he works, and other general details, but staff usually does not monitor or interact with all inmates sufficiently to note when subtle changes in cognition or memory manifest themselves. Work supervisors may note some early changes, but are unlikely to make a referral for evaluation until those changes are remarkable and of sufficient degree that they raise concern for the inmate's safety or job performance. Medical staff may see an inmate on an infrequent basis and of such short duration that subtle deficiencies are not noted. Often, only after a confrontation, disciplinary action, or behavior that is sufficiently unusual for other inmates to report it, does an individual in custody get a meaningful evaluation for dementia or cognitive impairment. Other inmates, not medical or custody staff, are generally the first to recognize the early stages of dementia. Discussion with current and former correctional administrators at the county, state, and federal levels confirm that, most frequently, an inmate or detainee is evaluated for cognitive decline after another inmate has voiced concern to a staff member.

Ray

Almost got into a fight with my cubicle mate this morning. He started making noise about how the cube stinks and that I need to get a shower and change my nasty sheets and get my clothes washed . . . Last time I went to shower, a big guy told me it was his shower and if I wanted to use it I had to pay him with commissary. Didn't want to fight, and didn't have a knife close by, so I just left . . . haven't been back. He's probably right about the sheets and clothes, but I just keep forgetting to get them over to the laundry when it's open. Got to find out again when they are open and get that done. In the meantime, will just avoid the cube mate.

Evaluation by medical or mental health staff generally includes the use of a brief instrument for the objective assessment of the presence of dementia (the Federal BOP uses the Mini-Mental Health Exam), and may require follow-up neurological assessment or medical imaging such as CT or MRI of the head, and laboratory results.

There are very few medications approved by the FDA for the treatment of dementia, most of which are targeted at Alzheimer's disease, and may be useful only at certain stages of the disorder. The most recently approved (aducanumab (aduhelm)) is the first new drug to receive approval for treatment of dementia in 20 years, and requires infusion every four weeks at an annual cost of more than $56,000. Other medications are much more moderate in cost, but may not routinely be available in a correctional setting. None of these medications are available on the national formulary of the BOP, for example, and require a multilevel approval for nonformulary use.

Ray

Got called over to medical today where some guy asked a lot of crazy questions, like when was the last time I took a shower, and did I know what day it was. Seems somebody thinks I'm crazy and needs to be looked at. At the end, says he's going to assign somebody to help me out, just to kind of look after me. With all this trouble lately, might not be a bad idea to have somebody watch my back, if I can trust him. Anyhow, his name is Joe, I think. Will see how it goes.

Strategies

As in the community, finding a way to humanely care for an individual with dementia or cognitive impairment so that they can live safely and securely, with some level of dignity, as well as the opportunity to function as nearly normally as they can, is not an easy task in prison. In most cases, no intervention is made until an individual causes some kind of disruption for staff and the orderly operation of the facility. Often, it is only after confrontation, disciplinary proceedings, or, most likely, complaints or concerns from other inmates, that one is meaningfully evaluated for cognitive impairment, and the search for some solution begins.

Many correctional agencies make use of inmate volunteers or workers who may be assigned as "companions" for a disabled inmate, assisting with simple activities of daily living. The level of care that an inmate companion may provide varies by correctional agency, as does the level of training and screening completed before assignment. In almost all cases, inmate companions can assist with dressing, mobility, eating, and other nonmedical activities. However, no matter how careful the screening, whenever one inmate is dependent on another for essential activities or services, there is always the potential for abuse or manipulation, and correctional administrators emphasize the need for ongoing monitoring and review of those who participate in these programs.

Mainstreaming elderly inmates and keeping them functioning in the general population of typical units and facilities as long as possible are common strategies. As long as sufficient support and security are provided, inmates with early-stage cognitive decline can function in that setting. Increasingly, however, with growing numbers of elderly inmates and the associated costs and risks of trying to maintain them in general population units, correctional agencies are creating specific units or facilities for elderly inmates who require frequent and ongoing medical or mental health intervention. With increased staffing and the associated medical costs, these units are expensive to operate, but generally provide a safer setting for the elderly. Some agencies, including the Federal BOP, provide units specifically for the cognitively challenged, including those with dementia, and have the capability of managing not only elderly inmates with dementia but also younger cognitively impaired inmates such as those who are severely intellectually disabled or who have suffered brain trauma or injury.

The use of typical half-way houses or residential reentry centers is often either not an option for those with dementia or for those with early-stage dementia, or may be extremely challenging. Those centers, often privately operated, are minimally staffed, do not generally have sufficient resources to support the cognitively impaired, and present a more complex living environment than prison does. Many inmates who are cognitively intact find such placement difficult, describing it as having one foot in and one foot out of prison, trying to live in the community with prison rules and regulations. In some cases, an inmate with early-stage dementia may be eligible for placement in a government-operated or -contracted long-term care facility, many of which have locked wings for the memory impaired.

Some agencies make use of open mental health wards or units for cognitively impaired inmates. Placement in a mental health facility for treatment may require the inmate to provide informed consent, and if not competent to make that decision, a court order may be required for such placement. The same may be true for psychotropic medications or other medical or mental health care.

Perhaps the most significant strategy for dealing with those with dementia is a strong advocacy. Not recognizing the changes that they are going through or understanding the progressive nature of decline, these inmates are often unable to seek needed help or possible solutions. They likely don't understand that they may be eligible for consideration for early release, how to request it, or what the entire process entails. They likely won't realize that alternative housing options may be available and how to request re-assignment, or even that they need it. A strong advocate for the elderly or for others who may become cognitively impaired can assist both inmates and correctional administrators in making timely and sound decisions that benefit both.

Joe (not his real name)

This is Joe. Ray can't write any more for now. He got up in the middle of the night, got dressed and headed for the unit door. Started banging on the door making all sorts of racket, the guard asked what he was doing. Ray said he didn't like this place, didn't belong here, and was going home. The officer tried to talk some sense into him, but couldn't, so they wrestled with him a little bit, then cuffed him and took him to the special housing unit. Last I heard, he is headed for a locked unit at the mental health facility. Too bad, he's not a bad old guy.

Conclusion

As in the community, effective management of those with cognitive impairment is extremely challenging in a correctional environment. All of the issues that exist in caring for these individuals in the community also exist in a correctional setting, but with an overlay of a very different sub-culture and overriding security concerns. Missing close family or caregiver interaction, inmates are more likely to be diagnosed much later in the progress of their decline, and resources to help them adjust to diminished cognition are much more limited. As they progress, inmates with dementia may present real security concerns and sufficient disruption that places them, other inmates, and staff in jeopardy.

• • •

With degrees from Emory University (BA, 1972) and Georgia State University (MEd, 1977), **Dr. Phillip Wise** started work with the Federal BOP as a psychology technician at the U.S. Penitentiary, Atlanta, in 1977. He managed a residential drug abuse treatment unit at Federal Correctional Institution (FCI) Fort Worth; taught firearms, self-defense, and policy at the Federal Law Enforcement Training Center; and held administrative positions in regional offices and the agency headquarters before serving as Warden at the Federal Prison Camp for Women in Alderson, West Virginia, and as Warden of the Federal Medical Center in Rochester,

Minnesota, where he was appointed to the Senior Executive Service of the United States. He was appointed as assistant director of the Bureau of Prisons with responsibility for Health Services in 1999, and retired from that agency in 2002. He worked for two years as vice president of a company that provided specialized medical care for federal, state, and local correctional facilities, and, since, has worked as a consultant on correctional medical issues, primarily with federal criminal defense attorneys on sentencing matters. Like many of us, he, too, has had personal experience dealing with a close family member suffering from dementia. Dr. Wise may be reached at psn@msn.com.

Citations available from author by request.

Chapter

15

Guardianships, Conservatorships, and Related Proceedings

Mary DeLeo, Esq.

The controversy of Brittany Spears' conservatorship alerted the public to the uses and abuses of this legal tool. The American Bar Association has long been an advocate for safeguarding the rights of the subject of a conservatorship as well as promoting the least-restrictive alternative.

Families of people with dementia may seek conservatorship as a vital tool for protecting their loved one as well as their loved one's assets. This chapter by attorney Mary DeLeo is a guide for the criminal defense practitioner. It will arm her with knowledge about the kinds of conservatorships, the strengths and weaknesses of each, and the procedure for obtaining them. The purpose for including this chapter is to alert the criminal defense lawyer to various issues that may impact the progress of a criminal case. Because this field is so complex, the criminal defense lawyer might do well to refer the family to a practitioner who specializes in it.

This chapter emphasizes, as does the ABA, that conservatorships deprive individuals of constitutional rights, and as such, should be applied wisely and compassionately.

• • •

Introduction to Conservatorships

This chapter is not intended to teach the criminal defense lawyer how to handle a conservatorship. It is assumed that the client or the client's family will engage an attorney who specializes in this area. Instead, this chapter is intended to serve as a general introduction to conservatorships and familiarize the criminal defense lawyer with the issues the client or their family will face when facing or under conservatorship.

Some things are of note: First, conservatorships (or guardianships, depending upon the jurisdiction) are governed by state law, and each state has its own system and procedural framework. It is beyond the scope of this chapter to review in-depth the conservatorship law for all 50 states. Instead, this chapter focuses on conservatorship law in California to introduce the practitioner to concepts likely to be encountered in any state's protective proceedings. The practitioner should carefully research the law in the state where the defendant lives, as that law is likely to be the controlling legal framework for any conservatorship proceedings.

Second, conservatorship law is not static. Indeed, at the time of this writing, there are several bills before the California legislature to reform the conservatorship structure. Motivated in part by public reaction in the form of the "#FreeBritney" movement, in which legions of fans of Britney Spears demanded that she be released from conservatorship, and in response to the Netflix film "I Care a Lot," in which an underhanded court-appointed guardian abuses her clients, these bills seek to add additional procedures and requirements to the existing conservatorship process to provide further protections for conservatees. Consequently, practitioners must be aware that the law in this area may be changing and ensure that they are accessing the latest and most up-to-date information.

Third, nomenclature is key. Not only does the name of the protective proceeding vary from state to state but also the term "dementia" is not consistently used, the reason being that "dementia" was replaced by the phrase "major neurocognitive disorder" in the latest version of the Diagnostic and Statistical Manual of Mental Disorders (DSM-V). This has led at least one state (California) to revise its probate code to replace "dementia" with "major neurocognitive disorder." A practitioner who is researching state law to determine whether that state has statutes specifically addressing placement and medication issues for demented individuals may overlook valuable information if he or she is not using the most up-to-date terminology.

Conservatorship Defined

Simply stated, a conservatorship is a legal action to appoint an individual to manage an incapacitated person's personal and/or financial needs. The incapacitated person's limitations may be mental, physical, or both. The person appointed as conservator is charged with making decisions in the best interests of the conservatee.

Although each state has some type of framework to institute protective proceedings for an incapacitated individual, the names given to that framework vary from state to state. In California, the term "conservatorship" is used to refer to a protective proceeding intended to protect an incapacitated adult individual, while "guardianship" refers to a California proceeding involving the appointment of a guardian for a minor child. In contrast, other states, such as New York, use the term "guardianship" when referring to the protective procedure for an incapacitated adult. To avoid confusion, counsel should familiarize themselves with the statue of the particular state with which they are dealing.

Types of Conservatorships

In California, there are several different types of conservatorships, depending on the circumstances of the individual needing protection:

- **Probate Conservatorships:** Probate conservatorships, called that because they are established pursuant to the California Probate Code, are of two types: general conservatorships and limited conservatorships.
    - **General Conservatorships:** A general conservatorship is established to protect an adult who is unable to provide for their personal needs, substantially manage their financial affairs, or resist fraud or undue influence. Cal. Prob. Code § 1801 (Deering, Lexis Advance through all 770 Chapters of the 2021 Regular Session). General conservatorships are often needed for elders who become impaired due to the limitations of aging. Major neurocognitive disorders such as dementia are a common reason for seeking a general conservatorship, and, where necessary, special powers can be obtained to place the conservatee in a secured-perimeter facility to prevent wandering and to permit the administration of anti-dementia medication to the conservatee. General conservatorships

also may be needed for younger adults who have become incapacitated due to injury or illness.

- **Limited Conservatorship:** A limited conservatorship is a particular type of probate conservatorship intended for developmentally disabled individuals who need assistance but who do not need the higher level of protections of a general conservatorship. Cal. Prob. Code § 1801(d) (Deering, Lexis Advance through all 770 Chapters of the 2021 Regular Session). Limited conservatorships are intended to preserve as much independence as possible for the limited conservatee. Unlike general conservatorships, pursuant to which the appointed conservator is granted a wide range of authority, the powers granted to the conservator in a limited conservatorship are tailored to promote the specific conservatee's independence, given the nature and extent of their disability. To qualify for a limited conservatorship, the developmental disability must have been begun before the conservatee reached age of 18.

This chapter focuses on probate conservatorships only, since those conservatorships are most often involved when the proposed conservatee is suffering from dementia. However, it is important for the practitioner to be aware of the other types of conservatorships that exist, and when they are used, to ensure that they are seeking the right type of relief. For example, if an individual suffers from both mental illness and dementia, and requires involuntary placement in a mental health facility, establishing a probate conservatorship, even with the special major neurocognitive disorder placement powers, will not provide the needed authority, as involuntary placement in a mental health facility can only be obtained under an LPS conservatorship.

Probate Conservatorships

In California, probate conservatorships are governed by Probate Code sections 1800 *et seq*. A petition for a probate conservatorship is typically brought by the person seeking to act as conservator of the proposed conservatee or by a relative or friend of the proposed conservatee who wishes another to act as the conservator. Occasionally, the proposed conservatee voluntarily brings a conservatorship petition on their own behalf, such as when the proposed conservatee suffers from a neurocognitive or physical disorder that will eventually result in their incapacity, or when the proposed conservatee has limitations that make it difficult for them to personally manage their own affairs. Where a voluntary conservatorship is sought, the court will grant the petition upon a showing of good cause. Cal. Prob. Code § 1802 (Deering, Lexis Advance through all 770 Chapters of the 2021 Regular Session). More common, however, is the conservatorship action initiated by the proposed conservator.

Probate conservatorships can be either a general conservatorship, typically established to assist an adult who is incapacitated due to aging-related impairments or by impairments caused by physical trauma or illness, or limited conservatorships, which are designed specifically for developmentally disabled individuals whose disability arose prior to age 18.

Threshold Questions in Every Conservatorship

The two primary questions in every action for appointment of a conservator are (1) is a conservatorship necessary, and (2) if a conservatorship is needed, who should be appointed as conservator.

First Threshold Question: Is the Conservatorship Necessary?

Even though a person may be mentally or physically impaired, a conservatorship may not always be needed. There are several alternatives to conservatorship. If the impaired individual will accept voluntary assistance, and that assistance is sufficient to ensure that the impaired individual's personal and financial needs are met, no conservatorship may be warranted. The existence of estate planning documents, such as a trust, power of attorney for financial management, and an Advance Health Care Directive, executed when the individual had capacity, typically will provide the designated trustee and agents with sufficient authority to avoid a conservatorship. Because a conservatorship is a drastic and expensive endeavor, one which deprives the proposed conservatee of many of their rights, a conservatorship should be considered a last resort, and not the first or only option.

Before filing for conservatorship, counsel should explore whether alternatives to conservatorship are available. Indeed, the Confidential

Supplement (one of the California Judicial Council forms that must be filed along with the petition for conservatorship) requires the petitioner to state whether any alternatives to conservatorship exist, and, if they do, why they are not sufficient to avoid the imposition of a conservatorship.

If counsel determines there is no viable alternative to conservatorship, counsel must then evaluate whether there is, or there is likely to be, sufficient evidence to proceed with a conservatorship action. Conservatorships are not imposed lightly and require considerable time and resources. Not prevailing on a conservatorship action can have drastic consequences, as where the proposed conservatee is the subject of undue influence, such a loss may embolden the influencer to further and greater exploitation. Because many conditions that underlie the need for the conservatorship are degenerative in nature, sometimes it is prudent to delay seeking conservatorship until counsel is reasonably assured that sufficient evidence can be brought before the court to meet the clear and convincing evidence burden.

Assuming that a conservatorship is indicated, counsel needs to distinguish whether the conservatorship should be a general conservatorship or a limited conservatorship. General conservatorships are intended to protect adults who are incapacitated due to aging-related impairments or other mental or physical impairments. In contrast, limited conservatorships, which are discussed elsewhere, are intended solely for developmentally disabled individuals whose disability arose before age 18. Notwithstanding, if the disability is so extensive as to warrant it, the court may order a general conservatorship over a developmentally disabled individual.

General Conservatorship

The criteria for imposing a general conservatorship (as opposed to a limited conservatorship, which is discussed in the next section) in California are set forth in Probate Code section 1801, subdivisions (a) and (b):

> "A conservator of the person may be appointed for a person who is unable to provide properly for his or her personal needs for physical health, food, clothing, or shelter. . . ." Cal. Prob. Code § 1802(a).

> "A conservator of the estate may be appointed for a person who is substantially unable to manage his or her own financial resources or resist fraud or undue influence. . . ." Cal. Prob. Code § 1802(b).

Conservatorships can be of the person, of the estate, or of both person and estate, depending on the circumstances and the assistance need by the proposed conservatee. Cal. Prob. Code § 1802(a)(1). For example, an incapacitated individual who has placed all of their assets in trust may need a conservatorship of the person, but not of the estate. Similarly, if a proposed conservatee is able to provide for their personal needs with voluntary assistance, but is unable to resist fraud or undue influence, a conservatorship of the estate only may be needed.

Although it is common for the same individual to serve as both conservator of the person and of the estate, it is not required, and the court can appoint separate conservators of the person and the estate.

Second Threshold Question: Who Should Be the Conservator?

Petitions for conservatorship must set forth not only the facts underlying the need for the conservatorship but also identify the proposed conservator. The proposed conservatee may object to the establishment of the conservatorship, to the appointment of the particular proposed conservator, or both; it is therefore important to ascertain exactly the nature and extent of the objections if the petition is contested. For example, in the case of a proposed conservatee being unduly influenced, the proposed conservatee may have no objections to the establishment of the conservatorship, but may want the influencer to be appointed as conservator instead of the proposed conservator identified in the petition for appointment. Or, the proposed conservatee may object to the conservatorship, but be willing to accept the proposed conservator in that role if the establishment of the conservatorship cannot be avoided.

The conservator may be one person or multiple people who serve as co-conservators. However, if two co-conservators are appointed they must act unanimously, which can lead to power struggles and disputes that may need to be resolved by the courts. If three or more co-conservators are appointed, then a majority must concur to exercise a power. Cal. Prob. Code § 1802(c)(1-2).

The conservator of the person and the conservator of the estate do not need to be the same person. However, the conservator of the estate is required to communicate "as necessary and appropriate" with the conservator of the person. Cal. Rules of Court, Rule 7.1059(b)(12).

The selection of the conservator is solely within the discretion of the court; however, the court will accommodate the proposed conservatee's wishes wherever possible, so long as the court determines the choice is in the best interests of the proposed conservatee. Cal. Prob. Code §§ 1810, 1812. A nomination of conservator contained in the proposed conservatee's estate planning documents, executed at a time when the proposed conservatee's capacity was unquestioned, typically carries substantial weight with the court. In the absence of a nomination by the proposed conservatee, Probate Code section 1812 sets forth a list of individuals who have priority of appointment as conservator, beginning first with the proposed conservatee's spouse or domestic partner, if any, followed by an adult child, then a parent, and then a sibling. If any of these individuals with priority of appointment does not wish to serve themselves, they may nominate a conservator and that nomination will hold the same level of priority, subordinate to the preference for any other parent, child, or siblings in that class. Cal. Prob. Code § 1812(c). If no family member is available or willing to serve, then a private professional fiduciary, licensed by the Professional Fiduciary Bureau under the Department of Consumer Affairs, may be the best solution.

Given the complexities of the rules regarding priority of appointment of a conservator and the court's commitment to accommodating the proposed conservatee's choice of conservator, if it is in the proposed conservatee's best interests to do so, great care should be given to the selection of the proposed conservator when filing for conservatorship. Proposing a conservator whom the proposed conservatee distrusts or does not get along with is almost sure to draw an objection, even if the proposed conservatee does not object to the establishment of the conservatorship itself. A trial over which sibling should be conservator, for instance, may consume considerable time and expense when a different family member, or even a private professional fiduciary, may be a better choice. Additionally, the court likely will require a conservatorship of the estate to be bonded, for the protection of the conservatee. Obtaining the appointment of a conservator only to then discover that they are not bondable is a waste of time and resources. Making sure that the proposed conservator is acceptable to both the proposed conservatee and the court is essential.

Special Powers Regarding Major Neurocognitive Disorders

Where the proposed conservatee suffers from a major neurocognitive disorder such as dementia, the petition may seek special powers in the form of the authority to place the conservatee in a secured-perimeter residential care facility for the elderly (e.g., memory care unit), and/or the authority to consent to the administration of anti-dementia medications and treatment for the conservatee. If the petition is seeking authority to treat the proposed conservatee with medication for major neurocognitive disorders and/or for placement in a secured-perimeter residential care facility for the elderly, then the health care evaluator must also complete the Attachment to Form CG-335, *Capacity Declaration—Conservatorship*, Only for (Proposed) Conservatee with a Major Neurocognitive Disorder, and indicate whether, in the health care evaluator's opinion, the proposed conservatee should be placed in a secured-perimeter facility and/or administered medication for treatment of a major neurocognitive disorder.

Once a petition for conservatorship, and the attendant pleadings, are filed, the court will set a hearing date. Prior to the hearing, a court investigator will be assigned to interview the proposed conservatee, their spouse, or registered domestic partner, relatives, and sometimes friends and neighbors, and also the proposed conservator.[1] During their interview with the proposed conservatee, the court investigator will inform the proposed conservatee of the nature, purpose, and effect of the conservatorship action, their right to attend the hearing, their right to a jury trial, their right to be represented by legal counsel if they choose, and their right to have counsel appointed for them if they wish. Cal. Prob. Code § 1826(a)(2). The court investigator will determine, among other things and to the extent possible, whether the proposed conservatee wishes to attend the hearing, whether they want to contest the conservatorship action, whether they object to the proposed conservator or prefer someone else to serve as conservator, and whether they wish legal counsel

1. Cal. Prob. Code § 1826, subd. (a)(1). If the petitioner is not the same person as the proposed conservator, the court investigator will interview the petitioner as well.

to be appointed for them. Cal. Prob. Code § 1826(a)(1-8). The court investigator will then prepare a written report of their findings, to be submitted to the court at least five days before the hearing of the outcome of the interviews. Cal. Prob. Code § 1826(a)(11-12). The court investigator's report is provided to the proposed conservatee, their spouse or registered domestic partner, their relatives within the first degree, counsel for the proposed conservatee (if any), and counsel for the petitioner. Cal. Prob. Code § 1826(a)(12).

If the proposed conservatee does not object to the conservatorship and does not wish to have counsel appointed for them, then the court may grant the conservatorship petition at the initial hearing. However, if the proposed conservatee objects to either the establishment of the conservatorship or to the proposed conservator, the court will set a trial on these issues. The court will also appoint counsel for the proposed conservatee, if they are not already represented. Cal. Prob. Code §§ 1470, 1471.

Although probate trials are typically court trials, conservatorship matters may be tried to a jury. The burden of proof for the establishment of a conservatorship is clear and convincing evidence.

If the court grants the Petition for Appointment of Probate Conservator, the court will issue an order appointing the conservator. In a general conservatorship, the conservator will be granted the authority under Probate Code sections 2350 through 2361 for conservatorship of the person and under Probate Code sections 2400 through 2595 for conservatorship of the estate. These powers can be limited or expanded by obtaining specific court orders; thus, if there is a need for additional orders or limitations on the conservator's statutory authority, the Petition for Appointment of Probate Conservator should contain those requests so that the court can rule on them, and, if granted, they can be included in the order of appointment. The court will also issue Letters of Conservatorship, which is the "badge of authority" that the conservator will use to establish with third parties their legal right to act on behalf of the conservatee.

As noted earlier, if there is a conservatorship of the estate, the court will likely require that the conservator be bonded in an amount sufficient to fully restore the conservatorship estate should the conservator commit misconduct. Cal. Prob. Code §§ 2300, 2320. Where the conservatorship is of the person only, typically a bond is not required. Cal. Prob. Code § 2322.

Authority and Duties: Conservatorship of the Person

If the conservatee suffers from a major neurocognitive disorder (e.g., dementia) and needs to be placed in a secured-perimeter facility to prevent wandering, or if the conservatee would benefit from treatment with medications for the disorder, the conservator must first obtain specific authority from the court for such placement and/or treatment. As noted earlier, this request can be included in the initial petition to establish the conservatorship or can be petitioned for separately, after the conservatorship is established, if the need for such placement and/or treatment arises after the conservatorship is established. To obtain these special powers, a doctor's declaration attesting to the need for such powers must be submitted to the court. *See* Cal. Judicial Counsel Form GC-335A, Attachment to Form CG-335, *Capacity Declaration—Conservatorship*, Only for (Proposed) Conservatee with a Major Neurocognitive Disorder.

It is important to note that a probate conservator does not have the authority under the probate code to place a conservatee in a mental health treatment facility against his or her will, to be administered experimental drugs, or to undergo convulsive treatment.[2]

If, while the conservatee had capacity, they executed a valid power of attorney for health care such as an Advance Health Care Directive, the agent under that power of attorney has priority over any other person in making decisions for the conservatee, even the conservator, unless the court has suspended the power of attorney. Cal. Prob. Code § 4685.

Termination

Once a conservatorship is established, it remains in place until it is terminated. The conservatorship terminates upon (1) the death of the conservatee; (2) a judicial determination that the conservatorship is no longer needed due to a change in circumstances;[3] or (3) the conservatee is relocated out of state and the conservatorship is transferred to the new state.

---

2. *Id.* § 2356. Powers such as involuntary placement in a mental health facility can only be obtained under an LPS hold or LPS conservatorship under Welf. & Inst. Code §§ 5150 *et seq.*
3. For example, where the conservatorship was established due to an incapacitation caused by illness, and the conservatee recovers.

Limited Conservatorships

A limited conservatorship is a special type of probate conservatorship and is designed strictly for adults with a developmental disability that was present prior to age 18. Cal. Prob. Code § 1801(d). Unlike a general conservatorship under which the conservator is granted a broad range of powers, the purpose of a limited conservatorship is to provide only that level of assistance to the conservatee that is needed to manage those personal and financial needs that the conservatee cannot do by themselves. *Id.* The express goal of the limited conservatorship is to "promote and protect the well-being" of the limited conservatee while "encourage[ing] the development of maximum self-reliance and independence," given the limited conservatee's limitations. *Id.*

Limited conservatorships differ from general conservatorships in certain key ways. First, a limited conservator only has those powers expressly granted them by the court and does not have the powers, absent express court order, to determine the residence of the limited conservatee, gain access to their confidential records and papers, control their financial resources, make medical decisions for them, or make decisions concerning their education. Cal. Prob. Code §§ 1801(d), 1828.5. Consequently, when petitioning for a limited conservatorship, it is important for the conservator to determine what powers are necessary and to specifically request those powers in the petition.

Second, the petitioner must give notice of the petition to the appropriate California Regional Center.[4] The Regional Center will then conduct an assessment of the proposed conservatee (with their consent) and file a report informing the court of the specific areas, nature, and degree of disability of the proposed limited conservatee. Cal. Prob. Code § 1827.5(c)(1). The Regional Center's assessment and report is in addition to the investigation and report conducted by the court investigator. The conclusions of the Regional Center as to the limited conservatee's ability to manage their own affairs, although not binding, can carry great weight with the court.

4. Cal. Prob. Code §§ 1822, subd. (e); *see also id.* § 1827.5. California Regional Centers provide a number of services to developmentally disabled individuals to assist them in leading independent and productive lives, including providing living arrangements, physical and occupational therapy, mental health services, job training and education, recreation and information and referral services. They also serve as advocates to help people with developmental disabilities get and keep government benefits.

Third, the court must inquire into the nature and extent of the general intellectual functioning of the proposed limited conservatee, evaluate the extent of the impairment of their adaptive behavior, and ascertain their capacity to care for themselves and their property. Cal. Prob. Code § 1828.5. The court then must expressly define the powers and duties of the limited conservator to permit the proposed limited conservatee to care for themselves or to manage their financial resources commensurate with their ability to do so. *Id.*

Limited conservatorships can become tricky if the limited conservatee begins to develop a major neurocognitive disorder, as it sometimes may be difficult to tell whether a behavior is the result of the developmental disability or a symptom of a dementia. The powers obtained in the limited conservatorship will likely be insufficient to provide the limited conservatee the protections they need if they develop dementia. The conservator may have to petition the court for further powers or for the appointment of a general conservator, to address the change in the limited conservatee's mental status. Because of the public policy in limiting a conservator's authority in a limited conservatorship, obtaining these additional powers can prove challenging and may involve a full evidentiary hearing on the issue. The practitioner should ensure that he or she retains a qualified medical expert who has expertise in both the developmental disability and major neurocognitive disorders so that the expert can provide evidence to the court that justifies expanding the conservator's authority over the limited conservatee.

Conclusion

Conservatorships are a valuable tool for providing protections to impaired individuals when estate planning documents do not exist or the impaired individual refuses to accept assistance from the agents appointed under those documents. However, because conservatorships deprive individuals of their constitutional rights, the process is (and rightfully so) complex and complicated, particularly for the practitioner who is new to the practice area. Understanding the concepts described in this chapter will assist the criminal defense lawyer in understanding the issues that may emerge for their clients who are facing or under conservatorship.

• • •

Mary deLeo is a shareholder with the law firm of Weintraub Tobin as part of the Trusts and Estates practice group in Sacramento, California. Her practice focuses on trust and estate litigation, trust and estate administration, conservatorships, fiduciary representation, special needs trust administration, and planning for incapacity.

Mary has successfully represented clients in trust and probate litigation controversies, including trust and will contests, beneficiary/trustee disputes, fiduciary abuse claims, accounting issues, financial elder abuse claims, public benefit eligibility issues, and a wide variety of trust and probate litigation. She also represents client in administering probates and trusts.

Mary is a member of the Trusts and Estates Executive Committee (TEXCOM) of the California Lawyers Association, where she has served as co-chair of the Legislation Committee for the past three years. She is a past co-editor in chief of the *Trusts and Estates Quarterly* and past co-chair of the Education Committee. She has been appointed as vice-chair of TEXCOM for 2022. Mary also was appointed to and presently serves on the Judicial Council of California Probate and Mental Health Advisory Committee, which makes recommendations to the Judicial Council of California for improving the administration of justice in probate matters involving mental health and developmental disability issues. She recently was elected to membership in the American College of Trust and Estate Counsel (ACTEC).

Mary is an avid speaker and author on a wide range of trusts and estates topics, including probate and trust litigation, financial elder abuse, and conservatorships. She can be reached at MdeLeo@weintraub.com.

Citations available from author by request.

Chapter

16

Dementia in the Legal Profession

Dr. Eric Y. Drogin

The practice of law is one where age and experience are valued and even revered. In particular, lions of the criminal defense bar hold groups spellbound at cocktail parties. At continuing legal education programs, audiences listen to war stories with rapt attention. Young lawyers eagerly sit as second chair with trial veterans. And lawyers themselves boast on their websites that they have practiced for decades.

Because of this admiration, we may be hesitant to acknowledge the cognitive decline in our colleagues. This chapter by Dr. Eric Y. Drogin describes the warning signs that we should be alert for. Then, following the Model Rules of Professional Responsibility, he analyzes the ethical implications of a criminal defense lawyer with dementia continuing to practice.

• • •

As years of dedicated professional service go by, counsel winds up encountering clients of every imaginable sort. Many of these clients have arrived at their present predicaments through a confluence of dire personal circumstances. New lawyers marvel at the mysterious complexity of these individual histories, while more experienced lawyers have progressed to the point at which they can hear some of the story and then predict the rest with surprising accuracy. In time, counsel learns the extent to which client adversity is essentially human adversity, and develops a degree of empathy born of experience that is not merely understood but is actually shared. So it can be when counsel, having represented countless clients with mental illness, is faced with a diagnosis of a condition like dementia.

The nature of dementia as a psychiatric disorder has already been discussed in this book in considerable detail (*see* Chapters 1, 7, and 9). It will suffice, at this juncture, to recall that dementia reflects an overlapping host of cognitive deficits that can include declines in executive function, complex attention, learning, memory, language ability, perceptual-motor ability, and social cognition—skills that comprise as neat a list as one might desire of what is necessary to function successfully as an attorney. American Psychiatric Association, Diagnostic and Statistical Manual of Mental Disorders 591–643 (5th ed. 2013). To find oneself diagnosed with dementia can be every bit as devastating personally as it is professionally. This chapter addresses how dementia can be detected, how it can affect counsel's practice, how preparations can be made for ensuring that the interests of clients are suitably protected, how assistance can be recommended, and how help can be obtained.

Warning Signs

As noted by dementia experts James Galvin and Carl Sadowsky, the well-regarded Alzheimer's Association maintains an updated posting of key warning signs that are applicable to all forms of dementia, citing these as "significant health concerns that should be evaluated by a doctor," and emphasizing further that "it's important to take action to figure out what's going on." James E. Galvin & Carl H. Sadowsky, *Practical Guidelines for the Recognition and Diagnosis of Dementia*, 25 J. Am. Board Fam. Med. 367 (2012); Alzheimer's Association, *10 Early Signs and Symptoms of Alzheimer's* (2021), https://tinyurl.com/Alzheimer10signs. Each of these signs is addressed here with annotations that relate them directly to counsel's various practical functioning as a legal practitioner.

(1) **Memory loss.** The sheer press of business and the uniquely detail-oriented work of legal practice call for multiple backup systems. Datebooks, calendars, smartphone alerts, secretaries, and co-counsel all have well-defined roles to play in ensuring that as little as possible is forgotten. Still, there are many things that counsel must be able recall on

their own, and not everything can be reduced to some form of written record for subsequent retrieval. The occasional slip is nothing to inspire any particular concern. However, persistent, consequential memory problems call for some form of professional attention.

(2) **Difficulty performing familiar tasks.** The law appears at times to be split equally between feverish improvisation and grinding, dull routine. In the latter instance, at least, counsel can take comfort from the notion that practice makes perfect. If tasks that have been performed almost reflexively for a number of years suddenly seem to require stepwise analysis, elaborate forethought, and laborious planning, it may be that simple fatigue is the culprit. Another suspect in this scenario could be burnout. Perhaps some time away from the office will cure these tendencies. If not, medical intervention should be considered.

(3) **Problems with language.** Hauling heavy files to the courthouse, visiting the jail, and pounding the table are all staple activities of the working legal practitioner, but what really keeps the referrals coming and clients smiling are counsel's way with words. Problems with language can involve receiving and encoding information as well as conveying it, and they can involve reading, writing, as well as speaking and hearing. Each of these discrete functions is conducted on the basis of complex interactions between different parts of the human brain, subject to disruption by the organic deterioration that forms the basis for dementia.

(4) **Disorientation to place and time.** If it really is the case that 80 percent of success is just showing up, then counsel's failure to know where to be and when is going to be a very significant problem indeed. To pursue this cliché just a bit further, clients are not paying for legal services that have at best a 20 percent chance of securing positive results. Not knowing where one is and what time it is are very easy problems to spot, and as a rule are not going to be attributable to boredom, overwork, or inattention. Dehydration can cause these difficulties, and so can delirium that occurs secondary to such factors as an unforeseen reaction to overprescribed or injudiciously combined medications. Dementia is another possibility that should be investigated promptly.

(5) **Poor or decreased judgment.** The life's blood of counsel's practice is the tendency of *other* persons to exercise poor or decreased judgment. Criminal lawyers understand how these lapses occurred in the past and strive to explain them. By contrast, business lawyers understand

how these lapses might occur in the future and strive to prevent them. Both functions require counsel to know how judgment should best be applied, in addition to which counsel will need to make quick, seasoned, well-informed decisions in order to best counsel's adversaries and hurdle a predictable array of procedural barriers. The lapses associated with dementia can prevent counsel from performing with requisite precision and speed, potentially to calamitous effect.

(6) **Problems with abstract thought.** Higher-order, integrated thinking is a critical asset to any form of legal practice involving complex matters. Dementia can involve a deterioration in executive functioning, as a result of which a viable case strategy may simply fail to materialize, much less be carried out in an efficacious manner. Counsel would never have gotten into law school, graduated from law school, or passed the bar examination without natural and subsequently well-honed talents in this regard. Abstract thinking ability involves skills that are far less likely to register via standard medical testing than they are on the basis of neuropsychological assessment, but professionals who conduct the former are ready, willing, and able to make referrals to professionals who conduct the latter.

(7) **Misplacing things.** When physicians misplace things—a scalpel, for example then the result is often regarded in terms of malpractice. For defendants in other contexts, the legal system turns to thoughts of theft or fraud. Counsel is comparatively unlikely to be faced directly with such consequences when a file, a phone number, or a set of keys is mislaid, but persistent problems of this nature can snowball to the point that far more serious errors can result. Family members with older relatives are used to gauging the potential for cognitive decline by a tendency to misplace things. So are physicians qualified to diagnose dementia.

(8) **Changes in mood and behavior.** There are many, many events in counsel's professional life that can work profound changes in mood and behavior. Seemingly unfair rulings. Overly lengthy, transparently gratuitous, or ostensibly random motions that are filed by the other side at the most inopportune of moments. Clients who fail to make appointments, show up in court, or pay. All of this is to say nothing, by the way, of similarly exasperating events in counsel's *personal* life. Counsel's mood and behavior may be contributing to errors that are misinterpreted as warning signs of dementia. They may also reflect counsel's reaction to problems that are *bona fide* warning signs of dementia.

(9) **Changes in personality.** At first blush, changes in personality may seem largely indistinguishable from changes in mood and behavior, at least from a lay perspective. The critical difference here is personality's manifestation as an interactive style, as opposed to mood and behavior symptoms that do not necessarily call for anyone else's involvement. One largely unrecognized aspect of this phenomenon is that it is not only negative personality characteristics that function as indicia of dementia. When counsel is suddenly unusually indulgent, interested, and kind, this may actually represent a relational shift that heralds some form of brain deterioration. Counsel will not, of course, urgently seek medical attention when newly and inexplicably well-disposed toward others, but it may will be worth checking to see if other warning signs are surfacing as well.

(10) **Loss of initiative.** This situation may play out in either or both of two different ways. Loss of initiative may consist of lethargy, and it also may consist of what could be considered a failure of nerve. Depression could be one viable explanation for this state of affairs, perhaps exacerbated by an unusual string of losses that are either personal or professional in nature. Dementia could be another viable explanation, possibly occasioned on one hand by counsel's failure to cobble together the insight and inspiration needed for decisive action, or on the other hand by a fear of failure that reflects a growing sense of deteriorating faculties.

None of these warning signs, in isolation or when combined, function as a guarantee of an accurate diagnosis of dementia. It is axiomatic that those who represent themselves have fools for lawyers, and something similar could justifiably be said of those who undertake to serve as their own doctors. The best reaction to suspicions of looming dementia will always be to seek the assistance of a qualified mental health professional.

Ethical Practice Obligations

As counsel is well aware from addressing such issues with clients—in labor, educational, substituted judgment, insurance, and other benefits assignment matters, as well as in criminal contexts—the mere existence of a mental health diagnosis does not automatically deprive one of substantive rights, including the ability to conduct a professional practice. This having been noted, such considerations are predictably a matter of degree. This may best be illustrated by means of a review of contemporary ethical practice obligations, for the purpose of reflecting upon what competent counsel needs to be able to do, and how intermediate to advanced stages of dementia might prevent counsel from meeting such obligations. Following are selected elements of the American Bar Association's Model Rules of Professional Conduct, annotated with comments relevant to dementia-related decline. American Bar Association, *Model Rules of Professional Conduct* (2020), https://www.americanbar.org/groups/professional_responsi bility/publications.

Declining or Terminating Representation

Most directly on point is Rule 1.16, which states counsel "shall not represent a client or, where representation has commenced, shall withdraw from the representation of a client," should it transpire that counsel's "physical or mental condition materially impairs the lawyer's ability to represent the client." The term "materially" is an understandably imprecise one, and the Model Rules do not define it. We've all had days when we failed to do our very best, perhaps due to a head cold or to nagging distractions in our personal lives. It is safe to assume that chronic, substantial, and disease-related disability would meet this standard. A subsequent portion of this chapter addresses how counsel can undertake to make good on this particular obligation.

Diligence

Rule 1.3 states in its entirety that "[a] lawyer shall act with reasonable diligence and promptness in representing a client." "Diligence" clearly pertains to counsel's ability to keep working away at the task at hand, while "promptness" calls for counsel to do so without undue delay. Dementia erodes not just the quality of one's work but also the degree to which duties can be addressed for a sustained period of time. Naturally, this in turn affects the speed with which projects can be completed on a timeline that satisfies clients and also that would be seen, one can only hope, to be properly expeditious in the eyes of one's state bar association. The unpredictably of case timelines would undercut the ability of counsel with dementia to set time aside for comparatively inactive days dedicated to rest and recovery.

Communications

Promptness is a notion that resurfaces repeatedly with respect to counsel's obligations concerning Rule 1.4. Counsel must "promptly" notify clients about "any decision or circumstance with respect to which the client's informed consent" will be necessary, and also must "promptly comply with reasonable requests for information," while also keeping clients "reasonably informed about the status of the matter." Here, a duty is being imposed that requires a suitably quick turnaround regarding issues that likely call for substantial deliberation, information retrieval, and responsiveness. Dementia militates against counsel's ability to persevere in each of these designated areas.

Duties to Former Clients

According to Rule 1.9, counsel should not, having formerly represented clients in one matter, "thereafter represent another person in the same or a substantially related matter" when the interests of new clients are "materially adverse to the interests" of prior clients. This situation can be cured when former clients provide "informed consent, confirmed in writing." Rule 1.9 also addresses similar situations in which former client conflicts might arise. Here, counsel is called upon to recall not only the identity but also the case details for former clients. There is also an obligation to balance the interests of former and new clients in a fashion that compares and contrasts their relative circumstances. Dementia can directly affect counsel's capabilities to gauge the advisability of taking on a supplemental criminal matter.

Client with Diminished Capacity

Under these circumstances, it is typically not just counsel who may be struggling. Clients with diminished capacity are described by Rule 1.14 as those whose "representation is diminished, whether because of minority, mental impairment, or some other reason." Counsel, whether diagnosed with dementia or not, is expected to "as far as reasonably possible, maintain a normal client-lawyer relationship" with such clients in criminal matters. Consultation with a broad range of "individuals or entities that have the ability to take action to protect the client" is encouraged, as is attempting "in appropriate cases" to seek "the appointment of a guardian ad litem, conservator or guardian." The incapacity of clients can, in effect, compound the incapacity of counsel when it is not just one but both of whom who are facing disability-related difficulties.

Expediting Litigation

Rule 3.2 states in its entirety that "[a] lawyer shall make reasonable efforts to expedite litigation consistent with the interests of the client." Counsel with dementia has what are in effect two separate but related duties here: acting expeditiously on the client's behalf, and also determining just what specific client interests may be in a given case. It can be exceedingly difficult to track such obligations simultaneously—or perhaps more to the point, to figure out how to accomplish one and then the other. Is it the needs of clients that will drive the speed with which counsel reacts to or takes the initiative concerning various case developments, or rather is it the rapid pace of criminal litigation that winds up determining how the shifting needs of clients are going to be evolving in real time? Counsel's ability to integrate these considerations is likely to be hampered quite considerably due to the presence of dementia.

Candor toward the Tribunal

Much is made in Rule 3.3 of the need for counsel to avoid making "a false statement of fact or law to the tribunal," and also to avoid any failure to "correct a false statement of material fact or law" that counsel has proffered earlier. In addition, counsel is obligated to "disclose to the tribunal legal authority in the controlling jurisdiction known to the lawyer to be directly adverse to the position of the client and not disclosed by opposing counsel." Of particular relevance to the situation of counsel with dementia is a qualification offered in each of these instances that such transgressions shall not be committed "knowingly." Although counsel's disability status may contribute to missteps that are not technically "knowing" in nature, this of course would not serve in criminal cases as a "safe harbor" regarding violations of other aspects of the Model Code.

Lawyer as Witness

On occasion, counsel may be called upon to testify about any of a range of different subjects, including the proper performance (or lack thereof) of another attorney's professional duties. Counsel is generally prohibited by Rule 3.7 from acting "as advocate at a trial in which the lawyer is likely to be a necessary witness." A number of exceptions exist, however, such as when "the testimony relates to an uncontested issue," when "the testimony relates to the nature and value of the legal services rendered in the case," or when "disqualification of the lawyer would work substantial hardship on the client." In any event, functioning as a witness can be every bit as helpful or damaging, in some cases, as anything counsel might be attempting to accomplish in a traditional advocacy role. Counsel with dementia is likely to be prone to memory problems what would complicate or rule out altogether the possibility of being truly useful under these circumstances, with the added twist that testifying as a witness in criminal matters may prevent some other, more capable person from assuming this role instead.

Truthfulness in Statements to Others

According to Rule 4.1, counsel must again avoid "knowingly" making two different forms of factual misrepresentation. First, counsel must not "make a false statement of material fact or law to a third person." Second, under certain circumstances, "when disclosure is necessary to avoid assisting a criminal or fraudulent act by a client," counsel must not "fail to disclose a material fact to a third person." Obligations to clients and to the tribunal are being expanded here to relationships that extend beyond the counsel-client dyad, and also to encounters that otherwise occur outside the specific context of legal proceedings. Here, counsel's task in criminal cases is hardly less complicated—and arguably more so—because it lies outside the purview of what counsel is usually expected to do, and because it is being performed with individuals with whom counsel is not typically expected to have developed a working relationship. Having to think on one's feet is a particular drawback for counsel with dementia, who may have become increasingly dependent on the option to rely upon routine, more familiar activities.

Dealing with Unrepresented Persons

Rule 4.3 addresses yet another context that, like those described in Rule 4.1, finds counsel functioning outside of traditional comfort zones. When counsel "knows or reasonably should know that the unrepresented person misunderstands the lawyer's role in the matter, the lawyer shall make reasonable efforts to correct the misunderstanding." Perhaps more than any other, this scenario draws upon counsel's ability to apply just the sort of social cognition skills—involving a suitable grasp of commonly accepted norms for human interaction—that persons with dementia are likely to find most challenging. Since counsel's obligation here is not tied just to what counsel in criminal cases "knows," but also to what counsel "reasonably should know," with respect to what someone else "understands," insight into the ability of others to take in and make sense of complex information is directly implicated.

These examples encompass less than 20 percent of the currently codified Model Rules, but presumably the point has suitably been made. Legal practice obligations hinge upon much more than simply the frequency with which counsel can win cases and the likelihood that clients will consider themselves suitably well-served by the process. Ethical duties become increasingly labyrinthine and burdensome, not due to the urgings of a mountingly hypersensitive network of watchdog groups and guild organizations, but rather due to the fact that new discoveries are constantly made about ways in which legal representation can go seriously wrong. Counsel with dementia, in addition to running afoul of the most basic practical requirements of criminal practice viability, may very well be ensnared in any of a slew of comparatively obscure guidelines that can prove no less injurious to clients and no less fatal to a professional career.

Planning Affirmatively to Protect the Interests of Clients

Given the often gradual onset and long-term progression of dementia, counsel—more likely than most others to have well-funded, adequately insured access to medical screening at frequent intervals—will often have time to develop an orderly, reasonably unhurried plan of normal conclusion and referral-based succession for current client matters. More difficult, for both financial and emotional reasons, will be the inevitable decision to avoid taking on new criminal matters. Word of this situation will quickly permeate the local professional community, often conveying the message that counsel is in some sort of trouble.

Not only is this a potential source of wounded pride, but it can also be seen as signaling a degree of vulnerability that may not bode well for counsel's attempt to wrap up successfully those criminal matters that are still capable of being negotiated or tried within practical and ethical boundaries. Similarly, such concerns can affect the decisions of criminal defendants to focus on these issues in the course of otherwise minimally supported post-conviction proceedings. It is advisable to consult with qualified medical personnel to double-check just what the predicted progression of skill deterioration is going to be, and also to get a sense from similarly experienced counsel how a disclosed condition of dementia stands to affect counsel's viability when pursuing a given matter in the pressure-cooker environment of an adversarial system. Is opposing counsel going to become more intractable with respect to settlement, or seek to delay matters to the client's detriment? Is the court going to second-guess counsel's judgment based on well-founded rumors of counsel's illness?

It will not always be the case that counsel will have much time to plan. If denial of patently obvious symptoms has delayed a decision to seek cognitive screening or subsequent medical attention, or if there has otherwise been a sudden onset of dementia, a decline in skills may have progressed to the point that events overtake counsel. It may even be the case that counsel has lost most or all meaningful opportunities to act at all by the time a diagnosis has been confirmed. For these reasons—in no way predicated upon the notion that counsel is lazy or irresponsible, but rather in simple recognition of the fact that anything is possible—counsel is best advised to draft, preferably with the assistance of a colleague experienced in both criminal practice issues and advanced directive matters, a "professional will." Elements are likely to include reference to, among others, the existence of the following:

(1) **An up-to-date listing of all current and prior matters.** It may come as a surprise to some lawyers to learn that not everyone maintains a "bottom line" list of open and closed legal cases. It may be that the rush of business is so gratifyingly fast-paced that counsel is perpetually trying to keep up with this most basic overall view of a practice's current obligations.

(2) **Progress notes for all current matters.** Chances are that it is not feasible that there is always going to be something about these matters of which counsel is aware, but that counsel has yet to find an opportunity to reduce to writing. This having been noted, counsel will need to make the time to keep files current to the extent that successor counsel can move forward expeditiously.

(3) **Coded access to all current and prior matters.** Physical files for the modern legal practice are kept under lock and key, and often require codes for padlocks that secure file drawers, or for compartments that contain file drawer keys. Electronic files will usually be encrypted individually or by their location in certain sectors of each computer's hard drive. Email applications frequently contain sensitive client information, as do cloud computing backup systems; these, too, will have passwords.

(4) **Designation of successor counsel.** Various preparations for counsel to refer cases in the event of incapacity will have considerably lesser effect if these are not accompanied by contact information for the lawyer—or lawyers—who are willing to step in. The efficiency of such transfers is greatly enhanced by the preservation and prior circulation of documents that certify counsel's willingness to transfer and successor counsel's willingness to accept. It may be worth considering some reference to this arrangement in client informed consent materials.

(5) **Location of files and authorized custodians.** Similarly, it is of little value to designate successor counsel when one's colleagues cannot find the physical and electronic files that form the basis for every contemporary legal action. Successor counsel cannot always spring into action immediately, and in some instances they may wind up being reluctant to serve or may otherwise be unavailable to do so. Until this issue can be resolved, it is best to designate another individual—preferably an office employee or some other person with a legitimate, compensated connection to legal services—who will watch over the working assets of the practice in the interim, including the "professional will" itself with its supporting documents.

Counsel's incapacity may wind up being temporary. Diagnoses are not always accurate, either in their identification of a specific condition or in their prediction of the progression of cognitive decline. For this reason, those undertaking to draft a "professional will" should consider including a mechanism by which counsel can regain possession, control, and the ability to practice on the basis of protected materials. Typically, this would include some form of medical certification of counsel's now-current status, predicated upon a finding that usual fitness-for-duty standards have been met. Before counsel and colleagues attempt to develop the "professional will," they are also best advised to determine what advice, guidance, or mandates have been provided by state bar associations—especially where the guild organization in question represents an "integrated" bar that both advocates for and controls legal practice in that jurisdiction.

In addition to whatever informed consent provisions may have telegraphed the possibility of counsel's subsequent incapacity, counsel will need to undertake to arrange direct meetings with potentially affected criminal law clients or their authorized representatives once a dementia diagnosis has been confirmed that reasonably stands to affect counsel's ability to execute representational duties effectively. This can be a very fraught and emotionally painful process for all involved. Counsel may wish to consult with a mental health professional to explore the best ways to convey such information, for counsel's own sake as well as for that of others. Written documentation of any such client conferences is highly advisable.

Recommending Assistance and Obtaining Help

Recommending assistance to one's colleagues at the bar is not an easy task, and it is not one to be undertaken lightly. Insinuations that fellow attorneys are not functioning at peak efficiency are likely to seen as a personal as well as professional affront. This observation is not meant to discourage intervention on another's behalf; rather, the message here is that some ways of going about this are better than others. Lawyers, after all, are typically in the best position to assess the performance of other lawyers, given the highly specialized nature of our work and the unique opportunities we have to witness each other's labors, in places, manners, and context not accessible to laypersons.

Leaping directly to a diagnosis—in other words, asking colleagues outright if they believe they suffer from dementia—is a method virtually guaranteed to inspire alarm, resentment, and perhaps outright rejection. So, along the same lines, is any line of inquiry that styles apparent difficulties as "symptoms." Counsel in almost every instance is not going to be a physician as well as an attorney. Lawyers are used to gauging their professional worth and efficacy in terms of performance. This is a relatable notion that can allow for more constructive and potentially successful interaction.

Someone may look tired, and why wouldn't they after the week we've all had? Counsel can share their own positive outcomes from a simple, perhaps long overdue physical exam. Wonders have been accomplished with a change of diet, a round of routinely prescribed medication, or maybe even the discovery of some nagging medical problem, attention to which can put the spring back into one's step. The extent to which criminal law counsel can ascribe good results to their own experience—or that of a mutual acquaintance—may serve to move things along in a helpful direction. More dire and readily apparent problems, of course, will inspire inquiries of greater urgency and far less subtlety.

The American Bar Association's Commission on Lawyer's Assistance Programs provides a wealth of free online resources that are not limited, in terms of either access or interest, to the programs themselves. This material includes articles that directly address the anxiety, depression, stress, and even panic that can be associated with declining mental and physical health—including that associated with dementia. American Bar Association, Commission on Lawyer Assistance Programs (2021), https://www.americanbar.org/groups/lawyer_assistance. Links are also provided that will enable counsel to contact directly every state bar lawyer assistance program in the country. These programs typically offer confidential advice for attorneys that includes referrals to employee assistance programs or individual practitioners skilled in providing services to persons with dementia.

The diagnosis and treatment of dementia are common enough that counsel need not contact a specialist in order to obtain initial medical guidance. This can be a very important consideration when making the decision to seek services, as insurance coverage for basic checkups in this regard may be far more quickly and easily confirmed. If initial suspicions about a dementia diagnosis are confirmed, counsel is likely to be impressed by the number of medical units and dedicated physicians who have chosen to specialize in this area. Organized medicine has been preparing to focus its own resources on these issues for decades, well aware that in time the so-called Baby Boomer generation would come calling—a generation that was never expected to take lightly any threats to its claim to eternal youth.

Conclusion

Day in and day out, criminal defense counsel solves problems for countless others who are experiencing some of the worst moments of their lives. This does not necessarily mean that counsel will always be able to recognize, understand, and solve problems for colleagues and for themselves. When it comes to dementia, warning signs—once learned—are both recognizable and understood as potentially serious. Ethical obligations concerning clients are among the most prominent reasons for seeking assistance. Help is available for colleagues, and help is available for us as well.

• • •

Eric Y. Drogin is a fellow of the American Psychological Association, a fellow of the American Academy of Forensic Psychology, a diplomate of the American Board of Professional Psychology, and a diplomate and former president of the American Board of Forensic Psychology. Dr. Drogin teaches on the faculty of Harvard Medical School, where he serves as the Affiliated Lead of Psycholegal Studies for the Psychiatry, Law, and Society Program at Brigham and Women's Hospital and participates in the Program in Psychiatry and the Law at the Massachusetts Mental Health Center and the Forensic Psychiatry Service at Beth Israel Deaconess Medical Center. Dr. Drogin received PhD in clinical psychology from Hahnemann University.

Dr. Drogin is a life fellow of the American Bar Foundation. He currently serves as immediate past chair of the ABA's Science & Technology Law Section. Dr. Drogin teaches as an adjunct professor of law and mental health for the University of New Hampshire's Franklin Pierce School of Law, as an instructor for the Harvard Law School Trial Advocacy Workshop, and as an honorary professor of law for the *Prifysgol Aberystwyth* (formerly "University of Wales") Department of Law and Criminology. He received his JD from the Villanova University School of Law.

Currently serving as associate editor of the *International Journal of Law and Psychiatry*, and formerly serving as editor in chief of the *Journal of Psychiatry & Law* and as co-editor in chief of *Psychological Injury and Law*, Dr. Drogin has authored or co-authored over 300 legal and scientific publications to date. His multidisciplinary practice encompasses mental health law, expert witness testimony, and trial consultation. Dr. Drogin describes himself as an avid musician, while conceding that "avid" is not synonymous with either "accomplished" or "well-received."

Dr. Drogin can be reached at eyd@drogin.net, and his website is www.drogin.net.

Citations available from author by request.

Suggested Works

The following list of suggested works is arranged according to chapter order. These categories are not airtight, and some resources listed in one chapter may be relevant to another. In addition to exploring the works cited in individual chapters, readers are encouraged to explore the articles and books written by various chapters' authors, many of whom are prolific writers.

Chapter 1 What Is Dementia?

Aaronson, A. L., Bordelon, S. D., Brakel, S. J., & Morrison, H. (March 2021). A review of the role of chronic traumatic encephalopathy in criminal court. *Journal of the American Academy of Psychiatry and the Law Online*, *49*(1), 60–65. Retrieved from https://www.ncbi.nlm.nih.gov/pmc/articles/PMC7979483/

Alisa. (July 2020). He's Not a Criminal, He's in Crisis. Retrieved from National Alliance on Mental Illness website: https://www.nami.org/Blogs/NAMI-Blog/July-2020/He-s-Not-a-Criminal-He-s-in-Crisis

Alzheimer's Association. (2021). *What Is Dementia?* Retrieved from https://www.alz.org/alzheimers-dementia/what-is-dementia#symptoms

Alzheimer's Society United Against Dementia. (2021). *Types of dementia*. Retrieved from https://www.alzheimers.org.uk/about-dementia/types-dementia

Bhandari, S. (March 31, 2020). What are the treatments for dementia? Retrieved from WebMD website: https://www.webmd.com/alzheimers/dementia-treatments-overview#1-2

Blatstein, M., Spence, F. F., Hurst, E. J., II, & Baird, M. (2021). Availability of treatment and rehabilitation in federal prison: The critical role of the presentence report. *The Federal Lawyer*, 42–52.

Bollinger, M., Stimson, S., & Gordon L. B. (2019). Caring for inmates in a specialized dementia unit in a correctional setting! Retrieved from National Council of Certified Dementia Practitioners website: https://www.nccdp.org/resources/caring-for-inmates-in-a-specialized-dementia-unit-in-a-corrrectional-setting.pdf

Civil Commitment of Dangerous Sex Offenders, Adam Walsh Child Protection and Safety Act of 2006, Pub. L. No. 109-248, Title III.

Cooper v. Oklahoma, 517 U.S. 348 (1996).

Doron, I., Werner, P., Spanier, B., & Lazar, O. (2017). The legal appearances of dementia in court rulings: Mapping the terrain. *International Psychogeriatrics 29*(5), 755–763. https://doi.org/10.1017/S1041610216002453

Drope v. Missouri, 420 U.S. 162 (1975).

Dusky v. United States, 362 U.S. 402 (1960).

Federal Bureau of Prisons. (September 2017). *Directory of national programs.* Retrieved from https://www.bop.gov/inmates/custody_and_care/docs/20170914_BOP_National_Program_Catalog.pdf

Federal Bureau of Prisons. (2019). *Care level classification for medical and mental health conditions or disabilities.* Retrieved from https://www.bop.gov/resources/pdfs/care_level_classification_guide.pdf

Federal Bureau of Prisons Health Services. (May 2020). *National Formulary Part I.* Retrieved from https://www.bop.gov/resources/pdfs/2020_winter_formulary_part_1.pdf

Federal Bureau of Prisons Health Services. (2020). *Winter 2020 National Formulary Part 2.* Retrieved from https://www.bop.gov/resources/pdfs/2020_winter_formulary_part_2.pdf

Ford v. Wainwright, 477 U.S. 399 (1986).

Insanity Defense, 18 U.S.C. § 17.

Liljegren, M., Naasan, G., Temlett, J., Perry, D. C., Rankin, K. P., Merrilees, J., Grinberg, L. T., Seeley, W. W., Englund, E., & Miller, B. L. (2015). Criminal behavior in frontotemporal dementia and Alzheimer disease. *JAMA Neurology.* doi:10.1001/jamaneurol.2014.3781

Lopez, R. (2020). Prisoners in US suffering dementia may hit 200,000 within the next decade—many won't even know why they are behind bars. *The Conversation.* Retrieved from https://theconversation.com/prisoners-in-us-suffering-dementia-may-hit-200-000-within-the-next-decade-many-wont-even-know-why-they-are-behind-bars-138236

Madison v. Alabama, 139 S. Ct. 718 (2019).

Melinosky, C. (2020). What medicines treat dementia? Retrieved from Web MD website: https://www.webmd.com/alzheimers/guide/medicines-to-treat-dementia

Mendez, M. F. (2010). The unique predisposition to criminal violations in frontotemporal dementia. *Journal of the American Academy of Psychiatry and the Law Online.* Retrieved from http://jaapl.org/content/38/3/318.long

Miller, D. (2020). Dementia and competency in United States courtrooms: A case law review (Master's thesis, John Jay College of Criminal Justice, City University of New York). *Academic Works*. Retrieved from https://academicworks cuny.edu/cgi/viewcontent.cgi?article=1157&context=jj_etds

Panetti v. Quarterman, 551 U.S. 930 (2007).

Pate. (December 2020). *Updated Compilation of Compassionate Release Grants*, The Federal Docket. Retrieved from https://thefederaldocket.com/updated-compilation-of-compassionate-release-grants/

Price, M. (June 2018). *Everywhere and nowhere: Compassionate release in the states*. Retrieved from Families Against Mandatory Minimums website: https://famm.org/wp-content/uploads/Exec-Summary-Report.pdf

Shugart, J. (January 2013). *When Frontotemporal Dementia Leads to Crime—Prosecution or Protection?* Retrieved from Alz Forum website: https://www.alzforum.org/news/research-news/when-frontotemporal-dementia-leads-crime-prosecution-or-protection

Chapter 2 Competency

American Academy of Psychiatry and the Law. (May 2005). *Ethics guidelines for the practice of forensic psychiatry*. Retrieved from https://www.aapl.org/ethics.htm.

American Psychiatric Association. (2013). Diagnostic and statistical manual of mental disorders (5th ed.).

Canevelli M., Valletta M., Trebbastoni A., Sarli G., D'Antonio F., Tariciotti L., de Lena C., & Bruno, G. (2016). Sundowning in dementia: Clinical relevance, pathophysiological determinants, and therapeutic approaches. *Frontiers in Medicine (Lausanne)*.

Cipriani, G., Danti, S., Vedovello, M., Nuti, A., & Lucetti, C. (2014). Understanding delusion in dementia: a review. *Geriatrics & Gerontology International*.

Colwell, L. H., & Gianesini, J. (2011). Demographic, criminogenic, and psychiatric factors that predict competency restoration. *Journal of the American Academy of Psychiatry and the Law*, *39*(3), 297–306.

Cooper, V. G., & Zapf, P. A. (2003). Predictor variables in competency to stand trial decisions. *Law and Human Behavior*, *27*(4), 423–436.

Cooper v. Oklahoma, 517 U.S. 348 (1996).

Craft S., Cholerton B,, & Reger M. (2003). Aging and cognition: What is normal? In W. R. Hazzard, J. P. Blass, J. B. Halter, J. G. Ouslander, and M. E. Tinetti (Eds.), *Principles of geriatric medicine and gerontology* (5th ed.). McGraw-Hill Companies.

Drope v. Missouri, 420 U.S. 162 (1975).

Dusky v. U.S., 362 U.S. 402 (1960).

Federal Bureau of Investigation. (2019). *Crime in the United States*. Retrieved from https://ucr.fbi.gov/crime-in-the-u.s/2019/crime-in-the-u.s.-2019/topic-pages/tables/table-38

Frierson R. L., Shea S. J., & Shea M. E. C. (2013). Competence-to-stand-trial evaluations of geriatric defendants. *Journal of the American Academy of Psychiatry and the Law*, *30*(2), 252–256.

Frierson, R. L. & Srinivasan S. (2018). Evaluation of elderly persons in the criminal justice system. In J. C. Holzer, R. Kohn, J. M. Ellison, & P. R. Recupero (Eds.), *Geriatric forensic psychiatry: Principles and practice*. Oxford University Press.

Gay, J. G., Vitacco, M. J., & Ragatz, L. (2017). Mental health symptoms predict competency to stand trial and competency restoration success. *Legal and Criminological Psychology*, *22*(2).

Heinik, J., Kimhi, R., & Hes, J. P. (1994). Dementia and crime: a forensic psychiatry unit study in Israel. *International Journal of Geriatric Psychiatry*, *9*(6).

Jackson v. Indiana, 406 U.S. 715 (1972).

Kaiser Family Foundation. *Population Distribution by Age: 2019*. Retrieved from https://www.kff.org/other/state-indicator/distribution-by-age/?currentTimeframe=0&sortModel=%7B%22colId%22:%22Location%22,%22sort%22:%22asc%22%7D

Lacro, J. P., Harris, M. J., & Jeste, D. V. (1993). Late life psychosis. *International Journal of Geriatric Psychiatry*, *8*(1).

Medina v. California, 505 U.S. 437 (1992).

Melton, G. B., Petrila, J., Poythress, N. G., Slobogin, C., et al. (2018). Competence to proceed. In *Psychological evaluations for the courts* (4th ed.), Guilford Press.

Morris, D. R., & Parker, G. F. (2009). Effects of advanced age and dementia on restoration of competence to stand trial. *International Journal of Law and Psychiatry*, *32*(3).

Mossman, D., Noffsinger, S. G., Ash, P., Frierson, R. L., et al. (2007). AAPL practice guideline for the forensic psychiatric evaluation of competence to stand trial. *Journal of the American Academy of Psychiatry and the Law*, *35*(4).

Nicholson, R. A. & Kugler, K .E. (1991). Competent and incompetent criminal defendants: A quantitative review of comparative research. *Psychological Bulletin*, *109*(3).

Rosner, R., Wiederlight, M., Harmon, R. B., & Cahn, D. J. (1991). Geriatric offenders examined at a forensic psychiatry clinic. *Journal of Forensic Sciences, 36*(6).

Scott, C. L. (2018). Evaluation of competencies in the criminal justice system. In L. H. Gold & R. L. Frierson (Eds.), *The American Psychiatric Association publishing textbook of forensic psychiatry* (3rd ed.).

Stout, R. G. & Farooque, R. S. (2008). Claims of amnesia for criminal offense: psychopathology, substance abuse, and malingering. *Journal of Forensic Sciences, 53*(5).

Wilson v. United States, 391 F.2d 460 (D.C. Cir. 1968).

Chapter 3 Restoration

Alzheimer's Association. (2021). *Facts and figures*. Retrieved from https://www.alz.org/alzheimers-dementia/facts-figures

Alzheimer's Association. (2021). *What Is Alzheimer's Disease?* Retrieved from https://www.alz.org/alzheimers-dementia/what-is-alzheimers

Alzheimer's Association. (2021). *What Is Dementia?* Retrieved from https://www.alz.org/alzheimers-dementia/what-is-dementia

American Psychiatric Association. (2013). Diagnostic and statistical manual of mental disorders (5th ed.).

Bureau of Justice Statistics. (2016). *Aging of the state prison population1993–2013*. Retrieved from https://bjs.ojp.gov/content/pub/pdf/aspp9313_Sum.pdf

Bush, S. S. (2014). Frontotemporal dementias. In K. J. Stucky, M. W. Kirkwood, & J. Donders (Eds.), *Clinical neuropsychology study guide and board review*. Oxford University Press.

Centers for Disease Control. (2003). *Morbidity and mortality weekly report, 52*(06), 101–106.

Cochrane, R. E., Laxton, K. L., Mulay, A. L., & Herbel, B. L. (2021). Guidelines for determining restorability of competency to stand trial and recommendations for involuntary treatment. *Journal of Forensic Science, 66*(4), 1201–1209.

Cullum, C. M., & Liff, C. D. (2014). Mild cognitive impairment and Alzheimer disease. In K. J. Stucky, M. W. Kirkwood, & J. Donders (Eds.), *Clinical neuropsychology study guide and board review*. Oxford University Press.

Danzer, G. S., Wheeler, E. M. A., Alexander, A. A., & Wasser, T. D. (2019). Competency restoration for adult defendants in different treatment environments. *Journal of the American Academy of Psychiatry and Law, 47*(1), 1–14.

Demakis, G. J. (2018). Assessment and competency to stand trial with older adults. In S. S. Bush & A. L. Heck (Eds.), *Forensic geropsychology*. American Psychological Association.

Frierson, R. L., Shea, S. J., & Craig Shea, M. E. (2002). Competence-to-stand-trial evaluations of geriatric defendants. *The Journal of the American Academy of Psychiatry and the Law*, *30*, 252–256.

Grisso, T., Steinberg, L., Woolard, J., Cauffman, E., Scott, E., Graham, S., Lexcen, F., Reppucci, N. D., & Schwartz, R. (2003). Juveniles' competence to stand trial: A comparison of adolescents' and adults' capacities as trial defendants. *Law and Human Behavior*, *27*(4), 333–363.

Grisso, T. (2014). Competence to stand trial evaluations: Just the basics. Professional Resource Press.

Heck, A. L., & Herrick, S. M. (2007). Geriatric considerations in restoration of competence to stand trial: Two cases of impaired cognition. *Journal of Forensic Psychology Practice*, 7(2), 73–82.

Heinik, J., Kimhi, R., & Hes, J. (1994). Dementia and crime: a forensic psychiatry unit study in Israel. *International Journal of Geriatric Psychiatry*, *9*, 491–494.

Kalbeitzter, R., & Benedetti, R. (2009). Assessment of competency to stand trial in individuals with mental retardation. *Journal of Forensic Psychology Practice*, *9*, 237–248.

Kruh, I., & Grisso. T. (2009). Evaluation of juveniles' competence to stand trial. In series: Best Practices in Forensic Mental Health Assessment. Oxford University Press.

Kruh, I., & Grisso, T. (2013). Evaluation of competence to stand trial in juveniles. In R. Roesch & P. A. Zapf (Eds.), *Forensic assessments in criminal and civil law: A handbook for lawyers* (pp. 222–236). Oxford University Press.

Medalia, A., & Freilich, B. (2008). The Neuropsychological Educational Approach to Cognitive Remediation (NEAR) Model: Practice principles and outcome studies. *American Journal of Psychiatric Rehabilitation*, *11*, 123–143.

Melton, G. B., Petrila, J., Poythress, N. G., Slobogin, C., Otto, R. K., Mossman, D., & Condie, L. O. (2018). *Psychological evaluations for the courts: A handbook for mental health professionals and lawyers* (4th ed.). Guilford Press.

Miller, D. (2020). Dementia and competency in United States courtrooms: A case law review. CUNY Academic Works. Retrieved from https://academicworks.cuny.edu/jj_etds/156

Morris, D. R., & Parker, G. F. (2009). Effects of advanced age and dementia on restoration of competence to stand trial. *International Journal of Law and Psychiatry*, *32*, 156–160.

Mossman, D., Noffsinger, S. G., Ash, P., Frierson, R. L., Gerbasi, J., Hackett, M., Lewis, C. F., Pinals, D. A., Scott, C. L., Sieg, K. G., Wall, B. W., & Zonana, H. V. (2007). AAPL practice guideline for the forensic psychiatric evaluation of competence to stand trial. *The Journal of The American Academy of Psychiatry and the Law*, *35*(4 Suppl), S3–S72.

Pirelli, G., Gottdiener, W. H., & Zapf, P. A. (2011). A meta-analytic review of competency to stand trial research. *Psychology, Public Policy, and Law*, *17*(1), 1–53. Retrieved from https://doi.org/10.1037/a0021713.

Polizzi, D., & Draper, M. R. (2015). Forensic psychology reconsidered: A critique of mental illness and the courts (1st ed.). Routledge.

Reisner, A. D. & Piel, J. L. (2018). Mental Condition Requirement in Competency to Stand Trial Assessments. *Journal of the American Academy of Psychiatry and the Law Online*, *46*(1), 86–92.

Reisner, A. D. & Piel, J. L., & Makey Jr., M. (2013). Competency to stand trial and defendants who lack insight into their mental illness. *Journal of the American Academy of Psychiatry Law*, *41*(85), 85–91.

Roesch, R., Zapf, P. A., & Hart, S. D. (2009). *Forensic psychology and law* (1st ed.). *Wiley*.

Schwalbe, E., & Medalia, A. (2007). Cognitive dysfunction and competency restoration: Using cognitive remediation to help restore the unrestorable. *Journal of the American Academy of Psychiatry and the Law Online*, *35*(4), 518–525.

Sperling, R. A., Aisen, P. S., Beckett, L. A., Bennett, D. A., Craft, S., Phelps, C. H., et al. (2011). Toward defining the pre-clinical stages of Alzheimer's disease: Recommendations from the National Institute on Aging Alzheimer's Association workgroups on diagnostic guidelines for Alzheimer's disease. *Alzheimer's Dementia*, 7, 280–292.

Stepanyan, S. T., Sidhu, S. S., & Bath, E. (2016). Juvenile competency to stand trial. *Child and Adolescent Psychiatric Clinics*, *25*(1), 49–59. Retrieved from http://dx.doi.org/10.1016/j.chc.2015.08.008.

U.S. Const. amend. XI., https://www.law.cornell.edu/constitution/sixth_amend ment

Wall, B. W. & Christopher, P. P. (2012). A training program for defendants with intellectual disabilities who are found incompetent to stand trial." *Journal of the American Academy of Psychiatry and the Law*, *40*, 366–373.

Warren, J. I., Murrie, D. C., Stejskal, W., Colweel, L. H., Morris, J., Chauhan, P., & Dietz, P. (2006). Opinion formation in evaluating the adjudicative competence and restorability of criminal defendants: A review of 8,000 evaluations." *Behavioral Sciences and the Law*, *24*, 113–132.

Wood, E. M., Lawson, K. M., Anderson, J. L., Kinney, D. I., Nitch, S., & Glassmire, D. M. (2019). Reasonable accommodations for meeting the unique needs of defendants with intellectual disability. *Journal of the American Academy of Psychiatry and the Law*, *47*(3), 1–11.

Zapf, P. A., & Roesch, R. (2011). Future directions in the restoration of competency to stand trial. *Current Directions in Psychological Science*, *20*(1), 43–47.

Chapter 4 Responsibility

American Law Institute. (1985). Model Penal Code: Official Draft and Explanatory Notes: Complete Text of Model Penal Code as Adopted at the 1962 Annual Meeting of the American Law Institute at Washington, D.C., May 24, 1962. Philadelphia, Pa.: The Institute.

Amjad, H., et al. (2018). Underdiagnosis of dementia: An observational study of patterns in diagnosis and awareness in US older adults. *Journal of General Internal Medicine*, *33*, 1131.

Callahan, L., et al. (1991). The volume and characteristics of insanity defense pleas: an eight-state study. *Bulletin. American Academy of Psychiatry the Law*, *19*, 331.

Cipriani, G., et al. (2014). Understanding delusions in dementia: A review. *Geriatrics & Gerontology International*, *14*, 32.

Cochrane, R., Grisso, T., & Frederick, R. (2001). The relationship between criminal charges, diagnoses, and psycholegal opinions among federal pretrial defendants. *Behavioral Sciences & Law*, *19*, 565.

Crime without criminals? Seniors, dementia and the aftermath: Hearing before the Special Committee on Aging, 108 Cong. 31. Statement of Donna Cohen, PhD. (2004).

Crime without criminals? Seniors, dementia and the aftermath: Hearing before the Special Committee on Aging, 108 Cong. 31. Statement of Senator Larry E. Craig. (2004).

Deutsch, L., et al. (1991). Psychosis and physical aggression in probably Alzheimer's disease. *American Journal of Psychiatry*, *148*, 1159.

Gassoumis, Z., Navarro, A., & Wilber, K. (2015). Protecting victims of elder financial exploitation: The role of an Elder Abuse Forensic Center in referring victims for conservatorship. *Aging and Mental Health*, *19*, 790.

Hashimoto, M., Sakamoto, S., & Ikeda, M. (2015). Clinical features of delusional jealousy in elderly patients with dementia. *Journal of Clinical Psychiatry*, *76*, 691.

Heck, A., & Vaulter, R. (2018). *Forensic Geropsychology: Practice Essentials*, 172.

Hoag, A. (2015, April 23). Saginaw township man who killed wife, sister-in-law found not legally responsible. *The Saginaw News*. Retrieved from https://www.mlive.com/news/saginaw/2015/04/report_trial_begins_for_former.html

Kahler v. Kansas, 589 U.S. (2020).

Keene, J., et al. (1999). Natural history of aggressive behavior in dementia. *International Journal of Geriatric Psychiatry, 14*, 151.

Liljegren, M., et al. (2015). Criminal behavior in frontotemporal dementia and Alzheimer disease. 72 *JAMA Neurol*, 295.

Liljegren, M., et al. (2019). Association of neuropathologically confirmed frontotemporal dementia and Alzheimer disease with criminal and socially inappropriate behavior in a Swedish Cohort. *2 JAMA Netw. Open e19026.*

Liljegren, M., Waldo, M., & Englund, E. (2018). Physical aggression among patients with dementia, neuropathologically confirmed post-mortem. *International Journal of Geriatric Psychiatry, 33*, e242.

Lindau, M., et al. (2000). First symptoms—frontotemporal dementia versus Alzheimer's disease. *Dementia and Geriatric Cognitive Disorders, 11*, 286.

Louis, C. (2015, April 29). Doctors worry that verdict in A.L.S. murder case could stigmatize the disease. *The New York Times*. Retrieved from https://www.nytimes.com/2015/04/30/health/doctors-worry-acquittal-in-als-murder-case-could-further-stigmatize-the-disease.html

Low, R. (2019, June 18). Aurora woman with dementia cited for trespassing after ringing doorbell. *Fox 31 Denver KDVR news*. Retrieved from https://kdvr.com/news/problem-solvers/aurora-woman-with-dementia-cited-for-trespassing-after-ringing-doorbell

Manes, F., et al. (2011). Decision-making in frontotemporal dementia: clinical, theoretical, and legal implications. *Dementia and Geriatric Cognitive Disorders, 32*, 11.

Mendez, M., et al. (2005). Acquired sociopathy and frontotemporal dementia. *Dementia and Geriatric Cognitive Disorders, 20*, 99.

Mendez, M., & Shapira, J. (2009). Altered emotional morality in frontotemporal dementia. *Cognitive Neuropsychiatry, 14*, 165.

Mendez, M. (2010). The unique predisposition to criminal violations in frontotemporal dementia. *Journal of the American Academy of Psychiatry Law, 38*, 318.

Mendez, M. (2011). Pathological stealing in dementia: poor response to SSRI medications. *Journal of Clinical Psychiatry*, 72, 418.

M'Naghten's Case, 8 Eng. Rep. 718 (1843).

Packer, I., (2009). Best practices in forensic mental health assessment: Evaluation of criminal responsibility.

Trevelen, E. (2015, February 11). Former deputy to plead mental defect in murders of wife, sister-in-law. *Wisconsin State Journal.* Retrieved from https://madison.com/wsj/news/local/crime_and_courts/former-deputy-to-plead-mental-defect-in-murders-of-wife-sister-in-law/article_af0e61fe-71a6-555a-91d3-a65f9b241da2.html

Trevelen, E. (2017, March 8). Andrew Steele, ex-deputy who killed wife and sister-in-law, dies of ALS. *Wisconsin State Journal.* Retrieved from https://madison.com/wsj/news/local/courts/andrew-steele-ex-deputy-who-killed-wife-and-sister-in-law-dies-of-als/article_ffdc71cd-c7aa-59cd-b76c-c6dc082e70b5.html

Tsai, S., et al. (1997). Delusional jealousy in dementia. *Journal of Clinical Psychiatry, 58*, 592.

Warren, J., et al. (2004). Opinion formation in evaluating sanity at the time of the offense: An examination of 5175 pre-trial evaluations." *Behavorial Sciences & the Law, 22*, 171.

Wood, S. & Lichtenberg, P. (2017). Financial capacity and financial exploitation of older adults: Research findings, policy recommendations, and clinical implications. *Clinical. Gerontology, 40*, 3.

Voskou, P., et al. (2018). Testamentary capacity assessment: Legal, medical, and neuropsychological issues. *Journal of Geriatric Psychiatry and Neurology, 31*, 3.

Chapter 5 Testing

Mace, N., & Rabins, P. (2021). The 36-hour day: A family guide to caring for people who have Alzheimer's disease and other dementias. Johns Hopkins University Press.

Mitrushina, M., Boone, K., Rozani, J., & D'Elia, L. (2005). *Handbook of normative data for neuropsychological assessment.* Oxford University Press.

Silbersweig, D., Safar, L., & Daffner, K. (2021). *Neuropsychiatric and behavioral neurology: Principles and practice.* McGraw Hill.

Smith, F., & Farias, G. (Eds.). (2018). *APA handbook of dementia.* American Psychological Association.

Strauss, E., Sherman, E., & Spreen, O. (2006). *A compendium of neuropsychological tests: Administration, norms, and commentary* (3rd ed.). Oxford University Press.

Chapter 6 Neuroimaging

Baskin, J. H., Edersheim, J. G., & Price, B. H. (2007). Is a picture worth a thousand words? Neuroimaging in the courtroom. *American Journal of Law & Medicine*, *33*(2–3), 239–269. Retrieved from https://doi.org/10.1177/009885880703300205.

Berger, A. (2002). Magnetic resonance imaging. *BMJ*, *324*(7328), 35.

Berti, V., Pupi, A., & Mosconi, L. (2011). PET/CT in diagnosis of dementia. *Annals of the New York Academy of Sciences*, *1228*, 81–92. Retrieved from https://doi.org/10.1111/j.1749-6632.2011.06015.x

Buckholtz, J. W., & Faigman, D. L. (2014). Promises, promises for neuroscience and law. *Current Biology*, *24*(18), R861–R867. Retrieved from https://doi.org/10.1016/j.cub.2014.07.057

Edersheim, J. G., Brendel, R. W., & Price, B. H. (2012). Neuroimaging, diminished capacity and mitigation. In *Neuroimaging in forensic psychiatry* (pp. 163–193). John Wiley & Sons, Ltd. Retrieved from https://doi.org/10.1002/9781119968900.ch10

Edersheim, J., & Wei, M. (2017). Neuroimaging and forensic psychiatry. In *The American Psychiatric Association Publishing Textbook of Forensic Psychiatry*. American Psychiatric Association Publishing. Retrieved from https://doi.org/10.1176/appi.books.9781615371914.lg07

Farahany, N. A. (2015) Neuroscience and behavioral genetics in US criminal law: An empirical analysis. *Journal of Law and the Biosciences*, *2*(3), 485–509. Retrieved from https://doi.org/10.1093/jlb/lsv059

Greene, J., & Cohen, J. (2004). For the law, neuroscience changes nothing and everything. *Philosophical Transactions of the Royal Society B: Biological Sciences*, *359*(1451), 1775–1785. Retrieved from https://doi.org/10.1098/rstb.2004.1546

Haynes, J.-D., & Rees, G. (2006). Decoding mental states from brain activity in humans. *Nature Reviews Neuroscience*, 7(7), 523–534. Retrieved from https://doi.org/10.1038/nrn1931

Herculano-Houzel, S. (2012). The remarkable, yet not extraordinary, human brain as a scaled-up primate brain and its associated cost. *Proceedings of the National Academy of Sciences*, *109*(Supplement 1), 10661–10668. Retrieved from https://doi.org/10.1073/pnas.1201895109

Jack, C. R., Knopman, D. S., Jagust, W. J., Petersen, R. C., Weiner, M. W., Aisen, P. S., Shaw, L. M., Vemuri, P., Wiste, H. J., Weigand, S. D., Lesnick, T. G., Pankratz, V. S., Donohue, M. C., & Trojanowski, J. Q. (2013). Tracking pathophysiological processes in Alzheimer's disease: An updated hypothetical model of dynamic biomarkers. *The Lancet. Neurology*, *12*(2), 207–216. Retrieved from https://doi.org/10.1016/S1474-4422(12)70291-0

Jones, O. D., & Shen, F. X. (2012). Law and neuroscience in the United States. In T. M. Spranger (Ed.), *International neurolaw: A comparative analysis* (pp. 349–380). Springer. Retrieved from https://doi.org/10.1007/978-3-642-21541-4_19

Kolanko, M. A., Win, Z., Loreto, F., Patel, N., Carswell, C., Gontsarova, A., Perry, R. J., & Malhotra, P. A. (2020). Amyloid PET imaging in clinical practice. *Practical Neurology*, *20*(6), 451–462. Retrieved from https://doi.org/10.1136/practneurol-2019-002468

LeMay, M. (1986). CT changes in dementing diseases: A review. *American Journal of Roentgenology*, *147*(5), 963–975. Retrieved from https://doi.org/10.2214/ajr.147.5.963

Leuzy, A., Chiotis, K., Lemoine, L., Gillberg, P.-G., Almkvist, O., Rodriguez-Vieitez, E., & Nordberg, A. (2019). Tau PET imaging in neurodegenerative tauopathies—still a challenge. *Molecular Psychiatry*, *24*(8), 1112–1134. Retrieved from https://doi.org/10.1038/s41380-018-0342-8

Logothetis, N. K. (2008). What we can do and what we cannot do with fMRI. *Nature*, *453*(7197), 869–878. Retrieved from https://doi.org/10.1038/nature06976

Morse, S. (2016). Actions speak louder than images: The use of neuroscientific evidence in criminal cases. *Journal of Law and the Biosciences*, *3*(2), 336–342. Retrieved from https://doi.org/10.1093/jlb/lsw025

Morse, S. J. (2011). The status of neurolaw: A plea for current modesty and future cautious optimism. *The Journal of Psychiatry & Law*, *39*(4), 595–626. Retrieved from https://doi.org/10.1177/009318531103900405

Pantano, P., Caramia, F., & Pierallini, A. (1999). The role of MRI in dementia. *The Italian Journal of Neurological Sciences*, *20*(2), S250–S253. Retrieved from https://doi.org/10.1007/s100729970006

Pasi, M., Poggesi, A., & Pantoni, L. (2011). The use of CT in dementia. *International Psychogeriatrics*, *23 Suppl 2*, S6-12. Retrieved from https://doi.org/10.1017/S1041610211000950

People v. Weinstein, 591 N.Y.S.2d 715 (N.Y. Sup. Ct. 1992).

Rushing, S. (2014). The admissibility of brain scans in criminal trials: The case of positron emission tomography." *Court Review*, *50*(2). Retrieved from https://digitalcommons.unl.edu/ajacourtreview/494

Slobogin, C. (1998). Psychiatric evidence in criminal trials: To junk or not to junk?" *William & Mary Law Review*, *40*(1), 1.

United States v. Gigante, 982 F. Supp. 140 (E.D.N.Y. 1997).

United States v. Kasim, No. 2:07 CR 56, 2008 U.S. Dist. LEXIS 89137 (N.D. Ind. Nov. 3, 2008).

Chapter 7 Early Onset Dementia/Frontotemporal Dementia

The Assocation for Frontotemporal Degeneration. (August 17, 2021). *Disease overview*. Retrieved from https://www.theaftd.org/what-is-ftd/disease-overview

Kerchner, G., & Rosenbloom, M. (2018). Frontotemporal dementia. In D. B. Arciniegas, S. C. Yudofsky, & R. E. Hales, *The textbook of neuropsychiatry and clinical neurosciences* (6th ed.) (pp. 487–592). American Psychiatric Association Publishing.

Liljegren, M., Naasan, G., Temlett, J., Perry, D. C., Rankin, K. P., Merrilees, J., Grinberg, L. T., Seeley, W. W., Englund, E., & Miller, B. (2015). Criminal behavior in frontotemporal dementia and Alzheimer disease." *JAMA Neurology*, 72(3).

Mendez, M. (2010). The unique predisposition to criminal violations in frontotemporal dementia. *The Journal of the American Academy of Psychiatry and the Law* ,38(3).

Rabinovici, G. & Miller, B. (2010). Frontotemporal lobar degeneration: Epidemiology, pathophysiology, diagnosis and management." *CNS Drugs*, *24*(5).

Rascovsky, K., Hodges, J. R., Knopman, D., Mendez, M. F., Kramer, J. H., Neuhaus, J., van Swieten, J. C., et al. (2011). Sensitivity of revised diagnostic criteria for the behavioural variant of frontotemporal dementia." *Brain*, *134*(9).

Shugart, J. (August 17, 2021). When frontotemporal dementia leads to crime—prosecution or protection? *The Center for Law, Brain & Behavior*. Retrieved from https://clbb.mgh.harvard.edu/when-frontotemporal-dementia-leads-to-crime-prosecution-or-protection

Wong, C., Merrilees, J., Ketelle, R., Barton, C., Wallhagen, M., & Miller, B. (2012). The experience of caregiving: Differences between behavioral variant of frontotemporal dementia and Alzheimer disease. *The American Journal of Geriatric Psychiatry*, *20*(8).

Chapter 8 How Can Lawyers Understand Medicine and Science While Representing People with Dementia?

Beran, R. G. (2009). The role of the expert witness in the adversarial legal system. *Journal of Law, Medicine and Ethics*, *17*(1), 133–137.

Healton, E. B., Treanor, W. M., DeGioia, J. J., & Girard, V. W. (2021). Training future health justice leaders—A role for medical-legal partnerships. *New England Journal of Medicine*, *384*(20), 1879–1881.

Howland W. (2020). Always a nurse: The legal nurse consultant. *Nursing Administration Quarterly*, *44*(1), 71–73.

Chapter 9 Working with Clients with Dementia

Boland, R., & Verduin, M. (2018). *Kaplan & Sadock's synopsis of psychiatry* (12th ed.).

Gold, L., & Frierson W. (2018). The American Psychiatric Association publishing textbook of forensic psychiatry (3rd ed.).

Hudson, D. (2018.) Lawyers and cognitive decline. In S. S. Bush (Ed.), *The APA Handbook of Forensic Neuropsychology*.

Kumaravel, A., & Drogin, E. (2020). Dementia: An overview for criminal law practitioners. *Criminal Justice*.

Lezak, M., et al. (2012). *Neuropsychological assessment* (5th ed.).

Melton, G., et al. (2018). *Phycological evaluations for the courts* (4th ed.).

Robert, A. (2021). Benching judges. *A.B.A. Journal*.

Weiss, D. (2021, May 12). As the legal profession ages, dementia becomes an increasing concern. Retrieved from https://www.abajournal.com/news/article /as-legal-profession-ages-dementia-becomes-an-increasing-concern.

Chapter 10 Working a Case

Armstrong, R. (2019). Risk factors for Alzheimer's disease. *Folia Neuropathology*, *57*(2), 87–105. doi: 10.5114/fn.2019.85929. PMID: 31556570.

Ebell M. H. (2009). Brief screening instruments for dementia in primary care. *American Family Physician*, 79(6), 497–498, 500. PMID: 19323363.

Chapter 11 Representing People on Death Row with Dementia

Caniglia, J. (2019). The graying of Ohio prisons: Number of older inmates continues to spike. *Cleveland.com*.

Dunham, R. (2020, July 8). INSIGHT: Vast majority on federal death row have significant impairments. *BloombergLaw.com*.

Dementia caused by chronic drug addiction (2020, April 1). *Recovery First Treatment Center Blog*.

The Dementia Society of America, https://www.dementiasociety.org/, provides useful information about the condition, symptoms, and causes.

Chapter 12 Working with the Expert

Amador, X. (2020). *I am not sick, I don't need help! How to help someone accept treatment* (20th anniversary ed.). Vida Press.

Cipriani, G., Lucetti, C., Danti, S., Carlesi, C., & Nuti, A. (2016). Violent and criminal manifestations in dementia patients. *Geriatrics & Gerontology International*, 16(5), 541–549.

Cipriani, G., Danti, S., Carlesi, C., & Di Fiorino, M. (2017). Old and dangerous: prison and dementia. *Journal of Forensic and Legal Medicine*, 51, 40–44.

Kim, J.-M., Chu, K., Jung, K.-H., Lee, S.-T., Choi, S.-S., & Lee, S. K. (2011). Criminal manifestations of dementia patients: report from the national forensic hospital. *Dementia and Geriatric Cognitive Disorders Extra*, *1*(1), 433–438.

Liljegren, M., Naasan, G., Temlett, J., Perry, D. C., Rankin, K. P., Merrilees, J., Grinberg, L. T., Seeley, W. W., Englund, E., & Miller, B. L. (2015). Criminal behavior in frontotemporal dementia and Alzheimer disease. *JAMA Neurology*, 72(3), 295–300.

Chapter 13 Jail and Prison Conditions

Aaronson, A. L., Bordelon, S. D., Brakel, S. J., & Morrison, H. (2021). A review of the role of chronic traumatic encephalopathy in criminal court. *Journal of the American Academy of Psychiatry and the Law Online*, *49*(1), 60–65. Retrieved from https://www.ncbi.nlm.nih.gov/pmc/articles/PMC7979483/

Alisa. (July 2020). He's Not a Criminal, He's in Crisis. Retrieved from National Alliance on Mental Illness website: https://www.nami.org/Blogs/NAMI-Blog/July-2020/He-s-Not-a-Criminal-He-s-in-Crisis

Alzheimer's Association. (2021). *What Is Dementia?* Retrieved from https://www.alz.org/alzheimers-dementia/what-is-dementia#symptoms

Bhandari, S. (2020). *What are the treatments for dementia?* Retrieved from WebMD website: https://www.webmd.com/alzheimers/dementia-treatments-overview#1-2

Blatstein, M., Spence, F. F., Hurst, E. J., II, & Baird, M. (2021). Availability of treatment and rehabilitation in federal prison: The critical role of the presentence report. *The Federal Lawyer*, 42–52.

Bollinger, M., Stimson, S., & Gordon L. B. (2019). Caring for inmates in a specialized dementia unit in a correctional setting! *National Council of Certified Dementia Practitioners.* Retrieved from https://www.nccdp.org/resources/caring-for-inmates-in-a-specialized-dementia-unit-in-a-corrrectional-setting.pdf

Civil Commitment of Dangerous Sex Offenders, Adam Walsh Child Protection and Safety Act of 2006, Pub. L. No. 109-248, Title III.

Cooper v. Oklahoma, 517 U.S. 348 (1996).

Doron, I., Werner, P., Spanier, B., & Lazar, O. (2017). The legal appearances of dementia in court rulings: Mapping the terrain. *International Psychogeriatrics, 29*(5), 755–763. Retrieved from https://doi.org/10.1017/S1041610216002453

Drope v. Missouri, 420 U.S. 162 (1975).

Dusky v. United States, 362 U.S. 402 (1960).

Eagles, C. C., Leach, J., & Amon, C. B. (2021). *Published appellate cases on "compassionate release" motions under § 3582(c)(1)(A).* (Federal Judicial Center, CLE material, June 30, 2021).

Ellis, A., & Allenbaugh, M. H. (2020, September). The state of compassionate release. *For the Defense, 5*(3), 51–55.

Federal Bureau of Prisons. (September 2017). *Directory of national programs.* Retrieved from https://www.bop.gov/inmates/custody_and_care/docs/20170914_BOP_National_Program_Catalog.pdf

Federal Bureau of Prisons. (2019). *Care level classification for medical and mental health conditions or disabilities.* Retrieved from https://www.bop.gov/resources/pdfs/care_level_classification_guide.pdf

Federal Bureau of Prisons Health Services. (2020). Winter 2020 National Formulary Part 2. Retrieved from https://www.bop.gov/resources/pdfs/2020_winter_formulary_part_2.pdf

Ferri, C. N. (2013). A stuck safety valve: The inadequacy of compassionate release for elderly inmates. *Stetson Law Review, 43*, 197–243.

Ford v. Wainwright, 477 U.S. 399 (1986).

Hamilton, K., Ferdowsi, S., & Arthur, R. (2021, March 18). Prisoners keep dying of COVID while "compassionate releases" stall in court. *VICE News.*

Insanity Defense, 18 U.S.C. § 17.

Liljegren, M., Naasan, G., Temlett, J., Perry, D. C., Rankin, K. P., Merrilees, J., Grinberg, L. T., Seeley, W. W., Englund, E., & Miller, B. L. (2015). Criminal behavior in frontotemporal dementia and Alzheimer disease. *JAMA Neurology.* doi:10.1001/jamaneurol.2014.3781

Lopez, R. (2020). Prisoners in US suffering dementia may hit 200,000 within the next decade—many won't even know why they are behind bars. *The Conversation.* Retrieved from https://theconversation.com/prisoners-in-us-suffering-dementia-may-hit-200-000-within-the-next-decade-many-wont-even-know-why-they-are-behind-bars-138236

Madison v. Alabama, 139 S. Ct. 718 (2019).

Melinosky, C. (2020). What medicines treat dementia? Retrieved from WebMD website: https://www.webmd.com/alzheimers/guide/medicines-to-treat-dementia

Mendez, M. F. "The unique predisposition to criminal violations in frontotemporal dementia." *Journal of the American Academy of Psychiatry and the Law Online*, (2010). http://jaapl.org/content/38/3/318.long

Miller, D. (2020). Dementia and competency in United States courtrooms: A case law review Master's thesis, John Jay College of Criminal Justice, City University of New York. *Academic Works*. Retrieved from https://academicworks.cuny.edu/cgi/viewcontent.cgi?article=1157&context=jj_etds

Federal Bureau of Prisons Health Services. (May 2020). National Formulary Part I. Retrieved from https://www.bop.gov/resources/pdfs/2020_winter_formulary_part_1.pdf

Panetti v. Quarterman, 551 U.S. 930 (2007).

Pate. (December 2020). Updated Compilation of Compassionate Release Grants, The Federal Docket. Retrieved from https://thefederaldocket.com/updated-compilation-of-compassionate-release-grants/

Price, M. (June 2018). Everywhere and nowhere: Compassionate release in the states. *Families Against Mandatory Minimums*. Retrieved from https://famm.org/wp-content/uploads/Exec-Summary-Report.pdf

Shugart, J. (January 2013). *When frontotemporal dementia leads to crime—prosecution or protection?* Retrieved from Alz Forum website: https://www.alzforum.org/news/research-news/when-frontotemporal-dementia-leads-crime-prosecution-or-protection

Types of dementia. (2021). Retrieved from Alzheimer's Society United Against Dementia website: https://www.alzheimers.org.uk/about-dementia/types-dementia

Chapter 14 The Reality of Daily Life for Someone with Dementia in Jail or Prison

Koller, D., & Bynum, J. P. W. (2015). Dementia in the USA: state variation in prevalence. *Journal of Public Health*, *37*(4), 597–604. Retrieved from https://doi.org/10.1093/pubmed/fdu080

National Institute of Corrections. (2004). Correctional health care, addressing the needs of elderly, chronically ill, and terminally ill inmates.

U.S. Department of Justice, Office of Justice Programs, Bureau of Justice Statistics, Bulletin. (January 2018). NCJ 251149, Prisoners in 2016, E. Ann Carson, Ph.D., BJS Statistician.

U.S. Department of Justice, Office of Justice Programs, Bureau of Justice Statistics Bulletin. (April 2019). NCJ 252156, Prisoners in 2017, Jennifer Bronson, Ph.D., and E. Ann Carson, Ph.D., BJS Statisticians.

U.S. Department of Justice, Office of Justice Programs, Bureau of Justice Statistics, Bulletin. (April 2020). NCJ 253516. Prisoners in 2018. E. Ann Carson, Ph.D., BJS Statistician.

U.S. Department of Justice, Office of Justice Programs, Bureau of Justice Statistics. (October 2020). NCJ 255115 Bulletin, Prisoners in 2019. E. Ann Carson, Ph.D., BJS Statistician.

Chapter 15 Guardianships, Conservatorships, and Related Proceedings

California Conservatorship Practice – CEB Handbook for Conservators, 2016 Edition – Judicial Counsel of California

Karlawish, J. (2021). The problem of Alzheimer's: How science, culture, and politics turned a rare disease into a crisis and what we can do about it. St. Martin's Press.

Law, R., & Peck, K. (2013). Alzheimer's and the practice of law: Counseling clients with dementia and their families. American Bar Association.

National Guardianship Association. (2016). *The fundamentals of guardianship: What every guardian should know*. American Bar Association.

Zalubowski, D. (2021, August 27). Inmates seeking release from COVID-hit prisons have next to no chance in this NC district. *The Charlotte Observer*. Retrieved from http://www.charlotteobserver.com/article253422724.html

Chapter 16 Dementia in the Legal Profession

Boland, R., & Verduin, M. (2018). *Kaplan & Sadock's synopsis of psychiatry* (12th ed.).

Gold, L., & Frierson W. (2018). The American Psychiatric Association publishing textbook of forensic psychiatry (3rd ed.).

Hudson, D. (2018.) Lawyers and cognitive decline. In S. S. Bush (Ed.) *The APA handbook of forensic neuropsychology.*

Kumaravel, A., Drogin, E. (2020). Dementia: An Overview for Criminal Law Practitioners. *Criminal Justice.*

Lezak, M., et al. (2012). *Neuropsychological assessment* (5th ed.).

Melton, G., et al. (2018). *Psychological evaluations for the courts* (4th ed.).

Robert, A. (2021). Benching judges. *A.B.A.J.*

Weiss, D. (May 12, 2021). As the legal profession ages, dementia becomes an increasing concern. Retrieved from https://www.abajournal.com/news/article/as-legal-profession-ages-dementia-becomes-an-increasing-concern

Index

A

B

C

L

M

O

P

R

S

T

U

V

W

Z